We'll Be Here For
the Rest of Our Lives

Paul Shaffer

WITH DAVID RITZ

WE'LL BE HERE FOR THE REST OF OUR LIVES

A Swingin' Show-Biz Saga

DOUBLEDAY

FLYING DOLPHIN PRESS

NEW YORK

FLYING
DOLPHIN
PRESS

FLYING DOLPHIN PRESS is a registered trademark of
Random House, Inc.

www.doubleday.com

Grateful acknowledgment is made to the following for permission to
reprint previously published and unpublished material:

Paul Anka: Excerpt from "My Way" parody by Paul Anka. Reprinted by
permission of Paul Anka.

Brew Music: Excerpt from "We're An American Band" by Don Brewer,
copyright © 1987 by Brew Music. All rights reserved. Reprinted by
permission of Brew Music.

LIBRARY OF CONGRESS CATALOGING-IN-PUBLICATION DATA
Shaffer, Paul,
We'll be here for the rest of our lives / by Paul Shaffer with David
Ritz. — 1st ed.
p. cm.
1. Shaffer, Paul. 2. Conductors (Music)—United States—Biography.
3. Musicians—United States—Biography. 4. Late night with David
Letterman (Television program) I. Ritz, David. II. Title.
ML422.S48A3 2009
784.092—dc22
[B]
2009005484

ISBN 978-0-385-52483-4

PRINTED IN THE UNITED STATES OF AMERICA

10 9 8 7 6 5 4 3 2 1

FIRST EDITION

For Cathy, Victoria, and Will

Contents

Acknowledgments

Paul thanks . . .

David Letterman, it's an honor to take it to the stage with you every night—a true friend ✳ David Ritz, you are the answer to the question, "What is hip?" ✳ Daniel Fetter, without whom I wouldn't know where "1" is ✳ Eric Gardner, wise and conscientious counselor; I couldn't imagine a better manager ✳ Suzan Evans Hochberg, my favorite rock and roll lawyer chick ✳ Chris Albers, writer to the stars, labor negotiator; who says working for me doesn't lead anywhere? ✳ Chris Schukei, news anchor, marketing genius; who says working for me doesn't lead anywhere? ✳ Jann Wenner, your knowledge and loyalty are unwavering ✳ Phil Hordy, my good friend, thanks for my street and hooking up the Order of Canada ✳ David Smyth, for the gig that entitled this book ✳ Susan Collins Caploe, what a voice! ✳ Joel Peresman, the rock CEO with the movie-star looks ✳ Joel Gallen, talent by the gallon ✳ Bob Anuik, lead Fugitive who sang the hell out of "Jezebel" ✳ Frank De Michele, first bass man (Fugitives) ✳ Peter Demian, second bass man (Fugitives) who taught me "Stand By Me" ✳ Ian Rosser, third bass man (Fugitives), designed his own electric sitar—it's a cool world ✳ Don Murray, original drummer (Fugitives) ✳ Tom Schiller, neither of us turned out to be gay ✳ Rhonda Coulet, sang beautifully at Belushi's memorial ✳ Rita Riggs, turned me out as an eyewear addict ✳ Tony Reid, the ring-bearer on the unicycle ✳ Barbara Gaines, exec producer, Thanks for the

Memories ✳ Maria Pope, exec producer, Dream Weaver ✳ Tom Leopold, the industry vet ✳ John Evans, dug "Love's Theme" as well ✳ Lee Gabler, my buddy in the Area of Responsibility ✳ Jude Brennan, exec producer, still doesn't know what "Act 1" is ✳ Michael Lichtstein, it's his "Day in Rock" ✳ Danno and Laura Wolkoff, rock Cleveland ✳ Alan Cross, a funny, funny man ✳ John Sykes, a dear friend who gave me some unforgettable gigs ✳ Matt Roberts, supervising producer and lyricist extraordinaire ✳ Margo Lewis, agent/organist—what a combo! ✳ Rob Burnett, swingingest CEO ✳ Jill Leiderman, does it all ✳ Senator Marian "The Babe" Maloney, dear family friend ✳ Her Excellency Governor General Michele Jean, with deep respect ✳ Rob Cohen, for the Sammy plaque ✳ Gabrielle Lappa, honours with a "u" ✳ Charlotte Igoe, had a Hammond as well ✳ Lee Richardson, for slipping me into that reception line ✳ The Stangles, Jerry and Sheila, thanks for the support

David thanks . . .

Paul Shaffer, "King of 'Em All, Y'all" ✳ Suzanne Herz ✳ Steve Rubin ✳ David Vigliano ✳ Peter Gethers ✳ Claudia Herr ✳ Stacy Creamer ✳ Emily Mahon ✳ Geoff Martin ✳ Helen Ansari ✳ Rob Kaufman ✳ My gang: Roberta, Alison, Jessica, Jim, Henry, Charlotte, Alden, James, Esther, Elizabeth, the great Pops Ritz and all the family, including Harry Weinger and Alan Eisenstock

We'll Be Here For
the Rest of Our Lives

1971.

The Brass Rail.

I'm twenty-one, and I've made it. I'm playing on Yonge Street, Toronto's main drag, where clubs like the Zanzibar and the Coq d'Or feature rockers like Rompin' Ronnie Hawkins and David Clayton Thomas. To be honest, though, the Brass Rail is a little farther up the street on a slightly less swinging block.

Doesn't matter. I'm thrilled to be here and I'm thrilled to be providing musical accompaniment for the nightclub's topless dancers. These girls may be a bit frayed around the G-string, but to me they're simply irresistible. I'm also happy to see that many of my college pals, who have never before bothered to hear me play, are out in force. In fact, they're so interested in my music that they're sitting at ringside tables. As for me, I'm caught in an exquisite dichotomy: embarrassment versus erotic stimulation.

It's a grind—literally for the girls and metaphorically for me. My grind is the stringency of the set requirements: seven straight hours, from 6 p.m. to 1 a.m., fifty minutes on, ten off. I bring on the

*dancers at the top of the set, when they do one number "covered,"
then two topless. After a few tunes from the band, they return at
the bottom of the set for more of the same. So at the end of this
long and beautiful/awful night, it's time to wrap it up.*

*"Ladies and gentlemen," I intone, playing to my friends, "let's
hear it once again for the very lovely, extremely talented Brass
Rail Topless Go-Go Dancers. The exquisite Donna. The enchanting Shanda. The delightful LaShana. The priceless Tiffany. And
the irresistible Bree. We love them madly. Well, that's about it for
us. We are the Shaf-Tones. Please come back and see us. We'll be
here for the rest of our lives."*

And the sound made me absolutely crazy. Then there was the certain knowledge that Dylan, the most important poet of our generation, was also a *landsman*. Bobby Zimmerman was a fellow Jew.

In the seventies, I had heard that Bob had returned to his Orthodox roots. Supposedly he was studying with a Hasidic rabbi in Brooklyn. Then came the rumors that our man Zimmy had ventured beyond the Old Testament into the New. I didn't want to believe it. I clung to the notion that once they cut the tip, you're always hip.

Yet there he was, onstage in Studio 8H at 30 Rock in the middle of New York City, singing "You Got to Serve Somebody." And I knew damn well that "somebody" sure wasn't Moses. I was bothered and bewildered. Dylan was bewitched.

"Can we lose the cross, Jerry?" I whispered in Wexler's hairy ear.

"Oh, I wouldn't say anything," he said in a panic. "Bob takes this shit seriously."

"I'm kidding," I said.

But I wasn't.

The rolling stone rolled on. The planet took several spins, and several worlds later I was amazed to find myself on nightly television as musical director of *Late Night with David Letterman*. Word came down that on this particular night there were to be two guests. The first was the flamboyant pianist beloved by audiences in Las Vegas, none other than Liberace. The second was Dylan. Liberace was there to cook, Dylan to play.

"Hey, Dave," I said at the top of the show, "what a night! Liberace cooking? In my book, that cat always cooks. And Dylan—I'm shocked. Did you know he went electric?"

"Calm down, Paul," Dave said.

Chapter 1

Dylan and Me

Bob Dylan was standing two feet away from me. It was the late seventies, and I was the piano player on *Saturday Night Live.* I was talking with his current producer, the legendary Jerry Wexler, as we watched Dylan rehearse his band. I was right where I belonged. Surely God had blessed me by putting me in this favored position. Only one problem: Dylan was wearing a huge cross.

So what was the problem?

A little background information: I grew up in an Orthodox synagogue. I also grew up at the end of Highway 61. My hometown of Thunder Bay, Ontario, Canada, is at the northern extreme of that storied road. Thunder Bay is where my close friend Wayne Tanner, one of the original Dylanologists, turned me on to the great singer/songwriter. His album *Highway 61 Revisited* was the Talmud to the Torah of my life. I learned Al Kooper's high organ line and Paul Griffin's piano part on "Like a Rolling Stone" note for note, sound for sound. The keyboard combination helped define Dylan's new sound.

And the sound made me absolutely crazy. Then there was the certain knowledge that Dylan, the most important poet of our generation, was also a *landsman*. Bobby Zimmerman was a fellow Jew.

In the seventies, I had heard that Bob had returned to his Orthodox roots. Supposedly he was studying with a Hasidic rabbi in Brooklyn. Then came the rumors that our man Zimmy had ventured beyond the Old Testament into the New. I didn't want to believe it. I clung to the notion that once they cut the tip, you're always hip.

Yet there he was, onstage in Studio 8H at 30 Rock in the middle of New York City, singing "You Got to Serve Somebody." And I knew damn well that "somebody" sure wasn't Moses. I was bothered and bewildered. Dylan was bewitched.

"Can we lose the cross, Jerry?" I whispered in Wexler's hairy ear.

"Oh, I wouldn't say anything," he said in a panic. "Bob takes this shit seriously."

"I'm kidding," I said.

But I wasn't.

The rolling stone rolled on. The planet took several spins, and several worlds later I was amazed to find myself on nightly television as musical director of *Late Night with David Letterman*. Word came down that on this particular night there were to be two guests. The first was the flamboyant pianist beloved by audiences in Las Vegas, none other than Liberace. The second was Dylan. Liberace was there to cook, Dylan to play.

"Hey, Dave," I said at the top of the show, "what a night! Liberace cooking? In my book, that cat always cooks. And Dylan—I'm shocked. Did you know he went electric?"

"Calm down, Paul," Dave said.

After Dave and Liberace worked up a soulful soufflé, Dylan came on with a borrowed band. Nonetheless, his three-song set was powerful. His "License to Kill" killed. Afterwards, I couldn't keep from knocking on heaven's door. I had to bond with Dylan.

When I stuck my head in his dressing room, I saw that he was with his lovely and talented girlfriend, singer Clydie King.

"Hi, Bob," I said and, offering Clydie a smile, quoted Dylan himself: "What's a sweetheart like her doing in a place like this?"

Bob nodded in my direction. He didn't say a word.

"You know, Bob, you grew up just 130 miles to the south of my hometown in Canada. We're linked by Highway 61. And I gotta tell you something else, man. Just like you, I spent my growing-up years with my ear pressed against the transistor listening to those faraway southern radio stations. Just like you, I learned to love rhythm and blues. And hey, Bob, how about that Bobby Vee? You played piano with him, I could sing both parts to 'Take Good Care of My Baby.' We're soul brothers."

I waited for his response, but none came. He just seemed to be staring into space. But I kept going.

"When you sang Roy Head's 'Treat Her Right' in rehearsal today, Bob, it sounded just great. I wish you'd record it."

Finally Bob looked me in the eyes. I'd obviously made a connection.

"Paul, do you think you could introduce me to Larry 'Bud' Melman?" he asked, referring to the lovable nerd who was a running character on our show.

I thought Dylan was kidding.

But he wasn't.

Years later, I encountered a different Bob at the Rock and Roll Hall of Fame induction dinner. This Bob enthusiastically grabbed his guitar and joined the post-dinner jam. His fellow jammers that night were, among others, Mick Jagger, Tina Turner, George Harrison, Ringo Starr, and Jeff Beck. Bill Graham and I were running the thing together. In those years there were no rehearsals. The jams were completely spontaneous.

As a finale, I called "Like a Rolling Stone." Dylan graciously took the mic and began to sing, backed up by Mick and Tina. After the second chorus, Bill came out and whispered in my ear, "Guitar cutting session." He wanted the guitarists to play against each other. I set them up—first Beck, then Harrison, then all the others. The guitar riffs were stupendous, but now it was time to get back to the song. I looked at Bob and gestured toward the mic. He stared back blankly. He clearly didn't know what to do.

I moved in next to Dylan, realizing I had to lay it out for him. He needed to sing. So instead of gesturing, I just whispered in his ear . . .

"How does it feel?"

Wow! I thought, *I'm directing Dylan to sing his own song with his own lyric.*

Then he got it. He went to the mic and sang with Zimmerman zest, "How does it feel . . . to be on your own . . ."

And with that, if you'll forgive the pun, our poet laureate got us out of a jam.

✦ ✦ ✦

Then came the Good Friday when Dylan crucified me, only to resurrect me on the Sunday. This passion played out on the

stage of Radio City Music Hall. In those years we would sometimes broadcast a Letterman anniversary special. And for the
tenth anniversary Dave wanted Dylan.

"Hey, Paul, Bob's agreed to come on," Dave said. "He'll play
with the all-star band you've put together. Who do you have this
year?"

"Carole King, Steve Vai, Chrissie Hynde, Doc Severinsen,
Emmylou Harris, the James Brown horns—and that's just for
starters."

"I'd love for Dylan to sing 'Stuck Inside of Mobile with the
Memphis Blues Again.' "

"Not sure it's enough of an anthem, Dave. This is going to
be monstrous. Do you know 'One of Us Must Know' from
Blonde on Blonde?"

"Not sure. Play it for me, Paul."

I slipped in the disc and within two bars Dave stopped me.
"No," he said.

We went back and forth until we landed on the inevitable. It
had to be "Like a Rolling Stone."

"You call Bob," said Dave. "You're the one who has the rapport with him."

"Right. Dylan loves me."

Dylan was hard to find. He lives on the road but is never
anywhere for more than a day. Finally, I tracked him down in
some motel in Des Moines and placed a call. When I told him
that we'd be honored if he'd play "Like a Rolling Stone," he
was lukewarm at best.

"That's a little obvious," he said. "There's gotta be something else."

"Dave and I really see 'Like a Rolling Stone' as our grand
finale."

The songwriter sighed. "It's a big catalog, Paul."

I was surprised to hear Bob Dylan sounding like music publisher Don Kirshner. Oh well, as an industry vet once told me, "It's all show biz. Totie Fields, John Coltrane—they're the same. Well, Totie could improvise."

"Tell you what, Paul. I'll be rehearsing my band in New York next week. Come by and we'll kick some things around."

When I showed up at the studio, Bob and the band were immersed in Paul Simon's "Hazy Shade of Winter." I'd later learn that Dylan dealt with writer's block by playing other people's songs. It loosened him up.

When they were done, he acknowledged me and indicated the piano.

"Let's try 'Rolling Stone,'" he said. I was pleasantly surprised. With the band behind me, I rose to the occasion. Paul Griffin would have been proud. Dylan was happy. It was on.

The next Friday, though, found me in something of a stew. Dylan had come to rehearse with my all-star band but, lo and behold, he needed to be gone before sundown. His long and winding spiritual road had led him back to Orthodox Judaism. He refused to play on the Sabbath. I had no time to waste. I placed him in front of the band and counted off. For reasons that were unclear, he refused to sing.

"Let's go again," I said.

This time he strummed his guitar a little, but nothing came out of his mouth.

I approached him gingerly. "What's going on?" I asked.

"I don't need this band to play my music," he said. "Me, I got four pieces. That's all I need. All this other stuff don't make no sense."

Panicked, I motioned to my assistant. "Get Dylan's manager over here," I ordered.

Jeff Kramer, Dylan's man, was an old friend. I spoke plainly. "Bob hates the band, Jeff. I don't know what to do."

"Just keep going," said Jeff. "He always does this."

But when I ran the tune the third time, Dylan still stayed silent.

So with the sun setting in the west, I called it a day. "Good *Shabbos*, Bob," I said as he left the stage. "See you tomorrow."

His exit left me in a state of uncertainty. I couldn't understand what was wrong. Carole King was wailing on that piano part. Steve Vai was channeling Hendrix on guitar. I was channeling Kooper on organ. What could be bad?

Saturday night arrived. We were to do a dress rehearsal before a live Radio City audience at 7 p.m., then the real show at 10. Lots of funny stuff in the first two acts. Then the third act: Bob Dylan singing "Like a Rolling Stone" backed by my superstar band.

Before Bob's entrance for the dress, I got an idea. While the band warmed up on "Everybody Must Get Stoned," I stood at his mic.

"Let me hear what Bob will hear," I asked the engineer.

I heard very little. It turned out Bob's monitor had nothing in it. The stage was so big, the hall so cavernous, all Bob had heard yesterday was a dull roar. No wonder he hated it. He couldn't hear it.

Then I went to work. "Give him some drums," I told the engineer. "Give him some bass. He needs to hear piano. Put some of my organ in there. Mix in a little guitar."

I did the best I could with the time that I had. At least now he had a halfway-decent mix.

When it came time for him to sing, I held my breath. His mouth moved, and some of that wonderful reediness came out, but I'd have to say he gave me only 30 percent.

Between the dress and air shows, Chrissie Hynde took me to Dylan's dressing room. If you're going to see Bob, let a woman lead the way.

"Everything okay, Bob?" I asked.

"It's sounding a little better," he said.

"Will you be able to sing?"

"Long as you can play."

Well, I did play. And so did the band. And, I'm happy to report, Mr. Dylan did sing. This time he gave me a more than decent 70 percent.

By the time I arrived at the after-party, Bob was already there. He and Chrissie had their guitars out and seemed to be in sync. I sat down beside him and asked, "How do you think it went?"

"Lemme be honest with you, Paul. When I'm in the hotel room at night, I flip on the show only to catch a glimpse of Larry 'Bud.' I've never really keyed in on you. But tonight, man, I saw that you know what you're doing. If I had realized this could have been something, I would have given more."

I looked at my watch. It was 2 a.m. Bob Dylan may have crucified me on Friday, but here, on Sunday morning, my soul was resurrected.

Over time, I've lost track of Dylan's movements in the spiritual continuum. I myself have remained consistent. I'm Jewish, I'm happy. I love the tradition. Like my favorite ball player, Sandy Koufax, I don't play on Yom Kippur, the holiest time of the Jewish year, the sacred Day of Atonement. Some of my musician friends, though, have had challenges surrounding this issue.

My buddy, the great trumpeter Lew Soloff, was playing with Blood, Sweat and Tears in Europe. He was actually walking on stage when a fellow band member happened to say, "Hey, Lew, I thought you were Jewish. Don't you know today's Yom Kippur?" Lew hadn't consulted his calendar and was caught in a quandary. It was one minute to showtime. He made a snap decision. "I'll play," he said, "but I won't improvise."

Another great trumpeter, Alan Rubin from *Saturday Night Live* and the Blues Brothers Band, once met me at the Fifth Avenue Synagogue on Yom Kippur eve—Kol Nidre night.

"Good *yom tov*, Alan," I said, "you're beaming."

"Who wouldn't be?" he said. "I just came from Caesar's Retreat."

"The massage parlor?" I asked.

"The whorehouse," he said. "Man, I was on. I made *love* to that chick."

With a voice that invoked the ages, the cantor sang, *"Kol Nidre...v'esorei..."*

Two years later, I was reading the New York *Daily News* when I noticed that Caesar's Retreat had been closed down and was the object of a grand jury inquiry. Records had been seized. Alan Rubin called to say that his name had been listed among the patrons and he was due to testify. I wished him luck. After his big day, I called him.

"How'd it go?" I asked.

"Well, Paul, they put me on the stand. The attorney was tough. He grilled me."

"What'd he say?"

" 'Mr. Rubin, do you recall patronizing an establishment by the name of Caesar's Retreat?' "

" 'Yes sir, I do,' I said. 'It was innocent fun.' "

" 'I understand that, Mr. Rubin, but why, sir, were you at this particular place at this particular time?' "

" 'Well, it was Yom Kippur eve, and I wanted to make sure I had something to atone for.' "

In my case, I have much to atone for. In order to understand that process fully, we must go back to the beginning.

Two Jews' Blues

Welcome to the Orthodox synagogue of my childhood, Shaarey Shomayim, a name that means "Gates of Heaven." I'm glad you could make it for this Tuesday evening affair. It'll be a short and simple recital given by two star bar mitzvah students who both happen to play the piano.

First up, Paul Shaffer.

Paul may be shy, but he's clearly a prodigy. He plays his Mozart sonatina with clarity and precision.

Next up, Paul's rival, Marvin Slobotsky. Paul expects Marvin to play a classical piece in the Mozartian mode. But Marvin surprises Paul. Marvin surprises everyone. Marvin breaks into "Jealousy," a flashy number made popular by that irrepressible Cuban, Xavier Cugat. Marvin plays the piece with a confidence that dazzles. Hearing it, you envision some macho male dancer dragging his scantily clad partner across the floor in a daring Apache dance. Slobotsky captures this extreme melodrama and, under his nimble fingers, brings the story to life. His rendition of "Jealousy" is a tour de force. As the congregants cheer wildly,

Paul can't help but join them, even as he himself is consumed with jealousy.

Before leaving, Paul overhears his mother's friend Yetti Helper whisper to her husband, Mendy, "That Marvin . . . he's our own Liberace."

For weeks Paul is resigned to the freezing-cold fact: He can never match Slobotsky.

But then comes a revelation. It comes, as do so many others, via the *Ed Sullivan Show*.

Paul and his folks are watching together as they do every Sunday night. Dad likes to point out the performers who are wearing good toupees and those who aren't. On this particular night, Tony Bennett sings "I Left My Heart In San Francisco."

"Rugsville!" exclaims Dad. "But it's a good wig and a great singer."

Next up—the piano playing duo of Ferrante & Teicher.

"Bad toupees," says Dad, "and schmaltzy piano players."

Dad's right. Ferrante & Teicher are bizarre-looking in their matching horn-rimmed glasses and matching wigs. They play in a Hollywood-meets-the-classics mode, very Mantovani. Their calling card—"The Grand Twins of the Twin Grands"— is certainly schmaltzy. So is their opening number, a Viennese waltz that, played in their four-handed style, has Paul yawning. But their second selection catches Paul's attention. It's "Exodus," the theme song from the movie of the same name. They infuse the composition with a kind of heroism that appeals to Paul and, even more importantly, will surely appeal to the members of Shaarey Shomayim. It's schmaltz for sure, but good schmaltz. Moreover, Ferrante & Teicher's interpretation is highly evocative. It paints a picture of the Promised Land.

Paul is determined to paint that picture himself. In the

movie, Paul Newman, the handsomest Jew since the beginning of time, is a Jewish freedom fighter. Leon Uris, the guy who wrote the book, is America's favorite Jewish novelist. In fact, *Exodus* is Jewish Hollywood to the max. Jews all over the world are embracing it. It doesn't matter that two of its stars—Eva Marie Saint and Sal Mineo—are not of Paul's spiritual persuasion; they've worked something out.

In short, *Exodus* is a great movie and "Exodus" is an equally great song. Paul has his vehicle.

Once the Sullivan show is over, Paul runs to the piano and begins to figure out "Exodus" by ear. It takes a while, but he masters the chords and Hebraic harmonies. He infuses the composition with the very heroism that fueled its creation. Paul views the theme as not merely the triumph of the Jewish people, but his own future triumph over Marvin Slobotsky.

Several weeks later, when the congregation is gathered for another musical evening, Paul is prepared. Marvin opens the recital with a repeat performance of "Jealousy." Paul expected as much. If it ain't broke, don't fix it. Marvin gives another dazzling performance.

Paul is thinking, *okay, now it's my turn.*

Paul's parents are sitting in the front row. Marvin Slobotsky is seated but a few feet from them. Paul feels his stare. Paul feels his glare. Fellow congregants occupy the remaining thirty-five or forty folding chairs.

Paul lifts his hands, attacks the keys, and goes to town. He has practiced this piece a thousand times and he owns it. It is his. He takes no prisoners, shows no mercy, puts into it every ounce of every emotion felt by every Jew since Father Abraham got the party started.

The result?

Tears streaming down his mother's face.

A proud smile on his father's face.

A hardened grimace on Marvin Slobotsky's face.

A satisfied Cheshire-cat smile on Paul's face.

Everyone standing and cheering.

And best of all, Yetti Helper's words to his mother: "That Paul of yours . . . he's our own George Gershwin."

Chapter 3

B3

A month passed—a month, I confess, during which I felt a sense of superiority. After all, I had bested the best.

It was Wednesday afternoon and I had just completed my bar mitzvah lesson. I was leaving the classroom when I heard a startling sound coming from that same social hall where Marvin Slobotsky and I had locked horns. I heard an elongated note that approximated a human cry. I stopped dead in my tracks, turned around, and went to find the source of the sound.

Marvin Slobotsky was playing an instrument that I immediately recognized. It was the Hammond B3 electric organ that belonged to Miss Noni Cooper, a well-known figure in our town. I had first encountered Noni in the ballroom of the Royal Edward Hotel, an establishment frequented by the city's professional class. The place had the look of England after the collapse of the empire. Every year that's where my parents would take me, their only child, to celebrate New Year's Day. It was tradition. Noni's organ performance was also tradition, as was the presence of her poodle, Princess Anne, named, of course, for the daughter of our beloved monarch, Elizabeth II. The princess poodle would sleep soundly as Noni played waltzes by Strauss and dusty old pop tunes from long ago: "Come Back to Sorrento," "Ah, Sweet Mystery of Life," "Beyond the Blue Horizon." At a certain point Mr. John McCullough, a handsome gentleman in a blue holiday tux, would step up and offer his version of "Moon River." I liked the sound of Noni's Hammond B3, skating rink reverb and all. And I have to admit that John milked "Moon River" pretty good.

But Slobotsky wasn't playing this Hammond B3; he was rocking it hard. In his hands, the two-keyboard organ sounded like an entire band, with sounds—deep moans and startling cries—that had an emotional punch that was very un-Noni.

"Paul, you've got a good ear," said Marvin condescendingly. "How can I make the upper keyboard sound like the lower one?"

With that, I sat beside him and began to tinker along, adjusting stops and drawbars, playing a lick, learning as I was doing.

"Listen to this," Marvin said. "Here's a sound that works great for Del Shannon's stuff."

I'd never heard of Del Shannon, but when Marvin launched into "Runaway" I recognized the song from the radio. Together we figured out the instrument—how to operate the stops and wooden pedals—and while he played the top keyboard, I played the bottom. Hours later, we were still jamming hard.

That night I was late for dinner, and Dad wanted to know where I'd been.

"In synagogue," I said.

"Doing what?"

"Rocking out on the Hammond B3."

"Your mother cooked a hot meal that's now cold, and you're rocking out on an electric organ?"

"I love it," I said. "The thing can almost talk."

"Forget talk," he said. "Eat! And don't be late again."

A couple of nights later, I was flipping through Dad's LPs. Al Hibbler. Oscar Peterson. Sarah Vaughan. Billy Eckstine. Ray Charles.

I pulled out the Ray Charles album called *Genius Plus Soul Equals Jazz.*

I dropped the record on the turntable and put the needle on "I've Got News for You." And there was that sound again. It was the Hammond B3 and Ray had it humming.

Naturally I immediately wanted a Hammond B3 of my own. In spite of their support of my music, my parents said this large, cumbersome, and expensive instrument was out of the question.

"But how am I ever going to learn it?" I asked.

My mother happened to have a friend with a Hammond. Her name was Yvonne Sherman. She was of the Christian persuasion, an upper-class lady with a house filled with antique mirrors, gold crosses, and fussy furniture.

Every time I went to Mrs. Sherman's, she invited me to sit at her organ. My mom requested that I play "Satin Doll." Dutifully, I did so. But when the Ellington ditty was over, I turned to the songs nearest and dearest to my own heart: "Any Day Now" by Chuck Jackson; "Happy Organ" by Dave "Baby" Cortez; the Four Seasons' "Save It for Me"—with its lovely organ solo— and the Seasons' "Candy Girl."

I viewed the organ metaphorically. It represented the universe in its entirety. The various drawbars were built to create the series of harmonic overtones. Manipulate them correctly and create harmony. Manage them poorly and cause discord. Such is life.

The organ wasn't there simply to be learned; it had to be understood. It was a mystery with many voices, many moods, many modes of expression.

"You're really spending a lot of time on that instrument," said Dad.

"I can't stay away from it," I explained.

"Nothing wrong with that, son. All the greats played the organ. Fats Waller. Count Basie. And of course Jimmy Smith."

I mentioned Ray Charles.

"No one plays it better than Ray," added Dad. "Ray's reason enough to keep playing the organ. Not that you'll be running into Ray Charles anytime soon, but if you ever do, you'll have something to show him."

Chapter 4

Running into Ray Charles

I leap ahead some fifteen years.

November 1977. In a few weeks I'd be turning twenty-eight.

Through the grace of God, I'd made my exodus from Thunder Bay. (Further details to follow.) It was the second season of *Saturday Night Live*, the hottest, edgiest comedy show to hit TV in decades. The cast—Aykroyd, Belushi, Jane, Garrett, Gilda, Laraine, and Billy Murray—was all abuzz because Ray Charles was not only appearing as a musical guest, but hosting as well.

Interesting: Lorne Michaels's original idea was to have Ray fill the musical slot only. When Ray heard the offer, he said, "That's cool, but why can't I be the host?" "There are a lot of lines to learn," his manager told him, "and you won't be able to read the cue cards." "There are a lot of notes on the piano," Ray told his manager, "but I've managed to memorize them. I think I can learn a few jokes." Lorne agreed and flew Ray to New York for the gig.

Howard Shore was musical director and I was the piano

player. I'd later enjoy a bigger role on the show, but during these early days I was your grateful and humble sideman. My humility was rewarded when Howard asked me if I would play Hammond B3 behind the first verse of Ray singing "Oh, What a Beautiful Morning."

Would I!

Would Gilbert work with Sullivan?

Would Sammy sub for Sinatra?

Would Dean play straight for Jerry?

What a moment!

What a dream come true!

What incredible pressure!

What irony!

It was Ray, of course, whose blues-soaked approach to keyboards served as my model. I loved others: I loved Ray's protégé Billy Preston, whose Sly Stone–produced album, *The Wildest Organ in Town*, I studied like the Bible; I loved Jimmy Smith, whose rendition of "The Cat" had all us would-be hipsters howling with delight; I loved the great Booker T. Jones of the MGs and the great Felix Cavaliere of the Rascals, two monster musicians whose licks I copped with great diligence. But Ray was different. Ray was the Genius.

Thus my motivation had never been keener. Nor had my nerves ever been more on edge. Our first encounter was the rehearsal onstage in 8H, the famous studio from which the show was broadcast. I arrived early to make certain the Hammond was up and running. The other band members, nearly as excited as I, filed in—our fearless leader Howard Shore, tuba player and baritone saxist Howard Johnson, and the rest. We waited a couple of minutes, chatting nervously about what it was going to be like to play with Ray. This was as up close and personal as it gets.

Led by his valet, Ray walked quickly to the stage. He was all business. He had with him members of his original small band from the 1950s, whose legendary status among musicians loomed nearly as large as Ray's.

Ray was in charge. He wanted to run through the opening number, "I Can See Clearly Now," perhaps his answer to his manager's skepticism about his inability to host. Seconds after the band began to play, Ray stopped us and said to Howard Johnson, "You're playing your tuba too high."

We began again.

Ray stopped us again.

"Still too high," Ray barked.

He snapped his head as he spoke, clapping his hands to stress his point. My performance anxiety, elevated to begin with, rose even higher when I saw how Ray dealt with my friend Howard. It took three tries before the Genius was finally pleased.

Next, my big moment. "Oh, What a Beautiful Morning."

The opening featured organ behind Ray's vocal. That meant I'd have a chance to improvise. The thought was equally thrilling and terrifying.

Ray counted off. The band was off and running, but I wasn't. I could hardly play, and when I did, the result was lame. Blues licks were my specialty—blues licks I had learned by studying Ray—but now, at this moment of truth, my blues licks sucked. I knew it. The band knew it. Ray knew it. Ray stopped the band.

"Organ!" Ray barked. "Play with some soul."

My heart dropped to the floor. Dead silence among my

bandmates. Time stopped. Then Howard Johnson, a great and valiant black man, spoke up in my defense. "He's got it, Ray," said Howard. "Let's just start again."

This time, in a split second, I reached far down into my soul, so far that I went all the way back to my dad's Ray Charles albums. I found the riffs and I delivered them. The Genius didn't smile, but he also didn't stop the band to criticize me. When we finished the entire song, the Genius turned toward me and said, "Yeah, that's more like it."

It was nothing like the congregation of Shaarey Shomayim giving me a standing ovation after I played "Exodus." It was better. Man, it was a whole lot better.

Chapter 5

With Your Kind Indulgence . . .

Let me introduce the beautiful couple that brought me into the world. I loved them both dearly.

How about it for my mother, everybody.

Mom was Shirley Eleanor Wood Shaffer, a native of Toronto and a gal of great dignity and class who dreamed of living in Paris's 16th arrondissement or Manhattan's Upper East Side. Mom was an antique collector. She was all about her delicate Crown Derby china, her love of Toulouse-Lautrec, and her fondness for a nice sipping sherry. She was an oil painter, a Bohemian du Maurier smoker, an exquisite host, and a doting mother.

Among my earliest memories is Mom at the piano. She had great style and poise; her touch was light; and when she played Gershwin and Chopin, I'd sit on the floor and lean my head against the piano leg, the sounds seeping into my little soul. At age six, she started me on piano lessons and I immediately began playing by ear. I worked out the black-notes-only William Tell Overture and was soon copying practically everything

I heard on the radio. Once I started playing, Mom stopped. It was as though her work was done. She never touched the piano again.

When it came to music, my mother also had a sense of humor that surely influenced my own.

Example:

At an alarmingly young age, her little Paul had fallen for rock and roll. After discovering the Ronettes and the Four Seasons, the yin and yang of his musical identity, he applied his classical piano training to the Top Ten tunes of the day. He learned them by ear and played them incessantly. The first single he bought was the Supremes' "You Can't Hurry Love," and his first LP *The Four Seasons' Golden Vault of Hits*. But Shaffer was never a record collector. He was a keyboard slugger whose interest focused on two-fisted duplications of the sounds he'd heard on the radio. He was smitten with the heroic confections of producer Phil Spector and the erotic cries of Phil's onetime wife Ronnie. It all came together in a song inspired by Ronnie and sung by the Four Seasons' high tenor Frankie Valli. Appropriately enough, the tune was entitled "Ronnie," and the lyrics had our young hero lost in a daydream of sweet romance: "I'll go on living and keep on forgiving because . . . you were my first love."

"Ronnie" was indeed Paul's first love. He had first seen her with the Ronettes singing "Be My Baby" on *American Bandstand*. Her high bouffant hair, her tantalizingly short skirt, her heavy mascara, and that voice—sweet as honey, wicked as sin. She was the very definition of feminine heat. He had learned to play "Ronnie" on piano, memorized the words, and ingested it whole.

"I'll go on living and keep on forgiving" became his mantra.

To his own spirited accompaniment, he sang the song over and over again. He rushed home from school to attack the piano so he could re-create the mood that set his imagination soaring.

"I'll go on living and keep on forgiving" was the sound that filled the Shaffer household.

He couldn't stop playing it, couldn't stop singing it, couldn't stop offering up this cry of teenage angst.

"I'll go on living and keep on forgiving," he emoted with even more impassioned conviction.

"For God's sake, Paul!" his mom shouted from the kitchen one day. "Forgive Ronnie already and come eat your lunch!"

＊ ＊ ＊

Meet my dad.

Bernard Shaffer, barrister, solicitor, notary public, respected civic leader, skilled litigator, and life of the party. He had a little temper on him, but a great passion for music—not just any music, mind you, but the most sophisticated jazz on the planet. Dad was a connoisseur. And although he liked his role as big legal eagle in the little nest of Thunder Bay, he, like Mom, felt the allure of brighter lights.

Example:

The Shaffer family is off to Vegas!

Young Paul is not yet a teenager, but fully aware of Sin City's well-advertised enticements. Most of those enticements are musical. This is the early sixties, the heyday of the Rat Pack. Sinatra is at his ring-a-ding-dingiest. Dean, Peter, and Joey are by his side, and Sammy has converted. All's right with the world.

When Bernard, Shirley, and Paul arrive, the sun is shining and the city is sparkling. Paul is riveted by the cabdriver's spe-

cial patois. The Desert Inn is referred to as the "D.I." The Tropicana is the "Trop." The Riviera is the "Riv." The language carries a magic of its own.

Walking into the Sahara, I'm galvanized by the ringing
sounds of the slot machines, but even more by the swinging
sounds of the band. My heart leaps at the sight of Louis Prima
performing in the open lounge. Louis's backup band is the
world-famous Witnesses led by tenor man Sam Butera. Prima's
duet partner is Keely Smith who, with her perfectly-in-place
black bangs and stoic facade, is the prototype for Cher. Louis is
singing "When You're Smiling" in his "Louis Armstrong meets
Dean Martin" voice. Then he's singing "Buona Sera," then
"Angelina," then he and Keely trade licks on "That Old Black
Magic." Riveted by the show, I refuse to move as my parents tell
me our bags are being transported up to our room and it's time
to freshen up.

When we reach the room, my father immediately scans the
Vegas entertainment guide and gets mad.

"The travel agent told me she was at the Sahara," he says.
"Now I see she's at the Riviera. Well, if that's the case we're
moving to the Riviera."

"Bernie," says Shirley, "we just got here."

My father doesn't care. "We're here but she's not. We're
leaving."

"Who's she?" I ask.

"The Divine One," he answers.

"Sarah, Dad?" I ask.

"Yes, Sarah," he says, pronouncing the name like a prayer.
"Sarah Vaughan."

Bags in tow, we check out of the Sahara and grab a cab for the
Riv. I love scooting around Vegas, especially in pursuit of jazz.

The Riv is cool, although inside it looks just like the Sahara. Another endless ocean of slots.

But that evening, the music in the lounge—Sarah's music—*is* different. It's a world away from Louis, Keely, and Sam. It's quiet; it's subtle; it swings gently, firmly, intoxicatingly; but mostly it emanates from a vocal prowess that, according to my dad, "creates the sound of honey-coated perfection."

I view the show not from my parents' table—kids aren't allowed in the lounge—but standing up on a raised area surrounded by a low railing that lets me see Sarah from afar. She is wonderful. My elevated position also allows me to lean over and stare into the deep cleavage of the waitresses, who are also wonderful.

Sassy Sarah sings a set of standards, the highlight of which is "Misty." The audience gives her a standing ovation, with Bernie and Shirley leading the cheers. Dad turns around to make sure I'm still there. He nods his head as if to say, "Son, take note. This is the music that matters." I do take note. I also see how Sarah, upon reaching the bridge, allows her pianist to seamlessly complete the vocal line as the spotlight moves from her to him. The Divine One disappears, only to return with an even more baroque lick. The audience is surprised and delighted. I understand that jazz and show business are not complete strangers.

Ironically, when we return to Thunder Bay I'll discover a different music by Sarah: "Broken Hearted Melody," her only record to reach the hit parade. Neither she nor my father liked the song—it wasn't jazz, it wasn't a Gershwin-style standard, it was mere pop—but I loved it. In fact, it opened up my ears. It had the same chord changes as Gene McDaniels's "Hundred Pounds of Clay" and represented an advance beyond the basic rock and roll song structure—four chords instead of three. Within days, I was rocking that fourth chord.

Back in Vegas, though, I was in love with Sarah's fabulous standards and the waitresses' fabulous bosoms. I figured this was surely the high point of my Vegas experience, but I figured wrong. As Steve Allen wrote, this was only "the start of something big."

Something big turned out to be something late. The notion of "late," incidental to some, loomed large in my personal mythology. It was in Vegas that I learned the inviolable axiom "the later the hipper."

"Take a nap," said my father, the day before we were scheduled to fly back to the frozen north.

"I want to go swimming," I said, thinking of the bikini-clad waitresses who served poolside.

"Then nap in a lounge chair," he urged, "because I have a special treat tonight."

"More Sarah, Dad?"

"No, a by-invitation-only late show that doesn't start till 1 a.m. It's the show Juliet Prowse does so other entertainers on the Strip can see her after they get off."

"And we've got seats?" I asked.

"Ringside!"

I've been told that Marcel Proust described the socialites in turn-of-the-century Paris with poetic brilliance. They say that Henry James captured high society on Washington Square in a way that will never be duplicated. I cannot compete with the literary masters of yesteryear, nor will I try. I invoke those names, however, only to let you know how I yearn to do justice to what I experienced that night at Juliet Prowse's by-invitation-only show that began, as her then-boyfriend Sinatra termed it, "in the wee small hours of the morning."

You know, there are show-biz buzzes and then there are show-biz *buzzes*.

This buzz hit me as soon as my parents and I got off the elevator. The slots were still ringing, the roulette wheels still turning, but there was a stream of energy even stronger than the gaming passion that flowed through the casino floor straight to the showroom. Despite the late hour, my state of fatigue had morphed into a state of high excitement.

As we entered the showroom, my dad shmeared the maître d' a twenty to seat us near the stage, but our table turned out to be in the rear. As Dad tried to better our position, my eyes were jumping out of my head. I was craning my neck so violently I nearly twisted my head off. I wanted to see stars. I did see stars, or at least I thought I did. Wasn't that Frank walking in with his famous confidant Jilly? Wasn't that Buddy Hackett, the comic from the Sullivan show? And hey, speaking of comics, wasn't that Fat Jack Leonard, whose take-my-wife jokes were my folks' favorites? That *had* to be Red Buttons. That *had* to be Shirley MacLaine. That *had* to be Bob Mitchum. "No," said Mom, "that's Van Heflin." I recognized—or at least I thought I did— Jerry Lewis, another early idol, whose yearly telethon became as sacred to me as fasting on Yom Kippur. "That's not Jerry," said Dad, "that's Jan Murray."

"I know the difference between Jerry and Jan," I said. "That's Jerry."

"Doesn't matter," said Mom, "they're all here."

Mom was right. The world was here. The world that remained unknown to the average man and woman was making itself known to me. The world of entertainers, usually hidden in dressing rooms and darkened limos, had, like a gorgeous woman stepping out of her clothes, suddenly exposed itself to me.

"Holy shit!" I heard someone behind me say. "It's the Great One! Jackie Gleason!"

As if being in the same room with so many stars wasn't enough, minutes before showtime we were ushered up to the ringside table Dad had coveted. We were practically in the spotlight.

We soon learned why. Opening comic Jackie Gayle needed a little kid as a foil. The waiter spotted me as a prime candidate and moved us up front.

Gayle called me to the stage. Surprisingly, I wasn't the least bit nervous. He asked me how many TVs we had in our house. I said, "One."

His joke depended upon our having more than one TV.

"Don't you have more than one?" he asked.

"No," I answered in a deadpan tone that rivaled Jack Benny's. "Just one."

And with that, I wrecked Jackie Gayle's act. He sent me back to my seat. He was glowering, but I was glowing. I was in show business!

When our salads arrived, the waiter asked me, "What kind of dressing, sir?"

Always a picky eater, I said, "No dressing."

"No dressing?" the waiter repeated. "That's the way to treat girls, not salad."

Mom shot the waiter a menacing look, as if to say, "Careful, this is a proper young Canadian you're addressing."

A few minutes later the orchestra swelled and Juliet appeared, covered from head to toe in feathers. Then, in a flash, the feathers fell and my life changed. My view of womanhood changed. Her moves, her curves, her bends and bounces had me soaring over the moon.

"Does she have to get undraped in every single number?" asked my mom.

"Please, God," I silently prayed, *"let her get undraped in every single number."*

God granted my prayer.

At the end of her last number, I looked at my little Davy Crockett wristwatch and saw it was nearly 3 a.m.

"Happy?" Mom asked me.

"Boy, am I happy," I said. "I've never been happier."

* * *

There were other happy out-of-town moments with my parents. If Vegas was one temple of entertainment for show-biz-loving Jews, the other was surely Miami Beach. It was there, in the splendor of the Eden Roc Hotel (close to the famed Fontainebleau), where we caught Billy Daniels, the over-the-top song stylist with the big-bottomed black voice. Don't let anyone tell you that Billy Daniels didn't know his audience. He closed with "My Yiddishe Mama." The Jews *plotzed.* His opening act: Myron Cohen. Cohen was king of the Jewish joke. But as my parents pointed out to me, the more Yiddish his punch lines, the more British-sounding his setups. Man, Mom and Dad were hip! And perhaps the greatest manifestation of their hipness came in the form of recreation and libation. They knew how to throw a party.

Let's go . . .

Chapter 6

Shaffer A-Go-Go

Cocktail parties were essential. In fact, social drinking and its ensuing merriment were Mom and Dad's way of coping with the Canadian climate. They lived their lives as they imagined Sinatra lived his. He had his clan; they had theirs. They had a party culture that involved a great deal of creativity. It also involved me.

There was, for instance, the beatnik party where Mom dressed in a leotard and Dad wore a beret. A hip singer and comic named Don Francks came all the way from Toronto to entertain. He covered songs by the jazz duo Jackie and Roy, in that cool vibrato-less style of crooning. Dad informed me that I was to learn bongos. "What's a beatnik party without bongos?" asked Dad.

I liked beating the bongos. In fact, I beat them night and day until Mom cut me off. "Stop beating the bongos and beat it down to the corner to get me a pack of du Mauriers."

When Dad got home, it was "Get back on the bongos. This beatnik party has got to swing wild."

To see my parents, respectable citizens by day, turn into make-believe beatniks by night was strange, especially when their behavior was fueled by my bongo grooves and Johnnie Walker Red. And especially when my father, before reciting the poetry of Lawrence Ferlinghetti, decided to break into his famous Al Jolson impression, falling on one knee and cryin' "Mammy" and "Swanee." Now I was accompanying him on piano. I did so with a degree of trepidation because, depending upon how many precisely proportioned martinis Dad had downed, my playing could throw him off. Other times, when he'd ask me to play a classical piece before, say, an important circuit court judge, I might not be completely prepared. This would incense Dad. He didn't hesitate to criticize me right then and there, as if he were cross-examining a witness in a court of law. I hated these public humiliations but dared not complain.

Don't misunderstand. In most ways my father was a sweetheart. He was also a hoot. While at the University of Toronto, he was a star in the collegiate follies and had worked with Wayne and Shuster, the great Canadian comedy team. He had dreamed of a career in show business, but the Depression hit and caution kept him home. Subsequently he called the courtroom his stage. I understood why he liked to ape Al Jolson and consort with Don Francks, whom he considered the Lenny Bruce of the Frozen Frontier. He wanted to entertain, to be noticed, to host his friends and peers with originality and humor. But Dad also struggled with a hidden rage whose source I could never trace. The cocktail party was a time when his complexities and contradictions might unexpectedly surface.

Mom anticipated such celebrations as eagerly as Dad. When she imbibed, her normally low-volume voice got loud and her laughter got raucous. Her transformation made me a touch uncomfortable. I preferred Mom to be plain ol' Mom, not the Mom who said to me, "Paul, your father and I are having a twist party. Can you find us a go-go dancer for Saturday night? We'll bring in a stage and it'll be absolutely marvelous."

It was a challenge. My folks had seen Chubby Checker on the *Ed Sullivan Show*. They knew about the Peppermint Lounge in New York City. But their real aim was to re-create Arthur, the trendy disco owned by Richard Burton's former wife, Sybil. That's where all the stars twisted the night away. My folks wanted to do the same and they reasoned—quite correctly—that a go-go dancer would spirit the party.

After some research, I managed to find a girl who, at eighteen, was a year older than I. She had appeared on a local TV dance show, and her name was Bonnie Carniato. Her costume consisted of a flimsy fringy skirt, a sparkly top, and the requisite white go-go boots. Her best attribute was her long legs. And, take it from me, the girl could twist. "Twistin' the Night Away" became the recurrent motif. I must have played the goddamn thing a hundred times.

"Fabulous party!" Mom exclaimed at 2:30 a.m.

I was exhausted. My fingers ached from banging out all those twist numbers. But Bonnie's appreciative fans wanted to keep on twistin'. How long, though, could I watch these middle-aged, overweight Canadians get down with their bad selves? *Get me out of here.*

"I got to get some sleep, Mom," I said.

"Just one more set, son."

Mom's dutiful son capitulated.

Finally, an hour later, the party pooped out. Dad handed Bonnie a fistful of Canadian dollars.

Bonnie thanked him. I walked her to the door and thanked her as well.

"Your parents are great, Paul," she said. "They throw a helluva party. And you could almost do this for a living."

* * *

Bonnie, bless her heart, saw my future.

It wasn't anything I could say out loud. But I did say it silently in the secret chambers of my heart. As I kept playing songs like the Ronettes' "Be My Baby," written by Ellie Greenwich, Jeff Barry, and producer Phil Spector, I saw myself flying on the wings of the music, flying over Lake Superior, over Lake Michigan, over the Motown studio in Detroit where the Sound of Young America rose up like a "Heat Wave" burning in my heart, flying over Alan Freed in Cleveland and Dick Clark in Philly, where the kids were lining up for *American Bandstand*, flying straight into New York City and landing at the feet of Ronnie Ronette herself. I'd try to speak, but the words wouldn't come. I was too timid, too unsure of myself. No Canadian manchild could hope to win the love of a lady who unabashedly demands, "Be My Baby." My flight would end. My dream would dissolve.

But the next morning I'd wake up and rush over to the piano and play the song. I'd play so loudly that the sound got all up in my ears. I'd close my eyes and, in the haze of my foggy morning mind, I could almost hear Ronnie saying, "Paul, come down to the States. Come down to Spanish Harlem, Knock three times to see if I'm home. Come down to where it's hot and sweaty and gritty. I'm waiting for you down here, Paul. I may not be of your faith . . . but we'll work something out."

One morning my reverie was broken by my mother shouting. "Start packing, Paul, we're leaving for the weekend."

"We can't leave," I said. "The Four Seasons are on Sullivan again Sunday night."

"Seasons come and go, son," said Dad, "but it's summertime. We're going to our cottage on the lake."

We often spent summer weekends lakeside. That was fine, except our cottage had no TV.

"I don't want to go to the lake," I said. "I want to watch Sullivan. The Four Seasons are going to do their new song, 'Rag Doll.' "

"You're already playing that 'Rag Doll' song. Isn't that the one where you bash the bongos on top of the piano?"

"Yes, that's how I duplicate the intro that's on the record."

"Well, so you have it down."

"I need to see them do it on TV," I said. "I've never seen the song performed and can't afford to miss it. I can stay home by myself."

"It's a family outing," said Dad. "You're coming."

I pleaded to stay with relatives; I pleaded for a plan that would have us home in time for Sullivan; I pleaded for a postponement of the trip. But all pleas fell on deaf ears.

Watching Canadian geese flying through summer rainstorms, I was miserable all weekend.

The storm in my heart, the one that stirred my soul as it had never been stirred before, had come earlier from watching the Seasons on Sullivan singing "Big Girls Don't Cry." My parents had no idea how riveting that moment had been to me.

Naturally it was in black and white. As the music started, singer Frankie Valli, guitarist Tommy DeVito, and bassist Nick Massi slowly began walking downstage in triangle formation.

Valli, who considered Sinatra the performer's performer, was almost conducting in a Frank-ish manner. The opening chords were chilling. The vocals were astounding, but my eye went to Valli's right, to the fourth Season, the group member who interested me most. This was the great Bob Gaudio, the co-composer, along with Bob Crewe, of their greatest hits. He stood behind a keyboard. I practically pressed my nose against the TV screen to catch every nuance of their presentation.

Later in life, I actually met Gaudio and pumped him for information. That's when he told a story that blew my mind: After writing "Who Wears Short Shorts" as a member of the Royal Teens, he had an offer to go on tour. But he was only fifteen and Dad said no, not until he graduated. Bob was crafty enough even then to arrange a meeting with his dad and the principal of his high school. After Bob eloquently pleaded his case, the principal made his pronouncement: "Mr. Gaudio, your son can finish high school anytime. An opportunity like this comes once in a lifetime. Let him go." Bob prevailed.

I didn't.

He wrote "Sherry." I only learned it. And back in the hot summer of my discontent, I couldn't even talk my parents into taking me home in time to watch the Four Seasons do "Rag Doll" on Sullivan.

"You'll get over it," my dad said. "It's no big deal."

"Yeah, no big deal," I said, but I never got over it. For me, the Four Seasons style was life changing. For my folks, it was just little Paul obsessed.

Meanwhile, the summer cottage party scene was in full swing, and my parents weren't about to cut it short. That Saturday night my folks were invited up to Bill Maloney's place. Bill, who became a Superior Court Justice, had an outdoor sauna.

Because Thunder Bay had a large Finnish population, saunas were a staple of the party scene. In fact, I was awakened at midnight by Bill himself, who insisted I join the party and bring my ukulele. Bill knew I could strum in the style of George Formby, the English music hall star whom George Harrison claimed as an influence. When I cleared the cobwebs from my head and got to the sauna, the liquor was flowing and, in no time flat, my parents were going pretty good to "Mr. Wu's a Window Cleaner Now." Bill and I had written special lyrics to "I'm Henry the Eighth I Am." Our parody was about Sulo the Steam Bath Man and included the line "every sauna was a Satana." I was especially proud of that line because "Satana" was a Finnish word that meant devil, as in "a devil of a good sauna."

Well, it was a devil of a good party—so good that our host, the Honorable Justice William Maloney, scooped up a dipper of boiling hot water and instead of pouring it on the hot rocks, poured it down his bathing trunks, scalding, if you will, *his* rocks. He was immediately rushed to the hospital. The next night, though, while the Seasons were singing "Rag Doll" on Sullivan, Maloney was back partying at his outdoor sauna— and so were the Shaffers.

✦ ✦ ✦

Once in a great while we would escape the deep freeze and vacation in warmer parts of the world. A most memorable trip unfolded in the Bahamas. We went to Nassau and stayed at the Royal Victoria Hotel. My dad, of course, was eager to hear jazz and discovered a club on the wrong side of the tracks. He took me and Mom to hear a hip revue where a big band wailed on "Slaughter on Tenth Avenue," complete with a smokin' Hammond B3 organist. Nassau'd gone funky, and I soaked it all in.

The next day Dad spotted Dr. Martin Luther King, Jr., by the pool. The great leader was in matching shirt-and-bathing-suit cabana attire. My father approached him and said, "My family and I greatly admire you and would be honored if we could take your picture."

"With pleasure," said Dr. King.

Dad snapped the photo. We all shook hands and went to the lounge chairs. A few minutes later, Dr. King entered the pool from the deep end while I entered from the shallow. Just like that, the dozen or so vacationers, white people all, who were in the pool suddenly got out, as if the water had been contaminated. Dr. King and I stayed in and swam for the next twenty minutes or so.

When I got out, my father took me aside and said, "We're changing hotels. I'm not staying anywhere the guests display this kind of racist behavior."

An hour later we checked out and headed for the Nassau Beach Hotel, a little outside of town. There we were given a lovely room with an ocean view. The next morning we all went for a swim. This time we ran into Harry Belafonte who, together with his daughter Shari, was about to take a dip. "May we have a photo, Mr. Belafonte," said Dad, "for the *kin-der?*"

"Of course," said the singer, who often sang in Yiddish. "For the *kin-der.*"

Decades later I was musical director for a charity concert produced by Joseph Papp. Belafonte appeared. I went up to him and said, "It's great to see you again, Mr. Belafonte. Last time was a million years ago at the Nassau Beach Hotel. We were all vacationing there."

"Impossible," said Belafonte. "I've never been to Nassau. You must be thinking of Sidney Poitier."

Oh God, I thought to myself, *I've committed some terrible racial blunder, confusing one famous black entertainer for another.*

Belafonte stood for several seconds, allowing me to die this slow death, before breaking into a smile and saying, "Just kidding. I was in Nassau, but I can't honestly say that I recall the Family Shaffer."

I was relieved.

When I told this story to my son, Will, who was nine at the time and studying the civil rights movement in school, he was puzzled and said, "Dad, how could Dr. King stay at that hotel when there were segregation laws?"

"Those laws were in the United States, son," I said. "That's why to vacation comfortably, he had to leave his own country."

Chapter 7

Did You Hear the One About the Ventriloquist and the Rabbi?

You hadn't lived till you'd watched Sullivan with the Shaffers. Back in the sixties, neighborhood kids would come over just for the experience of viewing the show with Bernie and Shirley, Thunder Bay's most sophisticated show-biz observers.

Sullivan brought us million-dollar stars; my parents' critiques of those stars: priceless. However, even though it was the musical stars that held my attention, I was also intrigued by Ed himself. It might have been his absolute squareness, especially in contrast to the hip acts he presented, that gave me an early understanding of irony. I immediately took to the concept. In fact, when Ed hosted the Beatles—the starkest possible contrast between an old-time presenter and a newfangled act—I was nearly as intrigued by his introduction as I was by their performance. After listening to it again and again, I memorized Ed's exact words and, to this day, give a credible impersonation of Sullivan—the nationally syndicated columnist for the *New York Daily News*—as he brought on the Fab Four:

"Well now yesterday and today our theater's been jammed

with newspapermen and photographers from across the country, and these veterans agree with me that the city has never seen the kind of excitement generated by these four youngsters from Liverpool who call themselves the Beatles. Now tonight you'll twice be entertained by them . . ."

"Twice be entertained"—that was one hell of a construction that Ed formulated, something like "twice cooked Chinese pork." In any event, the Beatles came out and tore the roof off the very theater where, three decades later, I'd be leading a band, and, from time to time, at the request of my boss, David Letterman, doing my imitation of Sullivan introducing the Beatles.

Back in the sixties, while Ed was presenting the Beatles to their hordes of screaming fans, he was also hosting an older generation—Sullivan's own generation—of entertainers. This included everyone from Kate Smith to Jerry Vale to Jan Peerce. Jan Peerce, the operatic tenor, was of special interest to the Shaffers because he once came to Thunder Bay to perform a recital. It was a grand occasion, and the city's Jewry, knowing Peerce was a.member of the tribe, invited him to our *shul* for a reception.

"Mr. Peerce," asked a member of our congregation, "would you be good enough to honor us with a musical selection?"

The great star looked straight in the man's eyes and said, "Sir, may I ask what you do for a living?"

"I'm a doctor."

"Well, Doctor," said Peerce, "if I were to invite you to my party and then ask you to take out my gallbladder, what would you say?"

The doctor said nothing.

Some years later, the good people of Shaarey Shomayim had the chance to be entertained by another celebrity whom we knew from Sullivan. Going from the sublime to the ridiculous, we would be hosting Ricky Layne and Velvel, a ventriloquist and his Jewish dummy.

Ricky and Velvel, like Myron Cohen, were among Sullivan's favorites. Ed had a fondness for Catskills chicken-soup humor, and of course my parents and I got a special kick out of Velvel, who actually spoke Yiddish. Starting in the fifties, Ed had been introducing middle America to the ways of funny Jews, thus preparing the country for an era when our brand of humor, from Woody Allen to Jerry Seinfeld, would prove popular with the masses. Back in the sixties, precisely because of Sullivan, Ricky Layne and Velvel were extremely popular. I was a fan. And when I learned that they would be coming to our synagogue to put on a show in support of an Israel bond drive, I was thrilled.

So was the whole town. Ricky Layne and Velvel were so massive, the Israel bond drive couldn't be contained. It had to be opened up to the goyim, including the mayor and the Pattersons, one of our city's leading families. The Pattersons were our Kennedys, and my parents were proud to be included in their social circle. I had even fancied one of the Patterson daughters when we were in our early teens, but I was too shy to make a move. I may have missed a golden opportunity to relieve myself of what would become a burdensome virginity.

On the eve of the bond drive, our *shul* was filled to the brim with Jews and gentiles alike. It was almost as if Ed Sullivan himself had come to Thunder Bay to present one of his favorite acts. But the irony was this: instead of Ed introducing the man and his dummy, the opening act was a Hasidic rabbi bent on selling Israel bonds.

I can't recall the name of the rabbi. But I can recall the power and passion of his plea for money. He was extraordinary, detailing the progress Israel had made while dramatizing the extreme danger the country still faced. When he was through, he asked for pledges, and though a few came dribbling in, they were modest. After all, this was Thunder Bay, not Manhattan. The rabbi wound up again and delivered another strong pitch, this time heightening the drama and raising the volume of his voice. The congregation responded, but only slightly.

The rabbi got pissed. *Real* pissed. He let go with a stream of vituperative accusations and flung insults at the integrity of Canadian Jewry. We were irresponsible. We were cheap. We were cowardly. We were misinformed. We were shaming our forefathers. We were shaming ourselves. And as the rabbi went a little nuts in his chastisements, his Yiddish-accented English grew more Yiddish. Seated next to the very goyish Pattersons, my assimilated parents slid down in their chairs, hoping this would soon end. But the more the rabbi's mission faltered, the less giving the crowd, the crazier the rabbi became. By the end, he was shouting in our faces and crying real tears.

During the ordeal, my eye had been on the dummy whose face peeked out of the case carried by Ricky. While the rabbi was ranting, I quietly slipped over to take a better look at the dormant Velvel, the very doll I had seen so often on Sullivan. Just then, the rabbi, still raging, concluded his pitch. I watched as Ricky leaned down under the table, brought the dummy out of the case and slipped his hand up Velvel's ass. Ricky looked at the man sitting next to him, the president of our congregation, and asked, "How the fuck am I supposed to do shtick now that this goddamn rabbi has reamed out the room?"

"Don't worry," said our president. "After that, we'll laugh at anything."

And we did.

Chapter 8

Here I Come to Save the Day

Ricky Layne and Velvel bring to mind Andy Kaufman. Both acts operated from a unique and bizarre perspective. Ricky Layne's was the first novelty act with which I had personal contact. Andy came much later in my life, but was perhaps the greatest novelty act of his time. Like Ricky, Andy had an alter ego. As it turned out, that alter ego bumped up against my actual ego.

My first encounter with Andy was during the debut of *SNL* in 1975; it was a performance that ignited Kaufman's career. As a painfully shy boy, he stood in front of a phonograph and simply dropped the needle on a record. Out came the Mighty Mouse theme. Rather than dance or even move, Andy simply stood there, like a little boy. At the chorus, though, he suddenly came alive and mouthed the words "Here I come to save the day." For those few seconds, he transformed into a superhero—his facial and body language pulsating with heroic masculinity—only to return to his listless state of awkwardness once the short chorus had ended. This strange little act was a sensation and put Andy on the map.

For a period, Andy went to any length to make audiences love him. In concert venues, he invited the entire crowd to join him for milk and cookies. Then he led them to a convoy of buses parked outside the auditorium—and off they went to a restaurant, where Andy would treat every last patron.

Conversely, or perversely, he went through another period where his solitary aim was to incur the audience's wrath. Now he wanted to be hated, and he succeeded by avoiding any semblance of entertainment in his act. All he would do was read a crushingly dull book out loud. The book would have no relevance. Andy would simply stand there and read until he was booed. When the booing stopped, people would start throwing things at his head. When the throwing stopped, the crowd would get up and leave. And when the last audience member walked out in disgust, Andy felt he had triumphed. He was hated.

His need to be despised darkened over the years. He got into the habit of insulting women and accusing them of inferior intelligence and strength. To prove his claim, he invited women to wrestle him onstage. Several were willing. In some cases the women—who may or may not have been shills—were injured, thus antagonizing the audience even more.

Andy Kaufman was a performance artist who trafficked in unpredictability. When he did a parody of a talk show, for instance, he placed his desk eight feet high so that he literally talked down to his guests. The piece was brilliant.

He was a semi-regular on the Letterman show in the early eighties. In a famous appearance, he showed up with wrestler Jerry "The King" Lawler. At one point, Kaufman began cursing Lawler, who, in turn, reacted violently. They lunged at each other, spilling Dave's coffee and scalding him. Andy looked to be seriously injured. Everyone was concerned for his health. But when he and Lawler were spotted having dinner later that same evening, we knew we'd been had.

Then came the week that Andy was scheduled to appear on Letterman two successive nights. The first night he would come on as himself, the second as Tony Clifton, his alter ego, a highly obnoxious Las Vegas–style lounge singer. He went so far as to have a latex application that altered his entire visage. In Clifton, he created a character who was not only abusive to the audience but to his accompanying musicians as well. One false note and Tony might attack you.

After his first night, Andy as Andy came over to me and said, "Tony Clifton will be here tomorrow. Now listen—he's notoriously tough on piano players. If you don't know your stuff, he's likely to punch out your lights."

"Oh, I can handle Tony," I said. "I've been backing lounge lizards my entire life."

"Well, you better have your shit together, Shaffer," he said, "or Tony will ream you a new asshole."

The next day I was careful to arrive early for rehearsal. Tony showed up at 2 p.m. sharp, in full regalia—shiny Vegas show suit, coal-black wig, latex mask, patent leather shoes.

"Okay, Shaffer," he said, "I don't know what I'm going to sing until I sing it, so you better fuckin' follow me or you'll wind up on the floor."

He started into a lounge medley where he threw a half dozen songs in my direction. I knew every one. When he skipped to the bridge, I was there with him; when he sang an extra chorus, I played the extra chorus; when he cut a lyric or improvised a verse, I didn't miss a beat.

"Damn, Shaffer," said Tony, "you know what you're doing."

"I try," I said.

"Well, you succeed."

When Andy played Tony, I sensed a sweetness that I never felt when Andy played Andy. In fact, I liked working with Tony Clifton a lot more than working with Andy Kaufman, whom I viewed with a degree of pity. During the actual show that night, the musical rapport between Clifton and Shaffer was silky smooth. The medley came off without a hitch.

Thereafter, Andy's career was marked by an increasing predilection toward pain. The pain became alarmingly real when he developed cancer and died tragically in 1984. He was thirty-five. Even now, though, there are those who say his death was the final hoax and that somewhere, in Indianapolis or Indonesia, he lives incognito as a plumber or rug salesman.

My fascination with Andy continued long after his premature demise. In fact, when his manager, Bob Zmuda, wrote a book about Kaufman, I bought it immediately. Imagine my shock, then, when I read Zmuda's description of Tony Clifton's appearance with me on Letterman. It wasn't Andy Kaufman who played Tony, said Zmuda; it was Zmuda himself who played Tony. Andy was home that night taking it easy.

How heartening to learn that Tony is indeed alive and well! If only the same could be said of Andy.

Chapter 9

Frank Sinatra Welcomes Elvis Back from the Army

A quarter century before Andy Kaufman, I was falling in love with the improbable and paradoxical nature of show business via our black-and-white TV set. What could be more unlikely than the joint appearance of Frank and Elvis?

Sinatra's television show was sponsored by Timex, and the guests included Peter Lawford, Joey Bishop, and Nancy Sinatra. Special lyrics by Sammy Cahn. It was the start of the sixties, the Rat Pack was swingin', and Frank was flying high.

I watched the show in wonder. In a duet with his daughter, Frank didn't sing, "You make me feel so young"; he sang, "You make me feel so old." In turn, Nancy replaced the line, "And even when I'm old and gray" with "And I don't need a dowry, Dad." Frank's lyrics also referenced Tommy Sands, Nancy's fiancé at the time. The whole thing made the audience feel like part of the Sinatra family.

But the segment of the show that moved me most was Frank and Elvis, the kings of warring universes, singing each other's songs. Frank did a big-band version of "Love Me Tender" while Elvis Elvis-ized "Witchcraft." Frank was constantly straightening his tie; Elvis had undone his. Frank was folding his arms; Elvis swiveled his hips. Frank was uptightsville; Elvis was loose as a goose. Frank was a good sport about it, but you couldn't help but feel that he saw the future of music and it wasn't him.

I was caught between these two worlds. And, to some degree, so was Elvis, who cited Dean Martin as an influence. Frank was my dad's man. My dad also loved Arthur Prysock, whom Elvis credited as another influence. I knew Prysock's one and only rock hit, "It's Too Late." My father knew it too but had little use for Elvis.

Without doubt, Elvis was a towering influence on future rockers around the world. Even in our frozen corner of Canada, we felt the heat. And although Elvis's post-army songs were certainly charming—who could resist his reading of "Follow That Dream" and the honky-tonk piano that rocked the chorus?—other artists spoke to me more directly. For example, I loved the Moody Blues. I especially loved their preorchestral singles rendered in an R&B vein: "Go Now" and "I Go Crazy." When I played those records, my dad would say, "That's a black group, isn't it?"

"No, Dad, they're English."

"I wouldn't have believed that anything English could be that hip," said my father. "When it comes to jazz, the English are so square."

"Well, they're not square anymore, Dad. There are these four youngsters from Liverpool who call themselves the Beatles. They're playing rock and roll and they seem to be changing the world."

I had wanted to change my world. I was tired of playing

the same old classical pieces for my high school assemblies. On the advice of my parents and teachers, I had always trotted out the classical numbers—a little Mozart, a little Chopin, a little Liszt—and played them with as much flair as the pieces would allow. The reaction from my peers was profound boredom. No one gave a rat's ass about Mozart, Chopin, or a little Liszt.

The fateful day came in spring when the ice had finally fallen from the hard shells surrounding our Canadian souls. That was the day I came to the auditorium prepared for what was clearly an act of revolution. And if that revolution had a slogan, it was simply this: *Fuck the classics.*

I had prepared for this moment for years. In fact, when I began duplicating records by learning all the parts by ear and banging them out on the piano with unchecked ferocity, Mom got annoyed.

"Paul," she shouted from the kitchen, "does it have to be so loud?"

"Mom," I retorted, "it's rock and roll!"

To her eternal credit, she never complained again.

That holy mantra—*Mom, it's rock and roll!*—resonated through every cell in my body as, on this day of days, I sat at the piano bench, mustered up all my courage, and launched into a take-no-prisoners version of "Pipeline," the instrumental romp made popular by the Chantays, a group of southern California rockers. The song had the new surfin' sound, set in a minor key that had me playing my own surf-piano version with an impassioned fever. At the end, the fever spread and my peers shouted with delight. Yes, Shaffer had delivered a knockout! Shaffer had delivered his fellow teens from the tedium of the classics!

Unbeknownst to me, sitting in the audience that day was a

certain Rick Shadrach Lazar. A year older, a decade hipper, Rick was the edgiest junior high schooler in Thunder Bay. He was of Assyrian descent, an exotic-looking kid with a dark complexion and pudgy build. He was deeply into music as a tenor saxist and later a drummer. He saw me as a kindred soul.

We were in high school before he introduced himself to me with a question.

"Wanna jam?"

Rick's employment of the felicitous word *jam* brought to mind an earlier episode in my childhood when Dad and I were watching Benny Goodman on Ed Sullivan. In the middle of a song, Goodman pointed to himself and then started to solo.

"It's a jam!" my father shouted excitedly. "They're having a jam session. The leader points to a musician—in this case him-self—who is spontaneously asked to improvise. Isn't that great, Paul?"

Yes, it was great: great to have a father with a firm under-standing of a fundamental jazz principle. That principle served me well when I took Rick up on his offer.

"Cool," said Rick. "Meet me in the music room after school."

Rick arrived smoking a cigarette. As he unpacked his sax, picked out his reed, and adjusted the horn, he kept smoking. In fact, he smoked and played at the same time, blowing a stream of white vapor into the instrument itself. His sax stunk of ciga-rettes.

"Do you know 'Take Five'?" he asked.

Fortunately, because of jazz-loving Bernie Shaffer, I knew the Dave Brubeck/Paul Desmond tour de force, a tricky num-ber if ever there was one. Rick stated the melody and nodded for me to follow. It was my first jam and I was limited to blues licks, à la Ramsey Lewis and his "In Crowd" rock-styled hits. Halfway through, Rick stopped, only to say, "Shaffer, you're still wearing your parka. Aren't you warmed up yet?" I took off my coat and got hot. The licks started cooking. It was fun and ended only when the janitor came in to say he was locking up for the night.

"Come over to my house," said Rick when we were through. "I've got some magazines to show you."

Rick had his own brand of cool. He didn't just have a bedroom in his parents' home; he had a self-contained basement apartment. The kid had a pad while still in high school. Against the wall, sitting under a James Brown poster, were two piles of magazines that climbed halfway to the ceiling: on the left were *Playboy*s; on the right were *Down Beat*s.

Rick riffled through his stash of LPs and pulled out one called *Paul Butterfield Blues Band.*

"Check out the notation on the cover," said Rick, pointing to a sticker that read, "Best enjoyed when played at full volume."

Rick cranked the volume and the music hit me hard. With stellar blues guitarist Michael Bloomfield crying over Butterfield's harmonica, I found myself in a field of music that was as thrilling as anything I'd ever heard.

Every young man needs a friend like Rick to cheer up his childhood.

Not long afterward, Rick Shadrach became Funky Ricky and recruited me as the keyboardist for his band, the Fugitives. Every Friday night we'd play a school dance, and every Saturday night we'd play the local hockey arena. It was freezing in there, but, hey, I was in a *band*.

When we unloaded the gear, the first pieces of equipment out of the trunk would always be the Beatle boots. Funky Ricky understood the importance of putting the fashion in the funk. The Beatle boots, imported from Toronto and featuring stylish Cuban stacked heels, pumped us up. The girls would have to notice.

But if the girls did notice, we certainly didn't hear about it. In truth, the girls didn't seem especially drawn to us at all— which led me to this sad conclusion:

Thunder Bay was the only place in the world where being in a band didn't get you laid.

In my beloved hometown, high school honeys did not hang around the bandstand; did not wink and flirt with band members; did not offer their young nubile bodies in appreciation of the music being played. In my beloved hometown, not only couldn't we musicians get the girls to lie down, we couldn't even get them to applaud. Here's how it worked:

The girls would gather together in the center of the arena. The boys would circle them, checking them out. The bravest among the boys would approach a girl.

"Wanna dance? No? Okay."

Shut down, the boy would shrug it off and move on.

This scene would repeat itself countless times. At evening's end, no more than six couples would be dancing, while the others continued to circle.

Meanwhile, the band worked in vain to get things going. I had confected a girl group medley that I was certain would excite the crowd. I seamlessly went from the Chiffons' "One Fine Day" to the Raindrops' (actually writers Ellie Greenwich and Jeff Barry singing their own song) "He's the Kind of Boy You Can't Forget" to the Exciters' "Tell Him" to the Crystals' "He's a Rebel." At the end of this ingenious string of songs, though, the action on the floor remained minimal and the response to the music nonexistent. Nothing but silence. Thunder Bay audiences were murder. Forget New York. If you could make it in Thunder Bay, you could make it anywhere!

Funky Ricky, a man ahead of his time, had a never-say-die attitude. He'd make the party rock if he had to invoke the great James Brown himself to do it. And, in fact, that's just what Ricky did. He'd break into his best JB mode with a killer version of "I Got You (I Feel Good)," slipping, splitting, and sliding his way across the stage. When we did Mitch Ryder's version of "Little Latin Loopy-Loo," before the last chorus Ricky and I would engage in a little hipster dialogue:

Paul: "We gonna try it once again and this time . . ."

Ricky: "This time we gonna rock out, Paul, baby?"

Paul: "Yeah, you right, baby, this time we gonna try to get a little more feeling, yeah, yeah."

And we'd kill—but then come off to silence.

We'd walk out into the frozen night air, schlepping our instruments to our cars. While other guys were in the backseat with their heated-up honeys, I was nestled up against my cold amp and numb portable organ.

That was rock and roll, Thunder Bay—style.

Before I left Thunder Bay, I did glean other valuable musical lessons. The Guess Who, for example, came through every winter on their way home to Winnipeg. These were the days before their original hits like "American Woman" and "These Eyes." To Thunder Bay audiences, the Guess Who was the ultimate cover band. That was good enough for my peers and, in truth, also good enough for me. I loved the Guess Who. Their version of "Penny Lane" sounded more like the Beatles than the Beatles. (Lead singer Burton Cummings was so proud of his authentic Liverpudlian pronunciation of the word *customer*—"in

Penny Lane the barber shaves another coostomer"—he'd say the word twice.) They did a moody "Moody's Mood for Love" that they learned from Georgie Fame. But most wondrous was their "Louie Louie" medley, a masterpiece of musical association. They began with the classic reading—the Kingsmen's version—and moved to the Kinks before launching into the Beach Boys' interpretation of the rock classic. The grand finale was their loving and faithful re-creation of the greatest show band in the world, Paul Revere and the Raiders. They performed the Raiders' act, starting with "Louie Louie," and then continuing into "Just Like Me," "Oo Poo Pa Doo," only to segue into a full twenty minutes of jaw-dropping fully choreographed rock-your-socks-off Raiders rock and roll.

Watching the Guess Who, I came to this conclusion: Not only was it enough to be a cover band, it was perhaps the highest calling. After all, if you could play music recorded by others, stay true to the original, and still add fire and flare, why not? The Guess Who's shows left me entirely satisfied.

Why write?

Why not just cover?

Besides, to cover is to pay tribute to the original artists who gave your psyche a deeper shade of soul. To cover them is to love them.

The Guess Who wasn't the only name band who made it to Thunder Bay. Our modest rock ensemble also opened for the Troggs, the red-hot English rock band. Before the Troggs, dressed to the nines in their Carnaby Street splendor, came out to entertain our local hockey arena music lovers, we Fugitives did our version of the Righteous Brothers' "You've Lost That Lovin' Feelin'." We sang the melody with as much hot soul as we could muster in the ice-cold arena. Reg Presley, head Trogg, was actually listening offstage and made it a point to stop us and say, "Hey, you guys are good."

"Why, thank you, Mr. Presley," I replied, feeling a bit like Jimmy Olsen addressing Clark Kent.

When the Troggs hit the stage, Presley introduced their first song.

"Here's a little ditty that was banned in Denmark." Then they broke into "I Can't Control Myself."

After that Presley said, "Our next number caused a scandal in Sweden." And with that, they played "With a Girl Like You."

"They threw us out of England," Presley continued, "when we performed this." Then they hit with "Night of the Long Grass."

The climax of the whole thing came when Presley said, "Here's the one you've been waiting for. This one scandalized the world." "This one," of course, was "Wild Thing," their signature scorcher.

The Thunder Bay crowd was convinced they had heard things that were strictly off limits. The Troggs devotees were pleased, but still not enough to applaud.

The lack of enthusiasm that my beloved hometown showed to musicians came at a dear cost. In other cities, pianists, saxists, singers, and guitarists were enjoying their first taste of sex. Because of their ability to rock and roll, certain, shall we say, favors were bestowed upon them. Women were only too willing to allow them entrance into their "hearts and souls." In Thunder Bay, we froze. There was something of a cruise scene on Saturday nights on our downtown's main drag, Victoria Avenue. I cruised but never conquered. I was too busy playing music. The truth is, I was a touch naive and shy when it came to the opposite sex. My passion was for music. Don't get me wrong; I was a red-blooded adolescent with raging Canadian hormones, but, alas, I had not yet tasted success in the sexual arena.

My senior year in high school 1967, though, God blessed me with a girlfriend, Judy. She had lustrous brown hair, a shapely figure, and an appreciation of my ability to play every Temptations song by heart. By then I had grown my hair long in the front. That may or may not have added to my appeal, but I could sure knock out any love song she mentioned.

Looking back, I see that Judy may well have been willing. She came to all my gigs. She watched me play my Rascals' covers. After I performed, if there was any applause whatsoever, it was Judy alone doing the clapping. When I took her home after the shows, we would kiss on her porch and, if her folks had gone to sleep, kiss on her living room couch. Kissing led to petting and, though I am not a baseball expert, I believe I may have made it to first base and was on my way to second when we heard her father loudly coughing from his upstairs bedroom. That was it.

"You can stay a little longer," said Judy.

I considered the offer. I tried to imagine the scenario of making it to third base and heading home. Exactly where would that happen? On the couch? On the floor? In either case, what would we do if Dad suddenly appeared? And besides, perhaps she had no intention of allowing me beyond second base anyway. Perhaps reaching home plate was simply impossible.

So at that moment I uttered words that have come back to haunt me decades later: "I've got to go," I said.

"You sure?" asked Judy.

"I'm sure."

What prompted my exit, though, even more than my uncertainty about hitting home, was the fact that the radio deejay who had promoted the dance was hosting an after-party—and I wanted to be there.

I wanted to be there because I realized even then that the good times—indeed the best times—happen after hours. The axiom learned in Vegas—the later the hipper—never left my consciousness, even when courting Judy. My friends like Wayne Tanner got funnier as the hour got later. And even if there was a possibility of a sexual coda at evening's end, I'd skip the coda in favor of getting back to the laughs. The truth is that I was most in love with the idea of being a late-night musician.

The Fugitives was the band that gave me my first taste of the road. To be sure, the road was abbreviated; it went no farther than nearby Terrace Bay, home of a gigantic Kleenex factory. It was there that our Ricky announced we couldn't hit the gig until he did what he called his "Triple S"—shower, shave, and shit. Wayne, who was along for the ride, said, "Funky Ricky's so funky he needs an equipment man to set up his shit."

Even the term "equipment man" was exotic to me. Everything about music and musicians was exotic. And if the erotic side of this exotic life was slow in coming, I figured there had to be a payoff.

Chapter 10

Sweet, Sweet Connie

Now before I leave you with the idea that I was a perennial loser in all matters sexual, I want you to meet sweet, sweet Connie.

Everyone knew her. My encounter with Connie came at the dawn of the eighties, at a time when I was unattached. If the seventies was the decade of debauchery, Connie, bless her heart, was determined to extend that happy era by offering her services to all those she deemed worthy. And Connie found many in the music biz worthy.

I am, of course, advancing my story—beyond Thunder Bay, beyond my college days and professional beginnings in Toronto and New York City—to a special moment when a group I helped assemble, the Blues Brothers, was on national tour. The genesis of that band will be dramatized for your reading pleasure at a later time in this narrative, including profiles of its stars. But first, Connie.

I met her in Memphis.

The Blues Brothers were on a tear. Our records were selling

millions. The first Blues Brothers movie was a smash. In their roles as Jake and Elwood, Belushi and Aykroyd had become rock superstars. We played to standing-room-only crowds in arenas across the country. What had begun as a comedy sketch had turned into a musical phenomenon. The fruit of our success was a succession of groupies who greeted us in every city.

Connie was more than a groupie. She was a specialist. When our caravan rolled into Memphis, we were told that she had driven all the way from Little Rock to meet us. What I didn't know—but quickly learned—was the etiquette governing her services. While the band members, and especially the stars, were her primary object, tradition dictated that she first win the approval of the crew; then she would be given entrée to the band.

Apparently she won that approval because at 2 a.m., after our show, I heard a knock at my hotel door. I was at the minibar, fixing myself a drink.

"Paul," she said, "it's Connie."

"Delighted to see you," I said. "Please come in."

A good-looking woman with a warm and friendly demeanor, Connie knew how to kick off a conversation.

"I loved your sitcom *Year at the Top.*"

That floored me. I had starred in an unsuccessful situation comedy that ran for only a few episodes. No one knew anything about it. But sweet Connie knew *everything* about it; she knew details from every episode.

"Would you like a drink?" I asked her.

"Sure."

I walked back to the minibar to fix her drink, and by the time I turned around, she had slipped out of all her clothes except her high heels and stockings and had spread herself across my bed like a *Playboy* centerfold. "Praise God!" was the one thought that came to mind. I was so surprised, so delighted, that I spilled my vodka tonic.

"Don't worry about it, Paul," she said. "Just get in bed."

I did as I was told. I soon saw that I was dealing with a master craftswoman. Her attention to detail was exceptional, and she handled her task with both confidence and cunning. I had absolutely no complaints.

When she was through, she said, "You need a Polaroid, Paul."

"I'm afraid I don't have a camera, Connie."

"Next time."

"I won't forget," I said.

Still in bed, she started reminiscing about her past. "I thought the glory days would go on forever," she said. "I thought Three Dog Night would keep showing up three times a year and the party would rock on forever."

"As long as we can make it to the show tonight," I said, quoting Grand Funk Railroad's "We're an American Band."

"You know that I'm actually in that song, don't you?" asked Connie.

"What do you mean?"

She quoted the first verse:

On the road for forty days
Last night in Little Rock put me in a haze
Sweet, sweet Connie, doing her act
She had the whole show and that's a natural fact

"You're *that* Connie?" I asked in amazement.

"Yes!"

"My God, you're royalty."

She was so pleased with my recognition of her status that she went to work again. This time I felt like I was being knighted.

After the second time around, she got up and started to get dressed.

"You don't have to leave," I said.

"I don't? Everyone always kicks me out when it's over."

"I wouldn't dream of kicking you out. You can stay if you want to."

"You're kidding," she said.

"I'm serious."

"Wow. I usually have to spend the rest of the night banging on doors to see who'll let me in. Sometimes I just sleep in the laundry room."

"Stay. Take off those nylon hose with the seams running up the back and the tears in all the right places."

"Most guys don't want me to take off my hose."

"I'm not most guys, Connie. I think you should make yourself comfortable. It's been a long day for you."

"You can say that again."

We fell asleep. The next morning I wasn't sure of the etiquette and wondered if I could offer her some kind of compensation.

"Oh, no," said Connie. "This is my calling. It's my pleasure. I have only one thing to ask of you."

"And what's that?"

"Take me on the band plane when you fly off today."

"I wish I could, but I can't. Seating is limited."

"I'll stay in the bathroom."

"That wouldn't be pleasant."

"Every time the boys had to use the bathroom, they'd be pleasantly surprised."

"I'm sure they would be, but FAA regulations are stringent. I know you understand."

"Will I see you on the next tour?"

"If there is a next tour."

There wasn't a next tour. But I've never forgotten sweet, sweet Connie, a rock-and-roll legend who knew that there was far more to pleasing a man than sex.

* * *

Back in the land of my coming of age, sexual liberation was nowhere to be found on the Canadian radar. What could be found, though, was another sort of liberation provided by music. I remember, for example, when I was still in high school, a band called the Vendettas—not to be confused, of course, with Martha and her Vandellas—who hailed from Sault Ste. Marie, a river city in Ontario even smaller than Thunder Bay, and had played Toronto but were stranded in TB. We opened for them when they played our hometown hockey rink. Their lead singer, Keith McKie, could pull off a pretty damn decent Ray Charles imitation. In his hotel room, McKie played me Ray's version of "I Believe to My Soul," explaining how Ray had sung all the harmony parts himself, thus replicating the Raelettes. I was enraptured by his Ray Charles knowledge, but even more drawn to his stories about Toronto, Ontario.

"Man," he said, "the R&B scene in T.O. is hot. Detroit pimps bring their girls up on weekends where those long-legged ladies work the bars. In some of those joints the music gets so funky you can smell it."

I wanted to smell it. I wanted to taste it. I wanted to get out of town.

For a boy of my ethnic and cultural background, there was but one way out: college. Fortunately, my dad's alma mater was the University of Toronto. That's where Bernard Shaffer saw me not only matriculating as an undergraduate but, following in his footsteps, going on to attend Osgoode Law School.

Fresh out of high school, I did not resist the plan. A lethal litigator, my father was no one with whom to argue. I knew better. But late at night, dozing off to sleep, I hardly dreamed of being called to the bar—at least not *that* kind of bar. Instead, my ear cupped to the radio, I heard the distant sounds of WLS all the way from Chicago, fifty thousand watts flying over the Great Lakes. I'd wait till 10 p.m. when the deejay announced the top three most requested songs in Chicagoland: the Beach Boys' "Good Vibrations," the Supremes' "Love Is Here and Now You're Gone," and the Young Rascals' "Groovin'," exotic sounds from exciting worlds of which I knew nothing—and yet I prayed they had a place reserved for me.

Chapter 11

The All-Time Greatest Pussycat of the World

As eager as I am to dramatize the highlights of my college years, I interrupt our narrative to introduce a passion that began well before my career as an undergraduate. To be sure, the passion continued during my time at the university, even as it continues to this day. It is a passion, but also a fascination and, to be candid, an obsession.

I am, in short—and will always be—obsessed with the marvelous yearly telethons put on by Mr. Jerry Lewis. I am a believer in his cause and a student of his methods. Mr. Lewis is, in short, an idol.

But even before beginning my paean to Jerry, allow me to declare my love of show-biz speak. It was Marty Short who pointed out that on the TV special *A Man and His Music*, Frank Sinatra said, "When a song lingers for many many years, it becomes what we in the business call a standard." I loved the way that sounded. To a kid like me, Sinatra's verbal swagger meant almost as much as Chuck Berry's twanging guitar or Little Richard's rollicking piano. Show-biz speak, as articulated by the masters (Frank was one, Sammy another) transported me to those magical kingdoms—Vegas showrooms and Hollywood studios—where over-the-top sincerity created personalities who loved themselves as much as we loved them. These were guys who didn't have much education but were determined to talk as if they had all gone to Harvard.

Jerry was a particular favorite, and I respected him deeply. I not only appreciated his comedic genius but understood that as a director he was an innovator and pioneer. It was Jerry, after all, who had invented video assist, the method that allowed the moviemaker to watch an instant playback in video rather than have to wait for the printed film.

But my regard for Jerry began years before I knew of his technical creativity. Jerry came to Canada on the wings of cable television, a welcome addition to what had been our one-channel choice, the deadly earnest Canadian Broadcasting Corporation, which specialized in unentertaining television. I don't want to put you to sleep with tales of our deadly boring shows, but I cannot resist at least naming a few. *Fighting Words* featured a panel of guests who had to guess a famous quotation from history. If that wasn't bad enough, after they identified it, they'd discuss it. The longest-running show was *Front Page Challenge*, where a panel had to guess the identity of someone associated with a famous Canadian headline. The "someone" always seemed to be a Russian spy who had defected to Canada. The same spy, shot in silhouette and speaking in an electronically altered voice, must have appeared on the show a dozen times.

Things picked up on the Canadian news front when Margaret Trudeau dated Ronnie Wood of the Stones. Canadians were also titillated that when Keith Richards was busted for drug possession, it happened on our shores. He got off when a Canadian fan, a blind girl, testified in his behalf. The judge softened and ordered Keith to put on a benefit concert. When Keith and Ronnie, as the New Barbarians, played for the blind, a Canadian wag, obviously no rock and roll fan, said they should have been playing for the deaf.

Canadians, myself among them, were thrilled when cable TV finally arrived, meaning we'd get to see the big three American networks. I was fixated on ABC. Their shows seemed poorly lit and had a makeshift look to them. *Shindig,* my rock and roll bible, came on after school, but Jerry Lewis didn't come on until 1 a.m. I had to prop my eyes open with toothpicks to stay up, but stay up I did. As host of his own talk show, Jerry had a hydraulic lift that rose up so he could work to the balcony. That's the kind of showman he was.

Some might call Jerry unctuous, but I found his brand of unctuousness attractive rather than repellent. In fact, I found it downright wonderful. Jerry always dressed in a tux because, as he said, he owed his audience no less. Jerry was so tux-centric he'd wear one even on Carson. When Johnny asked him about it, Jerry loved explaining why: "A garbage man has his overalls. A lawyer has his Brooks Brothers suit. In our industry, we have our tuxedos. It's our uniform."

When I came of age and found myself wearing a tux at an event I was hosting, writer Tom Leopold, my friend and fellow telethon devotee, wrote this line for me: "As Jerry Lewis says, every profession has its uniform. A priest has his vestments, a surgeon his surgical greens. Hef has that leather-studded jock-strap that he wears in the grotto . . ."

The greatest expression of unadulterated show-biz schmaltz was undoubtedly Lewis's fabulous telethon. I say fabulous because in one long weekend blitz we were treated to a candor best expressed when Milton Berle, once Jerry's opening guest, began by saying "Ladies and gentlemen, this telethon will give you an opportunity to see us as you do not normally see us. For this evening we intend to alleviate the mask."

I believed Uncle Miltie. I was convinced that his alleviation of the mask would give me a behind-the-scenes look at the stars who so completely captured my imagination.

Jerry was a benevolent autocrat. When it came to this special show, Jerry was proprietary—and rightfully so. The recipients of this charity were, after all, "Jerry's kids." Jerry began hosting telethons to benefit the Muscular Dystrophy Association of America back in the early fifties. And to those who say his devotion to the cause came as a result of his guilt for portraying physically challenged people in his act, I say, "Keep your cynicism to yourself!"

In 1966, Jerry expanded the telethon into a nineteen-hour show featuring his famous tote—telethonese for "total"—board. When the amount raised reached one million dollars, America celebrated as Jerry himself wrote the number *1* on the board.

In the early years, Jerry hosted from start to finish. Part of the thrill was seeing a man work himself to the point where he nearly passed out but never did. In later years, Jerry recruited others to help him, a group he called his "Pussycats." There was also the trio that Jerry dubbed the "Love Triangle": Jerry himself, Ed McMahon, and Chad Everett, a show-biz personality best known for the TV show *Medical Center*. Of course among all the Pussycats, Ed was special. He had a unique contribution that always impressed Jerry: Ed could predict the final tote.

"You're scaring me," Jerry would tell Ed. "You're a witch with these predictions."

"I'm always right," Ed would respond.

"If you're even close to being right this year," Jerry would say every year, "you got yourself a Jew houseboy for the next twelve months."

Ed would laugh his jolly Ed laugh, and at the end of the weekend, Ed's prediction would come uncannily close to the mark.

In telethon lore, no date looms larger than September 6, 1976, when, to the shock of the world, Frank Sinatra escorted Dean Martin to the stage, presenting him to his long-estranged partner and saying, "I think it's about time." Jerry and Dean embraced and shed tears before Jerry asked Dean, "So, are you working?" "Five weeks a year at the Megem," said Dean. "The Megem," repeated Jerry with a smile, and just like that, a new hip name for the MGM Grand Hotel in Vegas was coined. The Martin and Lewis rapprochement was realized.

There was a distinct dramatic arc to the telethons. They were, in fact, epics. To me, they had a Yom Kippur-esque feeling, with the tradition and the atonement and the suffering. It was all about the suffering. The kids suffer. Jerry suffers for them, even as he suffers to stay up hour after hour to bring in the money. All Jerry wants is a dollar more. Jerry might be in the middle of a speech about how this year he intends to "take off on" the press who have been accusing him of using charity for self-aggrandizement. Looking straight into the camera, Jerry adds, "And I'm enough of a showman to realize that if I tell you I'm going to take off on the press, you're gonna keep watching until I do."

With that, Ed breaks in. "Sorry, Jer," he says, "but it's time for a tote."

"Show me! Do me! Yeah!" cries Jerry.

The camera pans to the big board; the numbers flip and . . . yes! The tote has gone over $500K! Now Ed has some boiler-plate work to do. He thanks the unions who have allowed their members to perform free of charge on the show. Breaking from the acknowledgments, Ed braves new waters by singing special material: "Holiday for Strings" with lyrics written to thank the Theater Authority and its member unions.

"You pulled it off, Ed," says Jerry, tireless, grateful, unafraid to move deeper into the day and use all his considerable charm to raise more money for his kids. All Jerry wants is a dollar more. Other Pussycats are there to help. Some, like Norm Crosby, can't get prime-time slots and are glad to perform at 4 in the morning. I love staying up all night so I can catch some little-known Vegas lounge act. I'm especially charmed by the Treniers, who do their thing at 5 a.m. (I later learn that the Tre-niers cannot leave the Vegas lounges not simply because they love the ambience, but because, to put it politely, they have a special affinity for the game of Keno.) Meanwhile, Jerry is in the wings or perhaps in his dressing room catching forty winks on a couch. But Jerry always comes back. Jerry comes back every year. Frank never lets him down. And neither does Sammy. Sammy and his sui generis Sammy shtick are a huge presence on the telethon. Jerry's son Gary Lewis and his Play-boys are there to sing their new single "Too Big for Small Talk." (I can still play it note for note.) There are split screens that thrill us with the cross-continental nature of the spectacle: Jerry in Vegas, Buddy Hackett in Atlantic City. Jerry calls the stations that carry his telethon his "Love Network."

When I become an adult, I form my own "Love Network" with friends who share my affection for Jerry and his wondrous show. We indulge in a running commentary and analysis conducted simultaneously over the phone. My fellow telethon pundits are Martin Short, Harry Shearer, and Tom Leopold. Harry not only tapes the show so we can later review our favorite sections, he also gets the satellite feed, which means he reports on the rehearsals.

Earlier in life, before the formation of our "Love Network," I was proud to be a member of the Sammy Club, comprised of East Coast fans of Sammy Davis Jr. and, in particular, fans of his TV show *Sammy & Company*. In addition to Sammy simply being Sammy, the thing we enjoyed most about the show was Sammy's announcer, William B. Williams. His function was to pay the first compliment. "Sammy," Williams would say, "I hate to interrupt your conversation with the great Tony Curtis, but, if I could embarrass you for just a moment, on behalf of all of us who play your music, I must say that you, Sammy Davis Jr., you are the entertainer's entertainer." From then on, it was a frenetic compliment free-for-all—Sammy complimenting Williams, Williams complimenting Tony, Tony complimenting Sammy, and Sammy, the unrivaled king of compliments, complimenting the audience for their kind indulgence. (A year or two after the founding of our Sammy Club, I meet Tom Leopold for the first time. This happens in New York. He lives in L.A. and tells me there's a West Coast Sammy Club. He is taken aback when I declare in no uncertain terms, "I want this clearly understood. There is but one authentic Sammy Club, and it functions here on the East Coast. Yours is nothing but a copy." That statement cements my friendship with Tom.)

Back on Jerry's telethon, the weekend draws to a conclusion, and the marathon winds down. It is 2 p.m. in Vegas and 5 p.m. in New York when Jerry introduces the last big celebrity. It's the Desert Fox himself, the man fellow entertainers affectionately

call "the Indian" because of his part–Native American heritage. It's none other than Mr. Wayne Newton, who has come to
the studio with his own rhythm section.

"Wayne," says Jerry. "I can count on you. My kids can count
on you. And you're one of the great Pussycats of the World."

"No, Jerry," says Wayne, "*you* are the all-time greatest
Pussycat of the World."

Wayne breaks into Chuck Berry's "Promised Land," singing
about how he left his home in Norfolk, Virginia, and was taken
to the promised land. Jerry is transported, but Jerry is exhausted.
Jerry is also excited and grateful that the tote is well over a million. "This year was a close one," he says, "but you people came
through." Now it's time for Jerry to sit on a stool, pick up the
mic, and sing the closing song, "You'll Never Walk Alone."

Mr. Lou Brown, Jerry's longtime bandleader, is getting on in
years, but Jerry is loyal. Loyalty aside, though, Jerry is annoyed
with Lou—and tells him so on camera—when Lou misses
Jerry's cue to start the song. "I sing it every year, Louie," says
Jerry. "By now you should know—that's a cue."

Earlier in the evening, Jerry referred to Lou by his Yiddish
name, Lable. "Lable," said Jerry in jest, "are you ready for
Hesh?" Hesh is Yiddish for Harry. This was Jerry playfully introducing Harry James. From that moment on, Harry Shearer
began his every phone call with "Are you ready for Hesh?"

But there is no kidding around when it comes to "You'll
Never Walk Alone." On another night at another show, Jerry
wanders into the audience to interview a kid who does a Jerry
imitation.

"Do whatever you want, son," says Jerry.

The kid starts mocking Jerry's version of "You'll Never
Walk Alone."

Jerry stops him.

"No," the comic says firmly. "We don't joke around with that song."

Nor will I.

There are endless variations to the drama of Jerry asking for a dollar more. To be sure, the telethon is one of the enduring institutions in American show business. And of course Jerry Lewis sits at the center of that institution. Surely he is the celebrities' celebrity.

* * *

Decades later, I found myself in a place where I had met hundreds of celebrities. You might even say that I was suffering from celebrity burnout. And yet, when given the chance to have dinner with Mr. Jerry Lewis, I didn't hesitate to run out to John F. Kennedy International Airport and jump on the first nonstop to Vegas.

A little background information: My dear friend Richard Belzer had been befriended by Jerry. Richard was the link between Jerry and myself.

I had first met Jerry when he came on Letterman. All had gone well. After the show, he came over to me and whispered with a wink, "They aren't on to you yet, are they?" I took this remark as a compliment. Friends suggested he was actually saying that I was getting away with something—and that *he* was on to me. Whatever the interpretation of his cryptic remark, I was grateful for the attention.

That was in the eighties. Sometime in the new millennium Belzer told me, "You won't believe who called."

"Who?"

"Jerry Lewis!"

"For what reason?"

"He's a fan. He loves *Law & Order: Special Victims Unit*"—the show on which Belzer plays Detective John Munch—"and he wanted to discuss the production techniques we use."

Next thing I knew Jerry had invited Belzer to Vegas.

"How'd it go?" I asked Richard when he returned to New York.

"He bombarded me with questions about *Law & Order: SVU*. When it comes to the show, he's practically a groupie."

"Amazing."

"By the way, I told him that you were a fan and asked if you could join us for our next dinner out there."

"That's very kind of you, Richard. What did he say?"

" 'I love Paul. Bring him along.' "

Three weeks later Belzer and I were winging our way to Vegas. We met up with Jerry at his favorite Italian restaurant. He was already at his booth when we arrived.

"Glad to see you, Paul," said Jerry. "Do you like stone crabs?"

"I love them."

He ordered stone crabs.

"Do you like Maui onions, Richard?" he asked.

"Love them," said Belzer.

Jerry ordered the onions.

"I'm going to eat exactly half of everything that's placed before me," said Jerry, who had recently lost a great deal of weight. "That's my diet."

When it came time to order pasta, Jerry said, "They'll make the red sauce from the recipe I gave them." The restaurant also kept Jerry's special stash of wine close at hand.

As our conversation began, I couldn't help but speak in telethon-ese.

"Jerry," I said. "I've watched your telethon year after year. I study it. I make no secret of this."

Jerry didn't seem impressed. What's more, he really didn't seem to care. He was more interested in getting inside stories about *Law & Order: SVU* from Belzer. Acknowledging my interest in him, though, he did say, "I'll give you a complete set of my movies on DVD." And with that, he had his driver go back to his house and fetch the DVDs.

When the DVDs arrived, I thanked him profusely. "I will treasure these," I said.

"Richard," he said, "have I showed you the schedule I made up of the *Law & Order: SVU* marathons coming up? It's a very meticulous schedule."

"I haven't seen it, Jerry," said Belzer.

"Would you like to?" Jerry asked.

"Sure."

That prompted Jerry to send his driver back to the house to fetch the schedule. When the driver returned with paper in hand, Jerry carefully went over his viewing schedule, showing the countless hours he was devoting to watching each show, in some cases for the third or fourth time.

The rest of the evening consisted of Jerry discussing the technical aspects of *Law & Order: SVU*, the pans and zooms, the wide shots and close-ups. He showed little interest in me and could not have cared less about my encyclopedic knowledge of his telethons.

A week later when I was back in New York, an express envelope arrived from Las Vegas. Inside was a profile of me that had appeared some years before in *The New Yorker*. Attached to the article was a card that read, "With compliments from Jerry Lewis."

I thought it strange. Surely Jerry knew that I had seen the piece. Why was he sending it to me? Then I remembered that the author of the article had said something about Shaffer liking "telethon sleaze."

Oh God, I thought to myself, *Jerry feels like I've been making fun of him.* Our relationship, to quote the great standard song, had ended before it began. Not only had I not been able to impress him with my vast knowledge of his show business exploits, he was implying he never wanted to see me again.

Was this, in truth, an accurate reading of Jerry's attitude?

If you'll bear with me, I'll hold that question in abeyance. I'll get to more of my adventures with Mr. Jerry Lewis in due time. For now, though, we must pick up the thread of our story that has young Paul Shaffer, dutiful son, arriving at the University of Toronto to fulfill his destiny and do what has been done by hundreds of thousands of Jewish boys before him: get an education, become a lawyer, and make his parents proud.

Chapter 12

Nights in White Satin

Yes, I had a girlfriend in college. Her name was Virginia. She was lovely and coaxed me out of my virginity.

Yes, I was listening to progressive FM radio that played the Moody Blues and Spirit until Sly and the Family Stone hit with "Dance to the Music" and I was souled out again.

Yes, Ginny and I enjoyed loving nights in white satin, but, besides those, I was mostly bored with the college experience.

I took the required courses, I did reasonably well, but I did not connect with academia. I had hair down to my shoulders and a Fu Manchu mustache; I had music coming in and out of my ears; on solo piano I would play Laura Nyro's entire LP *Eli and the Thirteenth Confession*, from top to bottom. I was obsessed with the *Temptations Live!* record. After class, after getting back to the dorm and opening up my Sociology 101 book or philosophy text, I'd get into the bed and drift off to the sound of Dionne Warwick's "Make It Easy on Yourself." I was trying to make it as easy as possible. I spent most of my college years sleeping.

The one artist that woke me up and got me going—and, I

must add, has kept me going throughout my life——was the God-father of Soul, Mr. James Brown. James electrified me, as he electrified the world, beginning in my precollege years. I loved listening to the time-honored introduction rendered by Danny Ray, James Brown's formidable master of ceremonies.

"Now, ladies and gentlemen, it is Star Time. Are you ready for Star Time? Thank you and thank you kindly. It is indeed a great pleasure to present to you at this particular time the artist nationally and internationally known as the hardest-working man in show business.

"Bringing you such tunes as 'I Feel Good' . . . 'Try Me' . . . 'Night Train' . . . Million-dollar seller 'Lost Someone' . . . Very latest release 'It's a Man's Man's Man's World.'

"Yes, he'll make your bladder splatter, he'll make your knees freeze and your liver quiver. The star of the show, Mr. Please Please himself, soul brother number one, Mr. Dynamite, the man with the crown . . . James Brown and the Famous Flames."

Musicologists hail the sublime musical contributions of Mozart, Monteverdi, Beethoven, and Bach. Here in America we celebrate Louis Armstrong, Aaron Copland, Duke Ellington, and Charles Ives. The relative merits of musical geniuses are impossible to calculate. I won't try. I will only say that, for my money, James Brown is——as Arthur Conley calls him in his fabulous "Sweet Soul Music"——"King of them all, y'all."

It's the singing, yes: the pitch-perfect screams that penetrate your heart and freeze your blood. It's the dancing, of course: the spins, the splits, the grace, and the grit. It's the band: tighter and righter than any orchestra in the proud history of soul. It's the songs: the social messages, the sexual subtexts, the self-assertive anthems of a free black man in a white world. It's everything. James Brown is everything I love in music.

And while James's greatest songs were born before and during my days at the University of Toronto, and while I promised that I would give you a taste of that time and maintain some chronological order in this narrative, I must once again jump ahead, even as I slide back—just as James Brown might do in his act.

So dig me now, skip ahead to later. Then jump back, Jack, and do the Alligator . . .

✦ ✦ ✦

It's 2008. James is much on my mind because I have just returned from an auction at Christie's where I bought a number of choice items from the James Brown estate, including his Hammond B3 organ and a glorious cape worn by the man himself. As I will soon explain, the cape holds special significance for me. I was sad that James's finances required such a sale; but I was also grateful to have the chance to acquire and lovingly preserve pieces of his precious history.

My history with James began two decades before I met him in person. I met him on screen when he appeared in the famous T.A.M.I. concert film shot at Santa Monica Civic Auditorium in 1964. I saw it in Thunder Bay, at the local movie theater. When I heard it would be playing, I arrived at the only showing— Saturday morning at 9 a.m. By the time the film was over, I was a changed man. T.A.M.I. stood for "Teenage Awards Music International." The concert was wildly successful in defining the essence of teenage music for that era. Its director, Steve Binder, also directed *Shindig!* In fact, much to my delight, T.A.M.I. had the same shady lighting and Hollywood rock-and-roll feel as *Shindig!* I sat with my mouth open, my heart beating, blood coursing through my veins at twice the normal speed. I sat looking at Chuck Berry, the fiery opening act. Then came Gerry and the Pacemakers, a nod to the British Invasion. Motown stormed back with the Miracles literally getting down with "Mickey's Monkey." Then came marvelous Marvin Gaye. (I would later learn that Teri Garr was one of the background dancers and that Glen Campbell and Leon Russell played in the backing band.) Lesley Gore rocked pop's first women's lib affirmation, "You Don't Own Me." At this point I was convinced that it couldn't get any better. But it did. Jan and Dean were great. The Beach Boys were even greater. In fact, the Beach Boys were fantastic, even if Brian Wilson later insisted that they be edited out of the show because he thought their Kingston Trio–style outfits made them look like golf caddies. Next up, from the other side of the Pond: Billy J. Kramer and the Dakotas followed by Detroit's very own Supremes, whose delicious subtext was sex, sex, and more sex. How much more could I take? After Diana, Mary, and Flo came the burning sounds of the one-handed drummer Moulty Moulton and his Barbarians.

The most ferocious barbarian of all, however, appeared as the penultimate act. It was as though, for all their brilliance, the preceding artists had merely been warm-ups for this man. This man was James Brown. And his performance in this movie made time grind to a halt, and the world stop turning on its axis. Dogs stopped chasing cats. Cats stopped chasing birds. Lions lay down with lambs. Babies ceased crying. Women stopped weeping. And James Brown, in singing "Out of Sight," conquered the known world. From there he went into "Try Me" and "Prisoner of Love." But it was "Please, Please, Please" that tore the roof off and brought down the heavens. At the end of the song, a cape was placed on James's back. I sat in wonder.

Why the cape? What were they doing? James had fallen to his knees, and perhaps the purpose of the cape was to prevent a chill after his red-hot performance. But as he started to leave the stage, he threw off the cape and returned to the mic, singing another stirring chorus of "Please, Please, Please." The routine continued. He fell to his knees; a new cape was placed; then he got up and threw it off only to return to the mic. Again! And again! He couldn't stop himself. He couldn't stop returning to plead to his woman, "Don't Go." He was truly out of sight, only to get even further out of sight during his chaser, an instrumental version of "Night Train" during which JB left the ground and levitated like a dark angel in a waking dream.

The dream needed to end there, but, alas, it didn't. The Rolling Stones were the final act. The Stones weren't bad. The Stones were great. But the Messiah had already come and gone and, despite their love of R&B, the Stones simply couldn't deal with Mr. Dynamite. For the rest of his career, Mick Jagger would try to emulate the man who had performed before him, while the always-candid Keith Richards would admit that following JB was the worst mistake the Stones had ever made.

The best move I ever made was to perform with Mr. Brown on Letterman. His first appearance came in 1982 when we were on NBC.

"Mr. Brown," I said, "this is the honor of a lifetime. Just tell me what you'd like to play."

His answer astonished me. "What do you guys want to play, Paul?"

At the time, my World's Most Dangerous Band featured the great Will Lee on bass plus Steve Jordan, drums, and Hiram Bullock, guitar—three brilliant cats. I let the band pick the songs. Steve said, "Sex Machine" for the drumming. Hiram said, "There Was a Time" for the rhythm guitar. Will was cool with all of it.

On "Sex Machine," James wanted a fast tempo. That's the tradition of live R&B. It's all about energy. Steve Jordan, though, was a young buck who wanted to re-create the groove he'd heard on wax. He didn't quite understand that when you deal with the Godfather of Soul, you put the groove where *he* wants it. James won out and the funk got thick. He played his short keyboard solo and at the end of the song slapped me ten. I told him I wouldn't wash my hands for a week. During the break, as the band played a small portion of "I Got the Feeling," James took note.

When we were back on the air, James said, "Hey, Dave, you know what I'd like to do right now? Before you close, can we close with 'I Got the Feeling'?"

"Sure thing," said Dave. "Soon as we come back from one more break."

Once the commercial was over, we hit it: an unrehearsed full-blown version of "I Got the Feeling." The audience went crazy. Dave joined the James Brown Fan Club.

On James's second appearance, he wanted to bring his own drummer. He knew that Steve was brilliant, but James wanted full control—and that meant his own drummer. This was a delicate moment. Steve was my guy, and without him I knew we couldn't re-create the magic of James's first jam with us. On a personal note, I also knew Steve would be crushed to learn James was dropping him. Then, in a moment of inspiration, I remembered James's song from 1966, "Don't Be a Dropout," and his lifelong campaign to keep kids in school.

"James, I must tell you something about Steve," I said.

"What is it, Paul?"

"It'll kill him if he doesn't get to play. This kid stayed in school because of you."

There was a long pause before James came back with "Tell him he can play behind me. I'll bring my own drummer and we'll use both cats."

"That's great, James, Steve will be thrilled."

Steve was thrilled, until, during rehearsal, it became clear that James was dancing only to the beat of his own drummer. Steve gallantly laid out.

Then James had an idea for a musical ending. It was complicated, but pure JB. However, try as he might, James could not communicate it successfully to his drummer. Rehearsal time was running out. I had to do something.

"Godfather," I said, "with all due respect, it's one rim shot, followed by two, then three." My explanation enabled the drummer to execute James's notion. "Mr. Please Please" was pleased.

After the show, James had his man summon me to his dressing room. Mr. Dynamite was sitting under the hair dryer, his hair in curlers. As he spoke in his funky patois, I had to get on my knees—as would a subject to his royal liege—and get under the dryer with him in order to make out his words. "You gotta have a reserve drummer, Paul," said James, "because you never know what your regular drummer might do. In my band I got two drummers. Plus, my bass player can play drums, and I play drums if I have to. Get yourself a backup drummer.

"By the way, Paul," James added, "I have to give you credit, man."

"Why is that, James?"

"Because you have the *pressure of the time*. You got to do what you do in a flash. You got to turn on a dime. The *pressure of the time* is a bitch, and you handle it well, my brother."

No compliment has ever meant more to me.

Happily, the James Brown/Steve Jordan relationship was resolved in a sweetly satisfying way. A few months later, when the Godfather was asked by a magazine to name his favorite drummer, James mentioned the great Steve Jordan.

* * *

I mentioned the cape. The cape—and the routine where James throws off the cape—has a spiritual background. There is, of course, the famous Sam Cooke song, "Touch the Hem of His Garment," in which a sickly woman is healed by touching the garment of Jesus. Preachers used capelike garments in the churches that James visited early in his life. And when the sermons got good, and the preacher got to hollering, the clergyman would throw off the cloth, only to have it put back in place by an associate. Ironically, though, James told me he got the idea from watching the caped wrestler Gorgeous George.

Either way, the cape is more than a material object. It carries the spirit of James Brown who, in turn, carries the spirit of the Groove. Wearing the cape is like holding the Torah. Here's how I got called to the altar:

Blood, Sweat and Tears were great. Their first album—*Child Is Father to the Man*—came out in 1968, and I loved it extravagantly. The combination of big-band horns with funked-up rhythms and brassy vocals was original. The song that haunted me most from that first Blood, Sweat and Tears LP was Al Kooper's "I Love You More Than You'll Ever Know," a blues ballad of the highest order. Al sang it on the record. (The definitive version, though, would be cut in 1973 by the immortal Donny Hathaway.) Somehow I wound up with Al's original arrangement and started using it on Letterman after we moved to CBS. Once when I sang it during a commercial break, Dave commented, "Paul, that sounds like a James Brown kind of thing. I feel like I should put the cape on you when you sing it."

That's all I needed—dispensation from my rabbi—so I sang it and then, right in the middle of the song, went to center stage and dropped to my knees. Dave came out with the cape, draped it over me, and we performed the James Brown ritual.

The audience liked it and it became an ongoing bit. Every Friday night another celeb would put the cape on me. Cape handlers included Donald Trump, Heidi Klum, Nathan Lane, Bill Murray, Tina Fey, James Lipton, Jack Black, Governor George Pataki, Kareem Abdul-Jabbar, Whoopie Goldberg, and Ted Koppel.

* * *

The highlight, of course, was when the man himself, JB, came back to cloak me and show the world what the cape ritual was all about. He infused the drama with an intensity that rivaled Pagliacci.

After a couple of years, though, the cape had lost its glitter, and I searched for a way to retire it with grace. Around this time I had seen Paul Anka on *American Idol*, where he performed special lyrics to his "My Way" relating to the show's finale. And because I can never get enough special lyrics to "My Way," I asked Paul if he'd write a set for the cape's finale, and he readily agreed. So Paul Anka was the last to cover me with the cape after he sang:

My friend, let's not pretend, let's call an end
To something shoddy

You'd shout "roll tape," and stars would drape that crappy
    cape
On Shaffer's body
This has to stop, haven't you learned
Dave, have that shmata cleaned and burned
Paul is a proud Canadian, don't make him do that shtick
    again
If I were Paul, I'd say, "That's all"
And do it My Way.

While Anka sang, the cape, attached to pulleys, flew to the top of the set, as if ascending to the heavens.

Despite that final flight, though, the cape kept me grounded because James Brown kept me grounded—even decades before at college, when everything in me wanted to leave the ground.

College in the sixties.

The Rock Pile, a new club, opened in Toronto and booked world-class acts, including Procol Harum, the Chambers Brothers, Iron Butterfly, Brian Auger and the Trinity, featuring Julie Driscoll, and the Crazy World of Arthur Brown. Certain songs—like "Whiter Shade of Pale"—expressed the poetry of my own uncertainty.

The summer after freshman year, I convinced my parents to let me stay in Toronto by signing up for a course in musical arranging. It's a good thing I did because, besides piano lessons, that's the full extent of my formal training.

After being up all night with Ginny, laughing and loving and listening to music, I left her apartment sometime around 5 a.m. The sky was still dark, the streets deserted. The only sound was the whoosh of the street cleaner's brush. Walking through Yorkville, Toronto's Greenwich Village, I passed by the folk clubs and jazz spots. The customers were long gone. I was heading home when I noticed someone playing acoustic guitar on the stoop of the Grab Bag, an all-night deli. He was a Latin-looking cat. His sound startled me, but I kept on walking. After taking five or six steps, though, I had to stop. I turned around and walked toward him. He smiled and kept playing. I knew a little something about jazz, but this guy was way beyond jazz. He was improvising to a rhythmic pulse. He sent melodies soaring into space. He was playing scales and modes I had never heard before. They were mind-boggling. He went on for nearly a half hour.

"How do you do that?" I asked as soon as he was through.

"I let it go," he said. "I submit. Wanna try?"

Sure I did. Just as a beautiful Canadian sunrise gave light to the city, he and I made our way to a music room at the university that housed an upright piano. The guitarist introduced himself as Tisziji Munoz. His original first name was Michael. His lineage was Spanish and Puerto Rican, and he had grown up on the streets of Brooklyn. As a kid, he had been in gangs, and as a young man he'd joined the army, where he had played in a military band that, oddly enough, was filled with Coltrane freaks. Here he switched from his original instrument—congas—to guitar.

As Tisziji led me through his improvisational maze, he never offered a technical lexicon or, God forbid, a handbook. It was always "submit"—submit to the feeling, submit to the moment, submit to the power greater than thyself. He told me that my spirit was already free. It was just a matter of getting in touch with that freedom. When he spoke of seeking a Christ consciousness through the music, I couldn't help but be taken aback. Once a bar mitzvah boy, always a bar mitzvah boy.

"I don't mean crucifixion and resurrection," Tisziji said. "I mean responding to a source of love that is pure and eternal and without judgment or limits. You tap into that source, and the spirit shows you where to go."

That morning, my fatigue turned to excitement. We jammed together for well over three hours. I was fascinated. I couldn't have risen farther from my Motown/Phil Spector/James Brown foundation. My orientation was girl group pop, R&B, precise horn punches, and in-the-pocket blues grooves. My orientation was the earth. Munoz's orientation was the sky. "You gotta walk before you can fly, Paul," he told me. That's why he grounded me in standards. He taught me how to properly voice the tunes of my parents' generation, "A Foggy Day in London Town," "Body and Soul," "All the Things You Are." I knew them but could never realize them on piano until that morning. Tisziji taught me jazz from the inside out. And then, out we went, eventually leaving the standards and venturing into the unchartered territories of free jazz.

For reasons I still can't quite fathom, I was able to hang. I was able to follow his lead, or the flow of the spirit, and allow myself a freedom I had never known before. I liked it. Hell, I *loved* it. It wasn't precise. It wasn't a three-and-a-half-minute Top Ten tune. It was imprecise and it went on and on. Even the traditional chord changes employed by jazz musicians were abandoned. But somehow I could cope with that abandonment and, with Tisziji's guidance, float freely in his universe. I trusted the guy because I realized he heard things I didn't. His ears were open; his heart was open. When I followed his lead and abandoned my notions of song structure, I heard new sounds. I made new sounds. Improbably enough, I found myself inside the avant-garde jazz world of Toronto.

Munoz was my musical guru. Others, in turn, called Sonny Greenwich, another far-out guitarist, their guru. In fact, Sonny had a cult. Tisziji loved Sonny's musical mind. I became a member of Munoz's band, but I also learned a great deal from listening to Sonny, who was more of a melodist than Tisziji. Sonny played a version of "When the World Was Young" that made the world weep. Sonny knew the standards, and he strongly urged all respectable jazz musicians, avant-garde or straight-ahead, to develop a large repertoire of songs. I dug Sonny, but Munoz was my mentor.

Being inside this bohemian enclave was certainly stimulating, but I was also a college boy with college requirements. My major was sociology because I thought music would be too hard. I was also interested in how people related to each other. When I was told that fieldwork and a long paper were required for my deviant sociology course, I decided to step back from my role as a jazz avant-garde insider and take an outside look. I saw how I could use my time with Munoz for a dual purpose: I'd continue to learn from him musically and, at the same time, use that firsthand experience as research. That's how I came to write the term paper I called "A Sociological Analysis of the Subculture of Avant-Garde Jazz Musicians in Toronto, Canada, circa 1970."

My thesis soon became clear: just as I had learned earlier in my life that the later the hour, the hipper the humor, now I saw that for the avant-garde jazzman, the poorer his finances, the more respect he earned. For example, local jazz flautist Moe Kaufman, who in 1958 had enjoyed huge success with a single entitled "Swinging Shepherd Blues," was looked down on, precisely *because* of his hit. He was seen as a sellout. The academics called it inverse social stratification. All this intrigued me, and I was able to write my thesis, giving real-life examples and actual quotes from musicians with whom I played.

I was deep into the culture and, for a while, thought it would be my musical future.

I remember one night after a gig the cats and I were talking. Dave Decker, Munoz's drummer, was asking trumpeter Mike Malone a question.

"Hey, man, would you ever think about moving to New York and trying to play there?"

"No, man. Those cats down there—Ornette, Pharaoh, McCoy—they're so heavy, man, I could never hang."

"How 'bout you, Paul?" Munoz asked. "Would you ever consider New York?"

"Well, as a rock player I would, sure. Rock and roll's my thing."

But I was far from the world of rock and roll. This was the world of cosmic jazz. Yet even in that world, with all its spiritual enlightenment, all was not sweetness and light.

I was playing keyboards with Munoz at a coffeehouse near the university. This was the Vietnam era. Our appreciators included students, street people, and existentialists. Hippies in assorted colors and sizes sat in the audience. We welcomed all of them. As the evening went on, our music became freer, drifting from one planet to the next. In the process, several new planets were discovered. We were flying and taking the responsive listeners along with us on our journey.

Then, as if the coffee shop were an Old West saloon, the doors flew open, and in walked Sonny Greenwich with his cult of spiritual gunslingers behind him. He walked to the bandstand and, pointing to Tisziji, announced authoritatively, "You are not the Christ."

"I never claimed to be," Munoz replied.

"You are the anti-Christ," Sonny added.

"I am?" asked Munoz.

"Yes," Sonny went on, "I am the Christ."

Jesus Christ!

The audience sat spellbound, not quite understanding the magnitude or meaning of the confrontation at hand.

It wasn't long, though, before Sonny retreated. Having made such a divine claim, he did not see the need to restate his case. I must say that Tisziji reacted with sublime grace. He simply smiled.

Afterward, I realized I had witnessed a crucifixion. But a week later, when Munoz took me and the boys to play a gig in a majestic church on Bloor Street and kicked off with Pharoah Sanders's "The Creator Has a Master Plan," I saw the resurrection. Munoz transcended the ugly incident with Sonny and carried us to that place in the cosmos where pure peace prevails.

Chapter 13

Keeping North America Safe

My patriotism extends to two great nations: Canada and the U.S. Both countries have been good to me. And so it was without equivocation that, after having graduated from the University of Toronto, I took it upon myself to travel to far northern Quebec to make sure that the missile bases there, housing weapons designed to protect home and hearth, were indeed secure. I did this not with any military knowledge but with a firm grasp of the rock and roll piano. I played in a cover band supporting a variety show that provided entertainment for the officers and enlisted men. It was hard work, sometimes even treacherous work, but it had to be done. Music kept the soldiers sharp. Without hearing our inspiring version of "Raindrops Keep Falling on My Head," these brave Canadian military men might easily have lost their motivation and made a critical mistake.

Before I joined this band and began this noble trek, I had had a critical conversation with my father. Dad had come to Toronto on business during the end of my final semester before graduation. I was always happy to see him, and he was always happy in the certain knowledge that after graduation I would go to law school, just as he had done. We met for lunch in the dining room of the Royal York Hotel, a grand dame building in the center of the city. He asked how school was going and mentioned that he and Mom, along with several other relatives, were excited about attending my graduation ceremony.

"I presume your law school application is in," Dad said.

When I hesitated before answering, he knew something was wrong.

"Don't tell me you're not applying, Paul."

I was never one to tell my father anything he didn't want to hear. He was a good man, a strong man, a devoted dad. I didn't want to disappoint him, but my resolve was strong. My college experience had taught me one thing: I had to give music a try.

"I don't want to go to law school," I said.

"I understand, Paul, but consider this: in a few years you'll want the options that law school provides. Besides, there's also a respected practice I've established that could be yours."

I didn't want to say it to Dad—and didn't—but if the thought of my practicing law in Thunder Bay was my father's dream, it was my nightmare.

"I want to try this music thing," I said.

"And actually make a living as a musician?" he asked. "That's rough, son."

"I know it is, but I need to try. It's the one thing I'm passionate about."

"Passion doesn't equal income."

"I realize that, Dad. But if I don't try, I'll never know."

I expected my father to retaliate with ironclad arguments. He was, after all, a professional litigator. But much to his everlasting credit, he didn't respond, not for several long minutes.

Maybe he was thinking about his own passion for music; maybe he was thinking about his own unrealized ambition to be an entertainer; maybe he was thinking that I could do what he couldn't. Whatever he was thinking, his response was beautiful.

"You know, Paul, your mother and I figured you might say something like this. And . . . well, you're absolutely right. This is about you, not me. You need to give it a try. But also give yourself a time limit. If it isn't working after a year, reconsider. That sound fair?"

"Very fair."

When lunch was over and we walked out of the hotel, I kissed my father and said, "Thanks for understanding, Dad."

"I'm rooting for you, Paul."

A year.

I had a year to make a living making music.

✦ ✦ ✦

During my heroic missile base tour, one of my fellow entertainers was a young woman named Avril. She told me that when she got back to Toronto, she wanted to audition for *Godspell*, the theatrical musical. My girlfriend, Virginia, also wanted to try out. The composer, Stephen Schwartz, was personally listening to singers who hoped to get into the show. Both girls wanted my help; they wanted me to accompany them. I was happy to assist. But before I get to the part of my story where Shaffer meets Schwartz, I need to give you a glimpse into my life as a freelance musician in Toronto, desperate to make it. If not, a large pile of law books awaited me.

Toronto was the farthest point north on the southern chitlin' circuit. It was a soul town with lots of soul music. Hookers were in abundance. Johns were in abundance. Music lovers, who included both hookers and johns, were in abundance. Musicians were in abundance. Musicians who played the Hammond B3 organ, the soul instrument du jour, were in demand. The pay was low, but the sound was right. I loved the sound, and I didn't mind playing the raunchy joints. The raunch had flavor. Toronto had been favored by the presence of Jackie Mitoo, a well-known organist in reggae circles. Mitoo was the real deal, a brother from Kingston who put R&B through his fine Jamaican filter. His version of the Stylistics' "Betcha by Golly Wow" was one of the great revelations of my young life. He played the melody from start to finish with few flourishes. Just a great sound. He sang through the organ. This was, of course, several million miles away from my experience with Munoz. But one didn't cancel out the other. Both modes—the straight-ahead song and the far-out excursion—got me off.

Playing cover songs in cover bands suited me just fine, and my passion for that particular form of musical expression deepened. I was, after all, playing songs that I didn't simply like but loved. In fact, it was in Toronto in the early seventies that I developed a credo that has come in handy when, at critical times in my life, confusion threatened to cancel clarity: "What I do best is simply play songs I love."

To be in a funky bar band in a funky Toronto bar and play the Dells' "Stay in My Corner" and "Oh, What a Night" or the Dramatics' "Whatcha See Is Whatcha Get" and "In the Rain" was all I could ask for. And then to top it off with lovely topless dancers undulating right in front of my organ . . . well, these were stimulating times.

It was during these times that I first heard Wayne Cochran at the El Mocambo, a well-known Toronto rock club. As a kid in Thunder Bay, I was familiar with the Cochran legend, this singer from Florida known as the "white James Brown." He was said to have two drummers and cotton candy hair piled to the sky. He had a number of regional hits. I had heard "Going Back to Miami." (And later covered it with the Blues Brothers.)

The show was masterful. It opened with just a three-piece rhythm section—bass, guitar, and drums. No Wayne in sight. It was the bass player who killed me. He carved out a groove that could have made Richard Nixon boogaloo. He was the funkiest bass player I'd ever heard. (Later I'd learn he was the great Jaco Pastorius.) This groove kept grooving. The groove got groovier, and groovier, and so goddamn groovy that people were up and dancing while the horns came marching in from the back of the club. When they reached the stage it was horns up and out blasted a devastating version of Freddie Hubbard's "Mr. Clean." Then, on cue, a voice from heaven announced, "Ladies and gentlemen, *this* is Wayne Cochran and the C. C. Riders!"

I was already on the floor before Wayne came out. When Wayne appeared, Wayne killed. Wayne killed without a voice. His voice was shot, but it didn't matter. His soul was intact, and his soul made up for his voice. The pitch, the intonation, the enunciation—it all said one thing: *I am a showman whose ability to perform overwhelms all liabilities. I will win you over with my soul. I will soul you to death. My soul will prevail.*

Wayne's show was such a smash that the minute he closed I ran to the phone to call Funky Ricky.

"Wayne's as great as we imagined him to be," I said. "Even greater."

"I need every detail," Ricky demanded. "Don't leave out a fuckin' thing."

I didn't.

Which brings me to the first time I met David Letterman.

As this narrative continues, I'll put this meeting into some personal and—forgive my sense of self-importance—historical context. For now, it's enough to say that it was the early eighties, and I was being considered as the bandleader of Letterman's new post–Johnny Carson late-night talk show on NBC.

When I was ushered in to see Dave, the most affable of men, he asked me about my musical ideas for the show. I thought back to my days playing the topless bars in Toronto and said, "I'm partial to R&B and think it would be great to interpret the vocals instrumentally."

"Sounds good," said Dave. "I've always seen myself as Wayne Cochran anyway."

That was about the hippest thing I'd ever heard a talk-show host say.

* * *

Ten years earlier, in 1972, Avril and Virginia's request to have me accompany them for *Godspell* did not seem to be a life-altering opportunity. But my friends tell me that I'm a helpful kind of fellow, and in this spirit I agreed to play. I worried that the deadline established by my dad was nearing. In these past eleven months, I had worked steadily at clubs and with Munoz, but I wasn't really making a living. Something had to happen—and soon. I was only getting twenty dollars for this audition. But when it comes to music, I've always had the attitude that low-pay or no-pay, it's always good to play.

When we arrived, we saw that the auditorium was bustling with young performers waiting their turn. The audition line was long. Avril was called early. I went to the upright piano on stage, and Avril took her place before the mic. She sang the hell out of "Bless the Lord," a song from the show.

Virginia was next. Her number was Dusty Springfield's "I Only Want to Be with You."

From the dark void of the empty audience a voice rang out. "Very nice, young lady. Might I have a word with your piano player?"

I walked to the edge of the stage. A well-spoken man, also in his early twenties, approached me. He was well dressed and well mannered.

"I'm Stephen Schwartz," he said.

"Paul Shaffer."

"Paul, I like the way you play. You're a rock pianist, aren't you?"

"Try to be."

"Well, you are. And to be honest with you"—here he brought his voice down to a whisper—"my audition pianist doesn't quite get rock. He's a typical theatrical pianist with a light touch. I need that percussive feel that you seem to have. He doesn't understand that this is a rock musical and most of the aspiring singers are coming in with rock songs. How's your general knowledge of rock songs?"

"Good," I said. "Excellent."

"That's what I thought. Would you be willing to take his place and play for the rest of the auditions?"

"Of course."

"Just give me a few minutes to dismiss him."

As we all know, Lana Turner was discovered at Schwab's drugstore in Hollywood. Billie Holiday in Harlem. Don Rickles was discovered in Miami Beach. Stephen Schwartz discovered me in Toronto. What exactly, though, did Schwartz discover?

A guy who could bang out rock tunes and knew a helluva lot of rock tunes to bang. So when the next singer wanted to sing

"Roll Over, Beethoven," I was right there with him. Didn't need the music. And when the next gal sang "Respect," I was down. When a guy wanted "Heart of Gold," I gave him "Heart of Gold."

Stephen Schwartz, who had only recently found fame with *Godspell*, had discovered, at the very least, my talent as an audition pianist.

Toward the end of the afternoon, after I had accompanied at least two dozen auditioners, a skinny Jewish gal wearing floppy overalls came up to me and with an endearing lisp asked, "Do you know 'Zip-a-Dee-Doo-Dah'?"

"Sure," I said.

Her hair was in pigtails and her smile impish and irresistibly sweet.

I got into the Disney spirit, improvised a quick introduction, and then watched the young woman command the stage with such childlike charm we all realized we were watching a star. She was absolutely adorable; she danced and sang with such obvious sincerity that, when she was through, everyone—even her competitors—burst out into applause. I myself stood up and applauded. This was Gilda Radner.

Of course Gilda made it into the show. And so did Avril. Alas, Virginia did not.

At the conclusion of the long process, Stephen Schwartz came up to me and said, "Good job. How would you like to put together a band and become musical director of the show?"

I was speechless. Awestruck. Delirious.

This was it! Good-bye, law school!

When I told my dad that I had, in fact, gone beyond the topless bars and funky clubs of Yonge Street and had landed a legitimate job in the legitimate theater doing a legitimate musical, Bernie Shaffer, much to his credit, was nothing but proud. He didn't renege on his deal, and he didn't warn me that the show might not last.

"That's wonderful, Paul," he said. "Your mother and I will be there opening night."

The assignment, of course, represented an unexpected change. I had come to the *Godspell* auditions merely to make a few bucks. But I left with a whole new career direction. This wasn't playing cover tunes on the Hammond B3. Nor was it playing far-out jazz with Tisziji Munoz. This was inserting myself into the cutting-edge trend of the day, rock musicals. That *Godspell* had a Christian theme mattered not, especially when I heard Jewish Victor Garber win the part of Jesus. He sang like an angel. I felt like an angel had led me to this great gig. This great gig led me to a new circle of friends. And that changed everything.

Chapter 14

"You've Seen These, Then?"

With those words, Andrea Martin, perhaps the funniest of all the funny people who appeared in the Toronto *Godspell,* lifted her blouse and exposed her breasts. Her breasts were perfect, her delivery priceless.

That scene did not unfold in the show itself. It unfolded in the parking lot after she and other members of the cast had dined on spaghetti and cheap wine. In those days, we couldn't have cared less about the quality of the wine. We were more concerned with the quality of Andrea's breasts, humor, and indomitable spirit. Like all of us, she was hell bent on making it, and this musical, that we discussed night and day, was the vehicle.

At the same audition that saw Gilda win the part, two other stars emerged. They grew up together in Hamilton, Ontario, where they both graduated from McMaster University.

The first guy was Marty Short, who sang a Sinatra-styled version of "My Funny Valentine" that brought down the house. He was bursting with talent—impish, wildly irreverent, wholly unpredictable, and fueled by more energy than a souped-up Ferrari. At the time, however, he was driving a beat-up Beetle and wearing a John Lennon–style cap.

The second guy was Eugene Levy, who sang "Aquarius," but with a Perry Como cool. In fact, some time later, when Eugene started doing SCTV skits, he did a parody of "I Love the Night Life," the high-octane disco ditty by Alicia Bridges, as if done by Como. He'd sing as he reclined on a sofa, his head on a pillow, nearly dozing off as he yawned the lyrics "I love the night life, I love to Bogey . . ." Marty was subtle as a sledgehammer; Eugene actually *was* subtle. Both were hilarious.

After sadly breaking up with Virginia, I began living with Mary Ann McDonald, another cast member. Marty and Eugene shared a house at 1063 Avenue Road. Their home became Comedy Central. We'd gather there after the show for postmortem. We'd meet there at week's end for what Marty called "Friday Night Services"—and Marty isn't even Jewish. It was a nonstop gag and improv fest. We'd do impromptu skits, playing each other, ruthlessly parodying our own shortcomings. We became polished shtickticians.

Never mind Aquarius, this was the age of Living Theater. Off-the-wall antics were all the rage. Even within the context of *Godspell*, a retelling of St. Matthew's gospel, in between acts a cast member could come out and do unrelated and outrageous shtick. Marty, of course, was the king of outrageous shtick. Allow me to jump ahead some thirty years for an example of prime Short shtick.

The Janet Jackson One-Boob Super Bowl was the hottest story of the year. Marty was due to appear on Letterman. He phoned me and said, "Paul, I've been thinking about the Janet Jackson thing."

"Yes, Marty," I answered.

"Now, you've been with Dave for decades. You know him better than anyone. Do you think he'd mind if I came out wearing a pair of shorts?"

"Not at all," I said.

"And after I sat down, if I allowed just one testicle to pop out, that would be okay?"

"Of course," I said. "Dave would be delighted."

* * *

When I think back to the Toronto of the seventies, it becomes clear that Marty Short was inadvertently my life coach. He changed my vision of not only what it meant to *be* funny, but to *live* funny. Culturally, he was the bridge between my parents' culture and my own. For example, my parents loved Sinatra. So did Marty. But Marty, through an irony that both mimicked and adored the ring-a-ding-ding Sinatra style, made it okay for me, a rock 'n' roll kid, to embrace the Sinatra aesthetic. Marty showed me that life could be lived out in comedy sketches. Life might be tragic; catastrophe might be looming; but if we turn our little daily disappointments into funny bits—with setups and punch lines—we can beat back the blues and die laughing. Nothing keeps Marty Short from making you laugh.

Meanwhile, in our little world of Canadian show biz, I was delighted when Gilda threw a surprise party for my twenty-third birthday and gave it a fifties theme because I was known, even then, as a guy who loved the oldies. Gilda wore a poodle skirt and chewed a fat wad of gum, Eugene came as a greaser, and Marty as a nerd with his pockets stuffed with Kleenex. "Why Kleenex?" I asked. "Because in the fifties," he said, "everyone seemed to be carrying a lot of Kleenex."

A little later, Marty appeared in a serious play in Hamilton called *Fortune and Men's Eyes*. The story involved gay men in jail, which is why Gilda called it "Fortune and Men's Thighs." It was an arty drama with all the pretensions of the period.

Nonetheless, Eugene, Gilda, and I dutifully drove down for opening night. Marty had always spoken of Shakespeare's, his favorite restaurant in Hamilton, and insisted we eat there afterward. As we drove by Shakespeare's on the way to the theater, though, we saw that it was closed. When we arrived and took our seats, I saw that the actors were onstage and already in character. The atmosphere was solemn. After all, they were imprisoned. Marty was sitting on a bench center stage, assuming a deadly serious attitude. I marched down the aisle and approached him indignantly. "Marty!" I screamed. "Shakespeare's is closed! Do you hear me?" His head went down as he fought back the laughter; but he couldn't stop his lower body from shaking and soon lost control. There went the mood. Forget solemnity.

Back at *Godspell*, when Victor Garber left to shoot the movie version, Don Scardino came in from New York to take his place. Don actually moved into Victor's apartment. "I've sublet Victor's life," Don liked to say. Don did well in the role but after a while moved on. Then Eugene, a Jew like Jesus, got the part. The problem, however, involved hair, a big topic at the time. They claimed Eugene's chest was too hairy and insisted that he shave. Eugene said no. Chances are, Jesus himself was hairy as a bear. Besides, claimed Eugene, one has to maintain one's sense of dignity. He would not shave. Fortunately, a compromise was forged, and Eugene, as savior of mankind, wore a tank top during matinees so as not to scare the kids. The audience accepted him and Eugene was a hit.

A quick out-of-chronology aside for a glimpse into Eugene's humor. Eugene and I were in California. I was staying in L.A. at the Continental Hyatt House, lovingly called the Riot House by the rock stars who helped destroy it. My room overlooked the glamorous city. At the time, Eugene was living in not-so-glamorous Pasadena, and I invited him over. As we stood on the balcony and perused the landscape of glittering lights, I said, "It's Friday night. They're having 'Friday Night Services' in Toronto. Let's call the gang." Once we got our friends on the phone, Eugene began describing the scene in loving detail, rubbing in the fact that they were in Canada while we were in Hollywood. He talked about how Hollywood was overrun with stars. Then he'd say, "Look who just walked in the room. Why, it's Dick York." Dick York was one of the stars of *Bewitched*. Then Eugene added, "I can't believe it, it's Dick Sargent. Hey, you replaced Dick York on *Bewitched*. What are the odds?" But Eugene wasn't finished yet. "Can this really be happening?" he said. "I'm looking straight into the eyes of Don DeFore." DeFore played Thorny Thornberry, the ever-jovial neighbor on *Ozzie and Harriet*.

In the post–*Ozzie and Harriet* era of hippies and *Hair*, the producers of *Godspell* had to make sure the show didn't lose its edge. Once a choreographer/director was sent up from New York to whip us into shape. He assumed the demeanor of a guru. This, of course, was the era of gurus. He'd meditate; he'd medicate; he'd pontificate; he'd procrastinate; he'd speak of nuanced staging changes and subtle variations in delivering lines. He wore the robes of an ancient teacher. We were all impressed. As it turned out, though, the gentleman was using his guru figure shtick for a singular purpose: to get laid.

"Am I a guru figure?" I asked Eugene Levy.

"No," said Eugene, "you're more of a Jack Carter figure."

"Ah."

* * *

I'm not sure whether the guru figure was successful, but the show was successful enough to run for well over a year.

Chapter 15

"Where Are We Now?"...

... I ask the cabdriver.

"New York City, where the hell do you think we are?"

I've just flown into LaGuardia Airport. At 6 a.m. I caught the first morning flight from Toronto. Now it's 8 a.m. and the yellow cab, with me in the back gawking like a gringo, emerges from a tunnel and starts weaving its way through the canyons of steel.

I'm beside myself with excitement. I'm overcaffeinated and overtired. Last night I played *Godspell*, just as I've played it for the past eleven months, eight shows a week with four on the weekend. The band consists of only four members—myself and a bassist, drummer, and guitarist. Because Schwartz's score is so keyboard based, the weight is on me to bang it out and keep it moving. I have tremendous love for the show. I love the songs and the spirit and the fact that it allows me to demonstrate my technical prowess. I have it down cold and never tire of performing it.

(Even today, thirty-seven years later, whenever Marty Short

and I get together, I go to the piano, he stands behind me, and, for the next hour, we perform every single song in that blessed show. When our wives put us away in the old-age home, Marty and I will be performing *Godspell* there on a nightly basis.)

The show rekindles my energy. Last night, for example, after the curtain went down, I ran to a late-night gig with Munoz in Yorkville. And if that weren't enough, at 2 a.m. I hooked up with Lenny Breau, the remarkable jazz guitarist, for an after-hours jam. I didn't play with Tisziji or Lenny for money, but because my soul craved their inspiration. My body craved sleep, but after barely an hour of shut-eye, it had to head for the airport. Stephen Schwartz had sent me a ticket for a quick trip to New York City so I could play piano on the recording session for the sound track of the *Godspell* movie.

Nothing this big has ever happened to me before. This is not only my first trip to New York, it will also be my first time in a recording studio.

"This is my first time here," I tell the cabbie.

"No kidding," he replies.

He turns up his radio. "Walking in the Rain with the One I Love" comes on. This is Barry White's girl-group masterpiece with Love Unlimited. The soaring strings seem to contain all the romantic adventure of the city that awaits me. The song becomes the sound track to my trip.

Twenty minutes later, I notice that this cab ride is taking an awfully long time. It doesn't occur to me that the cabbie has taken me for a mark.

"Where are we now?" I ask.

"Spanish Harlem."

"Spanish Harlem!"

I look out the window and see my first brownstone. I think

of the lyrics about that red rose up in Spanish Harlem—it is a special one, it's never seen the sun. I see that beneath the brownstone there are steps leading down to a basement apartment. This architectural configuration thrills me. It's been in every New York detective show I've ever seen. I imagine that this is the very apartment that houses the rose. She reclines on a bed of cool cotton sheets and wears a sweet fragrance that I can detect, even in this passing cab.

"Where are we now?" I ask.

"The Bronx."

The Bronx! I crane my neck to get a glimpse of the roofs. I hear the Drifters telling me that on the roof's the only place they know where you just have to wish to make it so.

Fifteen minutes later, I ask, "Where are we now?"

"Park Avenue."

Park Avenue! There's the Waldorf Astoria! I remember hearing stories about Cole Porter living in the Waldorf Towers and composing "Down in the Depths of the 90th Floor" on the grand piano of his penthouse suite.

The cab keeps moving until I see that the neon lights are bright and feel the magic in the air. I don't have to ask where we are. We're boogalooing down Broadway! My heart is hammering. We stop at a red light and I glimpse the address: 1619 Broadway. Dear God, 1619 Broadway is the Brill Building, the place where virtually every great song of my childhood was written. I want to jump out of the cab and run into the building, looking for Jerry Leiber and Mike Stoller, Doc Pomus, and Morty Shuman. "Doc!" I want to shout, "I'm here." "Morty!" I want to scream, "I've made it to New York!"

By the time we pull up to Bill's Rehearsal Studio in midtown, the cab tab is fifty dollars, a fortune for me. I don't care. I don't regret having been taken for a ride—not when it's been the ride of my life. As I grab my bags, "Walking in the Rain with the One I Love" comes on the cab's radio again.

Inside, the first cat I see unpacking his gear is Ricky "Bongo Boy" Shutter, whose big drums were the defining sound of the *Godspell* cast album.

"We've heard of you, Paul Shaffer," he says. "Schwartz says that you're the guy who's tearing it up in Toronto."

Can I be hearing right? Has an authentic New York City musician actually heard of me?

Stephen comes in and greets me warmly. Then it's down to work. Because I've played the show hundreds of times, I am filled with confidence. The rehearsal goes well.

Lunch break.

Walking out of the studio with the guys, I look across the street and see the Cheetah, a famous club advertising upcoming appearances by Eddie Palmieri, Machito, and Tito Puente. Suddenly the city is pulsating with the baion beat of the Drifters singing "There Goes My Baby."

We eat at Thanos, a Greek restaurant, where I immediately notice the black-and-white signed celebrity photographs on the wall. My parents have told me that the Stage Deli has such photos, but now I ask myself: *Are there so many stars in New York City that every single restaurant has its very own collection of signed celeb pictures?*

I just can't stop staring. I look up and see Pia Zadora. Next to Pia is Gwen Verdon. Next to Gwen is Jerry Orbach. (A lifetime later, I will be the toastmaster at a Richard Belzer roast with Orbach on the dais. "Nice teeth, Jerry," I'll say. "But you know, these days they can actually make 'em look like real teeth.") Next to Jerry is Stubby Kaye. (My dad loved him in *Guys and*

Dolls.) Next to Stubby is Pat Henry. (My dad told me that when Pat opened for Sinatra with his stand-up routine, he'd put an alarm clock on a stool and say, "I'm setting it for twenty minutes. That's all the time Frank gives me.") Next to Stubby are the Platters, the doo-wop masters who sang "With This Ring," "Smoke Gets in Your Eyes," and "The Great Pretender."

When the food arrives, I'm too excited to eat.

After another three hours of rehearsal, Schwartz says, "Paul, I've arranged for you to use our producers' office tonight. There's a piano there where you can practice as long as you like." He's referring to my need to rehearse a long section where I'm to play fast-paced silent-movie-style piano.

Still going strong, I take a cab to the City Squire Hotel, where I check in, change, shower, and head out to the producers' office. It's at 1650 Broadway, the other legendary building where the great tunesmiths worked. I recall that 1650 was the address of Aldon Music, the publishing firm owned by Don Kirshner, the music mogul in whose tiny cubicles Carole King and Gerry Goffin, Barry Mann and Cynthia Weil, Neil Sedaka and Howie Greenfield all toiled, creating the sound track of my childhood. I walk down the hallowed hallways as if I'm in a cathedral. I find the producers' office, sit at an in-tune baby grand, and practice till midnight.

On the way back to the hotel, I stop at a newsstand and buy the *Village Voice,* where I see that the Ronettes will be appearing tomorrow night at the Brooklyn Academy of Music. Unbelievable! I'll be there.

Sometime around 1 a.m. I fall asleep, arpeggios rising and falling in my head.

Next morning I look at the slip of paper with the address of the recording studio. It says, "A&R 799" with the address "799

Seventh Avenue." I hail a cab, get in, and announce my destination, bristling with excitement. The cabdriver nods, drives a half block, and stops. He points back to a building with the huge number "799" looming over the door. Without my knowing it, Stephen had booked me into a hotel right across the street from the studio. I give the cabbie a buck and get out, feeling like a schmuck.

The studio is cavernous. This is the very room where Elton John cut his live album *11-17-70*. It is therefore sacred ground. I look around and see two hot-line phones on the wall. The first goes directly to Wolf's Deli, where hot pastramis and corned beefs can be ordered any hour of the night or day; the second direct line goes to Radio Registry, the premier booking service for New York studio musicians. In a few years I will be a Radio Registry subscriber. My life will revolve around Radio Registry. For now, it is enough to know that I am in a land where such a service exists.

The session goes well. On some numbers, Stephen Schwartz is on one keyboard while I'm on another. We match our playing to images on a giant theater-sized movie screen. If you screw up, no problem. Stop the tape, go back, "punch in," and do it again. I have never experienced anything like this before.

Lunch is at a coffee shop around the corner. Yet even in this, the most inconspicuous of eateries, there are fabulous celeb photos on the walls. There is George Maharis, who, of course, shot to fame on *Route 66*. There is also a photo of a smiling Jack Paar with his handwritten salutation, "Harry, no one does ham and eggs better. I kid you not. Jack."

(Jump ahead two decades: I am married to the sainted Cathy. We are living in the burbs outside New York City. Victoria, our first child, is an infant. Paar and his wife Miriam live nearby. We strike up a friendship. Marty Short is coming to town and must meet Paar. I have a backyard barbecue and, before the Paars arrive, Marty teaches me Paar's theme song from *The Tonight Show*. During the party, Paar puts Victoria on his lap and interviews her in his inimitable fashion. "How do you like your formula, sweetheart?" he asks. "Is this your preferred brand or do you have other favorites?" "Jack," I say, "tell Victoria, 'I kid you not.' " "Victoria," says Paar, " 'I kid you not.' " I'm thrilled.)

Later in the afternoon Jack speaks about his famous feud with Ed Sullivan over guest star fees. Jack explains, "The only thing that reconciled us was Ed's ability to secure tickets for my daughter Randy to see the Beatles." Marty and I know this story but act as though we're hearing it for the first time. At the end of the evening, just as Jack and Miriam are leaving, I go to the piano and play his theme song. The music stops Jack in his tracks. He tries to speak but can't. I see tears in his eyes. I kid you not.

At the end of the sound track recording session for *Godspell*, Stephen is satisfied. I've given him what he's wanted. I've passed another test. Some of the guys are going out for drinks and invite me along. I beg off, hurry outside, and grab a cab for the Brooklyn Academy of Music. Time is tight, and I desperately want to be there for the first song. Will they open with "Be My Baby" or "Walking in the Rain"? I tell the driver I'll give him an especially generous tip if he gets me there in time. He manages to dance through the traffic, zip over the Brooklyn Bridge, and arrive five minutes before the show's set to start. I tip him extravagantly. I run up to the box office, but the box office is closed. I misread the ad in the *Voice*. The Ronettes won't be here till next week. Next week I'm back in Toronto, where I never stop daydreaming of New York.

TOP: Portrait of the pianist as a young man.

BOTTOM: Bernard and Shirley Shaffer. I am nothing but the sum of their parts.

TOP: Paul, Marty, and Eugene—Three Canadian Musketeers.

MIDDLE: Don Kirshner to Paul: "Forget about contracts."

BOTTOM: Greg and Paul—torn from the pages of *Tiger Beat*.

TOP: Another Saturday night: the original *SNL* band. Top row, from left: Lou Del Gatto, Cheryl Hardwick, Howard Shore. Middle row, from left: Eliot Randall, Burt Jones, PS, Bob Cranshaw, Daoud Shawr. First row, from left: Lou Marini, Mauricio Smith, Alan Rubin, Howard Johnson, Tom Malone.

MIDDLE: Paul and Gilda.

BOTTOM: Belushi and Paul— Belushi as a Stones security guard, Shaffer as Kirshner; from an *SNL* sketch that never aired. (With Jane Curtin and Bill Murray, faces turned, at left.)

TOP: Paul, Jerry Lewis, and Belz in Vegas.

MIDDLE: From left: Sid McGinnis, Steve Jordan, PS, Eric Clapton, Will Lee. "Eric," I said, "I have the pressure of the time."

BOTTOM: Fats, Paul, Ray, and Jerry Lee—"Fats and Friends," New Orleans.

TOP: Ahmet, Yoko, Jann, Suzan Evans, and Paul at the opening of the Rock and Roll Hall of Fame in Cleveland, September 2, 1995.

MIDDLE: Paul and Phil Spector go back to Mono.

BOTTOM: "Nice tie, Bob."

TOP: "Steveland, don't let the Olympiads become an illusion." (At left: B. B. King.)

BOTTOM: Aykroyd—dancin', dancin', dancin', he's a dancin' machine!

TOP: Iraq—Biff, Dave, and Paul. Note the crossed sabers; note my terrified smile.

BOTTOM: Paul Shaffer and the CBS Orchestra, the best band in the land.
From left: Al Chez, Anton Fig, Felicia Collins, Will Lee, Tom "Bones" Malone,
Sid McGinnis, Bruce Kapler.

TOP: The enchanting Cathy.

BOTTOM: Family is everything.
Paul, Will, Cathy, and Victoria.

I can't forget the final words spoken to me by Schwartz before I headed out of the studio after that long day of recording:

"Paul," he said. "One way or another, I'll find a way to bring you here. You belong in New York. This is your town."

But how long would I have to wait? How would I ever find the patience? And would Schwartz really make good on his promise? Or had he made this same promise to dozens of musicians and then forgotten all about them?

How was I to know?

And in the meantime, how could I do anything but scheme, plot, and pray my way back to the big city where people never slept and the music never stopped?

Chapter 16

Blame Canada

Why Canada?

Why are so many brilliant comics Canadian?

What are the subtle reasons for this phenomenon?

My suggestion is this:

Canada is cold as hell. That means we stay inside and watch Canadian television. Watching Canadian television means watching the proceedings of the Canadian Parliament. Watching the Canadian Parliament means hearing the right honorable gentleman from Nova Scotia arguing about fishing rights. Later in the evening you'll be entertained by *The Plouffe Family,* in which the dad, Théophile Plouffe, a former provincial cycling champion, must come to terms with being a plumber.

Watching Canadian television makes sane children crazy. The only alternative, of course, is American television. So if you take the factor of the freezing cold that keeps us inside and combine it with the less than thrilling nature of Canadian TV, you wind up with a nation hungry for truly funny comedy. Thus

American comedy, no matter how goofy, is embraced whole-heartedly. We watch it, we study it, and then we watch it again.

There is, of course, the larger issue of Canadian culture. We have a British sensibility. Yet the paradox is this: that sensibility is not British enough to provide the chic urbanity of, say, London; yet it *is* British enough to cast a pall of boredom over our great nation. Far be it from me, however, to cast Canada in anything but a positive light. On a clear night in Thunder Bay, to venture outside and view the northernmost mountains of the Canadian Shield in all their breathtaking beauty—the rugged birch, the towering evergreens—is indeed an aesthetic experience of the highest order. If you like that kind of thing.

After experiencing the subzero evening, however, many of us ran back indoors and turned on the tube. That's where we escaped a culture and climate that chilled our blood and froze our spirit. It is for this reason that we not only became connoisseurs of American comedy, we actually invaded the United States, becoming participants—and in some cases innovators—in the high (or, depending upon your point of view, low) comedic art practiced by our neighbors to the south.

With your kind indulgence, I'd now like to offer something I call the Shafferian Theory of Selling Back Your Own Shit.

I came to the theory through music. In the sixties, England sold America's music back to America. Take the Rolling Stones—they loved American blues, absorbed American blues, repackaged American blues, and sold it back to America. Americans called it the British Invasion. But if it was an invasion, Britain was using musical weapons forged in the U.S.A.

In similar fashion, Canada sold American comedy back to America in repackaged form. Just as the English learned how to play blues from America, the Canadians learned how to be funny from America. Thus the Shafferian Theory.

When Canadian comedy careerists landed on U.S. soil, they had an edge. Many had toiled in the field of television production based on the English template. The CBC, the Canadian Broadcasting Corporation, was modeled on the BBC, our British counterpart that saw the producer/director as a single job function. Put simply, you learned to do it all. So when Canadian pros like Chris Bearde and Alan Blye landed in Hollywood, they were already whiz kids who were able to take over and run shows like *The Sonny and Cher Comedy Hour*. Other Canadians were equally active: Frank Peppiatt with *Hee Haw* and Dwight Hemion with Steve Allen's *Tonight Show*. Later, Lorne Michaels, a Toronto-born graduate of the CBC's rigorous boot camp, would make the biggest mark of all.

The Sell-Back-Your-Own-Shit Theory applies to performers as well as to producers/directors. When Second City, the famed improvisational comedy group from Chicago, opened its Canadian branch in Toronto in 1973, at the very same time we were knee deep in *Godspell*, they sent up two comedians, Brian Doyle-Murray and Joe Flaherty. Their job was to recruit and train. Second City, of course, was renowned. We knew their alumni list. They had trained, among others, Alan Arkin, Avery Schreiber, Joan Rivers, David Steinberg, and Robert Klein. Naturally Brian and Joe picked up the buzz surrounding *Godspell*. When Brian and I became fast friends, he was quick to tell me about his brother Billy back in Chicago, whom he said had fashioned the funniest takeoff on Allen and Rossi in the history of takeoffs. He also mentioned another Chicagoan named Belushi who was tearing it up with *Lemmings*, the National Lampoon musical in New York.

The *Godspell* and Second City crowds merged into one. Eventually Brian and Joe wisely raided our cast and hired Gilda and Eugene Levy. The merger became more intricate when Brian started going with Gilda.

Meanwhile, my stint at *Godspell* continued. When my rock guitarist quit, I immediately thought of Munoz as a replacement. Tisziji was unorthodox, but I thought he could cover it. I went to his house, where his wife told me that he was living in the Hare Krishna temple. To see him I must arrive at 7 a.m. because at 7:15 their all-day chanting and praying began.

Next morning I got myself out of bed and knocked at the temple door at 7 a.m. sharp. The man who opened the door had a fully shaven head, a white appliqué on his face, and a flowing orange-and-white gown covering his body.

"I'm here to see Tisziji Munoz," I said.

"Paul," he said. "It's me, Tisziji."

I took another look and yes, it *was* my man Munoz. I was shocked. It was too late. I had lost him to Krishna consciousness.

"I had wanted you to take over the guitar chair in the show for a while," I said, "but now I don't think it'll work."

"Of course it'll work," he said. "When should I start? Tonight?"

"Are you sure, Tisziji?"

"Believe me, Paul, it'll be beautiful."

And it was. For four months Munoz was brilliant in *Godspell.* Tisziji's music flowed just as freely as his flowing white-and-orange robes. It was that time in the history of entertainment when the rock musical allowed and even encouraged expansive freedom. Tisziji was all about freedom—later he'd call it "God Fire"—and though he was playing a suite of songs designed around a Christian narrative, he took the story further. All of us—musicians, singers, and audience alike—went along on his mystical merry-go-round.

At the same time, the arrival of Second City in our fair metropolis was anything but mystical. It was biting, satirical, sometimes sarcastic, but always hysterical. There was a formula. The first two acts of the evening were sketches molded in this Second City style and always ending with a musical number. That way the music would mask the sound of the waitresses collecting the tabs. The third act was a series of improvs based on a formulaic technique. The thing worked like gangbusters.

✦ ✦ ✦

Before Brian Doyle-Murray started going with Gilda, Marty and Gilda had been an item. One night, Mary Ann and I double-dated with Marty and Gilda to see Frank Sinatra Jr. at the Hook and Ladder Club. I tell you this to demonstrate our devotion to the Sinatras. We loved the kids as well as the father. In fact, I have a clear memory of Junior appearing on *Hullabaloo* sometime during my Thunder Bay childhood. He sang his bid for a rock hit, "Shadows on a Foggy Day." Marty, knowledgeable in all things Sinatra, knew the tune as well. So sometime toward the end of his act at the Hook and Ladder, when it didn't look like Junior was going to do the song, Marty and I yelled out, "Sing 'Shadows on a Foggy Day!' "

Junior turned to our table and gave us a demonic glare.

"Shadows up your foggy day," he said.

Allow me to advance the calendar and set the scene for when Junior appeared on Letterman:

It was the late eighties. Was (Not Was) had a hot new album, *What Up, Dog?* The big singles off the record were "Walk the Dinosaur" and "Spy in the House of Love." True to the Was

(Not Was) tradition of including a Vegas-y song on every album, they recorded Frank Jr. doing "Wedding Bells in Vegas" on *What Up, Dog?* After Junior gave a note-perfect performance of "Wedding Bells" on Letterman, I approached him in the dressing room to tell him how much I liked his "Shadows on a Foggy Day." "Make no mistake about it, Mr. Sinatra," I said. "Seeing you sing it on *Hullabaloo* is a most cherished memory from my Canadian childhood."

Junior was as stern as he had been at the Hook and Ladder Club in Toronto.

"That song nearly ruined my career," he said.

"How so?" I asked.

"I didn't want to sing it because it was about LSD. I did it anyway. But when they wanted me to do a follow-up—still *another* drug song—I flat-out refused. So they dropped me from the label."

Frank Sinatra Jr.—he just said no.

* * *

Back in the Toronto of the seventies, the original Second City club, in spite of its wealth of comedic talent, failed. Not to be deterred, the group opened again in a new and better location, the Old Firehall on Adelaide Street. Upstairs was a cabaret room where Marty Short performed in a revue called "What's a Nice Country Like You Doing in a State Like This?" Downstairs the Second City troupe included a wildly talented guy from Hull, Quebec, Dan Aykroyd, who shared my love for deep-dish rhythm and blues. Dan had a distinct genius for spoofing those lovingly ridiculous characters we had all seen on Canadian and American TV as kids.

The second Second City location did brisk business, and the

producers offered me the job of musical director. I loved the comedy but hated the pay, which was half of what I was making at *Godspell.* I turned it down, but made the scene incessantly.

Meanwhile, Brian Doyle-Murray had moved to New York. By then, he and Gilda were splitsville and Brian was carrying a torch.

"The only thing that's keeping me from killing myself," he said, "is Belushi. If I swallow the bottle of sleeping pills, I'll never get to see his Joe Cocker again."

"Enough already," I told Brian. "I'm coming down to see him for myself."

I flew in. On my very first night in the city Brian took me to the off-Broadway *Lemmings* show. Act 1 consisted of Second City–style sketches. Act 2 was a full-on parody of Woodstock. Chris Guest did a spot-on James Taylor. Chevy Chase was hysterical as a stoned-out drummer. But Brian was right; it was Belushi's Joe Cocker that brought the house down. He *was* the whirling swirling groveling growling English soul singer, showering the audience with beer, falling on his face, delivering a career-making caricature that's going to be remembered as long as our memories hold out. That same night Brian took me over to Belushi's place, where I met John and his wife, Judy. Doug Kenney was also there.

Doug had begun the *National Lampoon* magazine and *The National Lampoon Radio Hour.* He'd used his years at Harvard to develop a devastating wit and earned himself a place of high honor among the generation that was about to reshape comedy. Later, Brian got me a little work on the *Radio Hour* and I got to know Doug. You couldn't help but like the guy, even though you saw he had a dark side. When he died in the mountains of Hawaii in 1980, his demise was shrouded in mystery. Had he jumped to his death or merely slipped and fallen? His friends, who loved him dearly, said that he was looking for a place to jump, and slipped. They felt that the twist honored Doug, whose brilliant sense of humor was rooted in the morbid. I agreed when they said that Doug would have appreciated a joke about his own demise.

Meanwhile, back in the happier days of the seventies, Belushi and Doug were thick as thieves. And when Brian told John I was a piano player, John said, "I got a gig as Cocker in Jersey tomorrow. You can do Leon Russell. We'll do the whole 'Mad Dogs and Englishmen' routine."

"I wouldn't know what to do," I said.

"Bullshit," said John. "You put on one of those crazy top hats, stick your finger in the air, and you're Leon Russell."

I thought about it. I had Russell's piano style down. But I was intimidated by Belushi's bravado. Without even hearing me, John had more confidence in me than I had in myself.

"Sorry," I said, "I gotta get back to Toronto."

Eventually I'd hook up with Belushi. Before doing so, though, I needed a few more notches on my belt.

✳ ✳ ✳

Shakespeare's, Marty Short's favorite eating spot in Hamilton, had opened in Toronto, and Marty was thrilled. He just had to take me there.

Sure, we hadn't made it in New York, but in our minds we had made it in Toronto. We were in our early twenties; we were in show business; we could pay the rent; life had never been more glamorous.

Shakespeare's represented such glamour. What other restaurant in town had telephones at every booth? If only we had someone to call.

When the waiter came to take our order, he spoke in a European accent reminiscent of Sid Caesar in a skit from *Your Show of Shows*. He was hard to understand. When Marty pressed him to repeat himself, the waiter got angry.

"You are making fun of me," he said.

"I assure you, my good man, that we are not."

Marty's "good man" tone did not go over well with the waiter.

I tried to explain to the waiter that we were sympathetic to those who had come to Canada from foreign shores and would never dream of belittling them. My explanation fell flat. The waiter got even more incensed. To prove his literacy in our language, he burst out with a line that, to this day, Marty, Eugene, and I often repeat to each other when we want to get a laugh.

"If you . . . come to my house," declared the waiter in a state of high indignation, "I will show you *books!*"

＊ ＊ ＊

At our still-going-strong "Friday Night Services," Marty told a story about meeting Richard Burton after a performance of *Camelot.*

"I was young and nervous," Marty said, "and somehow found myself backstage after one of Burton's more brilliant interpretations. I was in line to shake the great man's hand. It was a long line, and the wait made me that much more apprehensive. When I finally stood there face to face, I managed to say, 'Sir, I've always admired your work.' I figured he'd smile and I'd move on. But for some unknown reason, he engaged me in conversation. In that elegant English accent of his, he said, 'Young man, didn't you think that the reverb in the back of the hall was distracting?' I was so overwhelmed by the power of his celebrity that all I could reply was 'Thank you.' "

When Marty was through telling the story, Eugene said, "Marty, it wasn't Burton you went to see. It wasn't Burton who told you that stuff, it was Shirley MacLaine."

"Yes," said Marty, "but I don't *do* Shirley MacLaine."

* * *

We all still wanted to do New York.

After *Godspell* closed, I learned that a show at Manhattan's Public Theater was looking for a rehearsal pianist. Naturally I jumped at the chance. I was told that if rehearsals went well, I'd have a shot at being the musical director. The production was called *More Than You Deserve*.

And it was.

It began with Marty rushing me to the Toronto airport in his VW Beetle. I had managed to book the last plane out for New York. If I missed this flight, I'd miss the first rehearsal and be out of the running. I'd seen that every New York rehearsal was full-on; miss the first one and you're dead. Marty put on his John Lennon cap and played the part of a harried taxi driver who spoke in an Indian/British accent. "Don't worry, don't worry," he kept saying. "I get you there in plenty time."

But unfortunately Marty hadn't cared for his Beetle the way he had cared for the woman who would turn out to be the love of his life, the wonderful Nancy Dolman, a talented actress and another member of the *Godspell* company. His relationship with Nancy was in superb shape. His car was not. On the way to the airport the accelerator pedal snapped free of its connecting cable, and, just like that, the Beetle stopped.

"Get on the floor, Paul," Marty urged, "and pull that cable out with your fingers. That's the only way we're going to get going. You'll have to be my accelerator pedal."

For the next half hour, as we wove in and out of traffic, I was crouched on the floor, responding to Marty's exhortations. "More gas, Paul!" "Less gas, Paul!" "Lay off it, Paul!" "Lay on it, Paul!"

Miraculously, I arrived in time to catch the flight, with my fingers bleeding all the way to New York City.

Joseph Papp, who ran the Public Theater, had hired Jim Steinman to write a rock score for *More Than You Deserve*. It was an unsettling parody of *South Pacific* set in the troubled times of the Vietnam War.

I gave it my all, but halfway through the rehearsals, Steinman fired me. He didn't think I had the right feel for the music. I was bummed, but what could I do? It was back to Toronto, back to Marty's beat-up Beetle, back to the occasional gig with Tisziji Munoz. Part of me just wanted to up and move to New York, but that would require a union card, and I couldn't get a union card without having worked in the United States for at least six months. And I couldn't work in the United States without a union card. Catch-22.

I settled in and helped Marty's Nancy and my Mary Ann put together a show band called *Synergy*. They were both extremely lovely and talented women, but the *Synergy* didn't last.

I wasn't encouraged about my prospects. How could I be? I'd just been fired as a lowly rehearsal pianist. I didn't have the right papers to get to New York. All I had to look forward to were the "Friday Night Services" at Marty and Eugene's house. It was during one such service that the phone rang. It was Jim Steinman from *More Than You Deserve*.

"I was wrong to let you go," he said. "We need you."

I was in New York the next day.

Chapter 17

Jilly Loves You More Than You Will Know

STARRING . . .

MARTY SHORT AS FRANK SINATRA

EUGENE LEVY AS DEAN MARTIN

GILDA RADNER AS SHIRLEY MACLAINE

DAVE THOMAS AS CAESAR ROMERO

PAUL SHAFFER AS SAMMY DAVIS JR.

I was back in New York conducting *More Than You Deserve.*
My loyal friends came to town to see me in my august role as
musical director. For some of them, this was their first time in
the big city. The gang included my dear buddy Dave Thomas,
who took over Eugene's role in *Godspell* when Eugene became
Jesus.

To celebrate my sweet success at going from rehearsal
pianist to musical director, we planned an after-show dinner
at Jilly's.

At this point, we had all learned from Marty that life should be lived out in comedic bits. According to Shortian philosophy, life could be nothing more or less than a series of hilarious sketches. Marty was our Chairman. So when we decided to dine at Jilly's, the watering hole owned by Jilly Rizzo, Sinatra's best friend, we tried to take on the aura of the place and go in character.

"Marty is our Chairman," said Gilda. "There can be no doubt. Marty's Frank."

Agreement all around.

"And you, my dear," I said, "you must be Shirley MacLaine."

"If I'm Shirley," said Gilda, "Eugene is Dean."

"And if I'm Dean," said Eugene, "you must be . . ."

"Mr. Sammy Davis Jr.," I said.

"But what about me?" asked Dave Thomas.

A pause. Then our response in unison: "Caesar Romero."

"Do I have to be Caesar Romero?" Dave protested.

"Yes," ordered the Chairman. "You have no choice."

Thus the casting was set.

When we walked in, our first instinct was to look around to see if Frank himself might be there. After all, he did drop in from time to time. But there was no Frank in sight. In fact, the place was practically empty. Yet despite the dearth of patrons, an eight-piece band was onstage swinging.

"Groovy, man," I said in Sammy-ese. "If Frank shows, the cats are warmed up and ready to wail."

We stayed in character during dinner, zinging one-liners associated with each of our roles.

Marty kept saying, "Jilly's is my bistro," only because it was the caption under Frank's caricature on the cocktail napkins.

Then when Marty, as Sinatra, ordered Sinatra's drink, a Jack Daniel's, the waiter asked, "On the rocks?"

"Yes," Marty said, ". . . relaxed."

The waiter had no idea what Marty meant. In truth, we were completely unfamiliar with New York and its sophisticated ways. We weren't hipsters after all; we were Canadian squares. But that didn't stop us.

We rewrote the names of the dishes on the menu to coincide with Sinatra associations. Dave Thomas, in recognition of Frank's collaboration with Antonio Carlos Jobim, called his dish "Lobster Jobim."

Like all of us, Gilda was fascinated by how Sinatra had yelled out "Six!" in the middle of one of his live Vegas shows. No one knew why. Nonetheless, we picked it up and mindlessly shouted it out at any opportunity. "Six!" we loved to scream. Therefore, when it came time to write the name of her dish, Gilda, with a watch-this attitude, printed "Oysters (6)."

Another menu story: This time it was Harry Shearer, Tom Leopold, and me heading down from Hollywood to Orange County to see the Righteous Brothers. Here's the menu we came up with, as we kept in mind the producer of the group's biggest hits:

The Phil Spector Wall of Onion Rings
River Deep Dish Pizza
Unchained Medley of Wild Mushrooms
You've Lost That Lovin' Filet Mignon
Be My Baby Asparagus

Back at Jilly's in New York City, we kept hoping. So what if Frank hadn't walked through the front door? He was probably in the back room at a table charming some wild doll. In one way or the other, the Chairman had to be present; we felt his spirit.

When the waiter brought the check and we reached into our pockets for money, Marty's Canadian change spilled all over the floor. Marty on all fours, picking up his Loonies, was hardly Sinatra suave. But it didn't matter. By then we were loaded. We walked out humming "The Tender Trap."

Out on the street, I looked up and there, right there across from me, were the blazing lights of the Roseland Ballroom, a blast from the ten-cents-a-dance swing-band past. New York continued to be a dream.

The show itself had been a nightmare. In attempting to update *South Pacific*, the creators of *More Than You Deserve* did it in the grossest way possible. The production was replete with graphic gore and bloody decapitations. One song asked, "How'd You Like to Marry a Man Without a Face?" Bloody Mary was raped in her wheelchair by a soldier using a bayonet. (Years later when I met Papp, I told him, "I was once musical director of *More Than You Deserve*, and every night when I left the theater I was..." "Sick," Papp completed the sentence for me. "Yes," I said. "Me too," he confessed.)

In spite of its unredeemable flaws, the show had an interesting cast. Fred Gwynne, famous for *The Munsters*, was the star. Mary Beth Hurt, then married to William Hurt, was the much-abused Bloody Mary. A young Meat Loaf sang his ass off. After four months of previews, though, even Meat Loaf's rare vocal talents couldn't save the show. The damn thing opened and closed in one week. I had no regrets. I was proud of the fact that, after an initial struggle, I had learned the highly complex classical-style rock score. I was glad that the one-week run gave me a union card. I was happy not to have to see Bloody Mary get raped again. But it didn't feel great having to schlep back to

Toronto. I wanted to linger a while longer in New York. Hell, I wanted to *live* in New York.

＊ ＊ ＊

I went back to Mary Ann, who had waited patiently for me. I helped put together an experimental theatrical piece in which she starred—*Hey, Justine,* a musical about being open sexually. Later, Mary Ann wrote an article that included details of our sex life for *Maclean's,* the most popular magazine in Canada. Talk about being open! I didn't know I'd been sleeping with an investigative journalist. Mary Ann's description of my lovemaking was, well, a mixed review at best. Hey, she was more open than I.

Mary Ann's openness was the downside of *Hey, Justine.* The upside was the fact that the producer slipped a saxophone player into my band named Howard Shore. Howard would change my life. More on that later.

＊ ＊ ＊

More good news came out of the blue.

Stephen Schwartz called.

"Paul," he said, "do you believe in magic?"

I didn't hesitate for a second. "Who doesn't?" I said.

"Good. Because something magical is about to happen. I've found a fellow Canadian of yours, Doug Henning. He's a hippie-looking kid with long hair. He's cute and he's charismatic and he does a more casual kicked-back kind of magic. I've written a whole show around him, a full-blown musical called *The Magic Show* and I need you on piano."

"Will this happen in Canada?"

"I know how much you don't want to leave Canada," said Stephen with sarcastic glee, "but I'm afraid we're opening the show at the Cort Theatre on Broadway. It'll be hard on you, Paul, but you'll have to move to New York."

"That's a helluva sacrifice," I said, "but one I'm willing to make. I'll be there tomorrow."

Chapter 18

"Love's Theme"

It starts with soaring violins. They sail around the isle of Manhattan; they chase the stars over the Bronx and Brooklyn; they anchor on the docks of the West Side, where the bass and drums and guitars find a funky groove that grounds us.

"Love's Theme" is pure elegance. For me, the Barry White instrumental ushered in the era of my New York, where I would finally find everything I was looking for—music, glamour, and comedy, all squeezed into this overcrowded crime-ridden city. Remember, this was presanitization and pre-Disneyization. This was down-and-dirty get-mugged-in-Central-Park New York. And I loved it.

By the way, I did get mugged. I made this critical mistake: I went out at eleven at night with the pure motive of window-shopping. True New Yorkers only go out with a specific destination and walk purposefully toward it. On this night, I had no purpose other than to take a break and stroll down Upper Broadway. A man approached me. "Got a quarter?" he asked. "Sure," I said, reaching into my pocket. "Keep your quarter, buddy," he barked. "Give me all your fuckin' money. I got a gun in my pocket." I looked perplexed. He went on, "I don't wanna do this, but I got to. I'm a junkie. Gimme the money." "Oh man," I said, more disappointed in him than anything else. I didn't really think he had a gun but didn't want to chance being wrong. I gave him three hundred bucks—another critical mistake, walking around with so much cash—and he ran. I felt violated but also knew that I had endured a rite of passage. From then on, I walked with purpose and destination; I was a real New Yorker.

A little earlier, when I first moved down from Toronto, Stephen Schwartz had invited me to stay with him in the vanilla suburbs of Connecticut. He had a comfortable guest room and could not have been more hospitable. He thought staying in the country and traveling into the city each day would ease my transition.

What Stephen didn't know, and what good manners kept me from saying, is that I loathe the country. Nature is not my friend. As Marlon Brando told Eva Marie Saint in *On the Waterfront*, the crickets make me nervous. I want the city. I need the city. Get me to the city. Each morning, then, when Stephen drove us in, I waited for that moment when we crossed over the river and entered the island of Manhattan. The second we were on the West Side Highway, I relaxed. I breathed in the putrid air and felt good about myself and the world. I felt ten million people moving in ten million different directions and could feel that finally I had a direction of my own. I loved the stop-and-start traffic. I loved the great wash of yellow taxis. I didn't mind dogs relieving themselves on fire hydrants and sirens screaming from ambulances. The city made me feel safe. The city made me feel good.

How in the world could anyone live in the burbs? I asked myself.

Why in the world would anyone live in the burbs?

I'll never live in the burbs, I vowed.

* * *

The Magic Show was a hit. Doug Henning was an avatar of a new style. Schwartz's rockish score was lively. I played in the pit band, which, in fact, wasn't in a pit at all; we sat some fifteen feet above the stage. And it was a kick.

The guitarist, Gerry Weiner, shared my love for R&B and Maestro White's orchestral approach to deep soul. He and I would get together and play "Love's Theme" with such crazed enthusiasm that we'd jam on that one song for well over an hour. We'd get to grooving so hard that we'd start screaming like idiots.

Then we learned Barry White himself was coming to town. That's all we needed to hear. "Love's Theme" became an even greater obsession. Just as Orpheus's guitar summons the rising of the morning sun, in the mythopoetic Brazilian movie *Black Orpheus,* so were we summoning Barry White by playing "Love's Theme."

During the heady weekend of Barry White anticipation, we used our high energy to write a Maestro-motivated song, "I Never Want to Lose Your Love," that actually got recorded by Paul Davis a few years later on his *I Go Crazy* album. That happy occurrence, however, was incidental to the great event itself: The Maestro live and in person. Barry was magnificent. And so was his conductor, who wielded a dramatically long glitter-encrusted baton while wearing a short kimono with a fierce dragon on the back.

⁕ ⁕ ⁕

I spent a year working *The Magic Show*.

Doug was as cautious as he was brilliant. Everyone in the production was required to sign a pledge that said we'd never reveal the secrets to his tricks. Because we had a behind-the-scenes look at his act, we saw how he worked his magic. After a couple of shows, I was hip to all his tricks except the one called "Houdini's Metamorphosis." That was one I could never figure out.

Meanwhile, the hotter the show became, the more women went wild for Doug. He became a chick magnet. Even my dear friend Gilda fell for him. One day she invited me to lunch. We met at an Upper West Side café. I could see she was despondent.

"What's wrong?" I asked.

"Doug didn't call," she said.

"What? What are you talking about?"

"I had a date with Doug."

"Come on, Gilda," I said, "you didn't fall prey to the magic of illusion, did you?"

"Actually, I did. We slept together."

"And . . . was it magical?" I asked.

"It was nice," said Gilda, "but it was a week ago and he hasn't called. I guess I'm just part of his disappearing act."

Even though I had genuine brotherly feelings for Gilda, like almost all the guys in her circle I had a little crush on her. I was protective and, hey, a little jealous. As a result, I was pissed, so pissed that I carefully told her the secrets behind every one of Doug's tricks. Except, of course, for Houdini's Metamorphosis. I still didn't know how the hell he did that one.

The truth is that I always liked Doug. He was really a sweetheart. Turned out he also had a deeply mystical side. He fell head over heels in love with Transcendental Meditation and became tight with the Beatles' guru, the Maharishi Mahesh Yogi. He went back to Canada, where he ran for public office on some sort of yogic platform. A friend of mine told me what ultimately happened to him. "Doug got cancer and knew he could heal himself through TM. And he didn't go to a doctor. So he died." Poor Doug.

* * *

My New York turn-ons were two: the music scene and the comedy scene. They both came together when Christopher Guest and Brian Doyle-Murray asked me to write and perform with them on the fifth National Lampoon album, *Goodbye Pop,* a suite of musical parodies. I was stoked because back in college when I heard the first National Lampoon record, I was convinced it was the hippest thing since Nichols and May. Who else would do a bit with Bob Dylan as a TV huckster hawking *The Greatest Protest Hits of the Sixties?*

On *Goodbye Pop,* David Hurdon, Chris, and Gilda performed a song I co-composed called "Kung-Fu Christmas." It became a classic, at least among the three people who bought the album. Musically, the song mirrored the silky-smooth soul sounds of the Stylistics, the Dells, and the Dramatics:

> *There's a man comin' today with lots of loot*
> *He got a pimp-mo-sleigh, a red and white fur suit*
> *He's a super-fly guy, and he's awful cute*
> *He's about to arrive bringing jingle-bell jive:*
> *Santa Claus makin' the Soul Train scene*
> *Slickin' down his beard with Afro Sheen*
> *Christmas Eve comin' with its last minute bustle*
> *Santa tells the elves, "You gotta 'Do the Hustle'…"*

You better be bad, and that means good
So Santa bring you somethin' that's really Hollywood
Diamond in the back trimmed with holly
My girls are workin' the street and I'm feeling jolly
Pimpin' bad daddy in Super-Fly clothes
Selling Joy to the world in her panty hose

On the fade, Chris and Gilda improvised:

CHRIS: *Hey baby, I'd like to do something extra special for you this Christmas... I thought maybe I'd buy you a big house in the south of France.*

GILDA: *Oh, I don't want to live in France.*

CHRIS: *Well, why don't I buy you a big glass-bottom boat then, honey?*

GILDA: *Oh darlin', I don't want no fish lookin' up my skirt.*

CHRIS: *Well, baby, let me ask you, what do you want for Christmas?*

GILDA: *Oh baby, I just want a Kung Fu Christmas!*

Some days later, the phone rang.

It was Howard Shore, the saxophonist from *Hey, Justine,* the Toronto musical I had conducted.

"I'm musical director of this new comedy show," said Howard, "and I'd love to use you on piano."

"What's it called?"

"*NBC's Saturday Night.*"

Chapter 19

"Which of These Coffees *Is* the Fresher?"

Much mythology surrounds *NBC's Saturday Night*, or, as it was rechristened in 1977, *Saturday Night Live*. In the history of American comedy, *SNL* has its place. You could even argue that it looms large in the history of American youth culture. It certainly reflected the age from which it emerged. In the mid-seventies, we were transitioning from the Age of Aquarius to the Age of Indulgence. Our hippie styles hadn't disappeared as much as they had morphed into something more materialistic. We realized we needed to work, and yet we hadn't lost our antipathy to the establishment and its old ways. Thus came a new kind of comedy concoction. I was privileged to watch it happen.

I must say, though, that my primary role was the same as the one I assume today on Letterman. It is, after all, who I am. I'm the piano player. In Canada I accompanied topless dancers. On *SNL* I accompanied a new generation of crazy comics. Howard hired me because I knew many of those comics. He understood that I could rehearse them and help them develop musical material. Like Howard and Lorne Michaels, the show's producer, I had been rigorously trained in the hard-knocks school of Canadian comedy.

Howard had gone to summer camp with Lorne near Toronto, where they'd produced amateur musicals. After much success in Hollywood, Lorne was about to make his big move.

I cherish my years with Lorne. I saw him as a visionary. He understood irony—and ironic people—as well as anyone. Early on, he told me, "Paul, when you say one thing, you mean two." He had me pegged.

I felt that I had him pegged simply by observing this scene:

It was late one night early in the first season. Gilda and I were taking a short break from rehearsing a number. Gilda, always the most helpful of friends, noticed me at loose ends trying to complete my immigration form. She took it upon herself to sit down and type out the five-page application. I felt much better.

That's when Lorne appeared, oblivious in his imperious manner. Two pots were sitting on burners, each filled with coffee. Lorne looked at the pots and, musing to himself, asked, "Which of these coffees *is* the fresher?"

I thought to myself, *This guy speaks in some sort of comedic pentameter. Interesting cat.*

I found myself doing two gigs at once: Lorne's and *The Magic Show.* But even before that double duty, a third opportunity came along that took me to L.A. in the mid-seventies. I was chosen to costar in a sitcom.

Don Scardino, a former Jesus Christ in *Godspell* and a good friend, hooked me up. He recommended me for a show called *Hereafter.* I liked the premise: three old vaudeville guys sell their soul to an agent, who is the devil. In return, they get to be young again and form a rock and roll band. Don and I were in the band along with Greg Evigan. There were plans, independent of the show, to actually record and tour the band, also called Hereafter.

What differentiated this pilot from the usual pie-in-the-sky Hollywood project was its two producers—Norman Lear and Don Kirshner. Lear was king of television comedy and Kirshner was the famous music mogul of Brill Building fame. He was currently hot, with a national TV show called *Don Kirshner's Rock Concert.*

Kirshner fascinated me. An hour after I landed in Los Angeles, Kirshner had me over to his bungalow at the Beverly Hills Hotel. He sat in a green floral chair facing a TV playing tapes of his rock concert show. Donny, as everyone called him, spoke a mile a minute. His New York brogue had a nasal edge that could scare young children. He spoke so fast, your head spun. His pitch, a mingling of the past and future, had a way of pumping up the present.

His machine-gun banter went something like this:

"Forget about the Monkees. Forget about ten million records sold worldwide. Forget about I made the Monkees. I got them their producers. I got them their writers. With the Carole Kings and a kid named Davey Gates who came back later with a band called Bread and a 'Baby I'm a Want You,' but that's not the point. The point is, you'll be bigger than the Monkees. Your band Hereafter is gonna make the Monkees look like chimps. I did it before, I'll do it again, I'm doing it now! You want to talk to Norman Lear? I pick up a phone, you talk to Norman Lear. Norman Lear wants a hit band in a hit show, he picks up a phone and calls me. I call you. You write a hit song, I pick up a phone and call a Jeff Barry. Jeff produces the hits. Jeff Barry with an Ellie Greenwich and a 'Be My Baby,' forget about it with the Phil Spector Wall of Sound and the whole symphonic whatever, it's over. You go off, you write a song, you need a sound, give it to me, that's what I got my Jeffs for. Call me when you got the song."

Scardino and I went off to write a song tailor-made for the show. We called it "Like a Rising Star." A few days later we were back at Kirshner's bungalow. When he heard it, he went into overdrive.

"I got to tell you, Paul, I love the song," he said. "When a Neil Diamond came in with an 'I'm a Believer' for the Monkees, I said, 'Neil, I love the song.' In the studio, with my Jeffs and a Micky Dolenz and the *shtumies* we gave him with a doo-doo-doo, I knew we had a monster. But your song—bigger than the Monkees. I pick up a phone, I call a Norman Lear, I play him the song, he loves it, it's over. 'Like a Rising Star' with a new group, are you kidding? We're going straight to the top."

With that, Kirshner picked up a phone and called his wife, Sheila.

"Sheila," he said, "I forgot to tell you that I ran into Steve and Eydie at the Polo Lounge. They hadn't seen me in a long time. They said, 'Kirsh, with the thinness with the tan and the whole California bit, you look terrific.'"

When the High Holy Days came around, I wanted to go to services, so I called my new rabbi, Don Kirshner, and asked for suggestions.

"You got two choices," said Kirsh. "First, there's Alan Blye, your Canadian *landsman*. He's the cantor at the Temple of the Performing Arts. Choice number two is that we go to *shul* with Steve Lawrence and Eydie's mom. Eydie's going to Liza's wedding at Ciro's. She's marrying Jack Haley, Jr."

"I had no idea you were so close to Stevie and Eydie," I said.

"Are you kidding? I gave 'em 'Blame It on the Bossa Nova' and 'Go Away, Little Girl.' "

Meanwhile, Kirsh kept assuring us that we would be the Monkees, but bigger. "Norman Lear picks up a phone and you're the Beatles," Donny said.

Then a problem: Don Scardino didn't want to sign the contract. Don had done some serious acting, starting in childhood, and didn't want to give Kirshner and Lear first call on his services. In Scardino's view, that would hinder his acting career. Meanwhile, I hadn't signed the contract either because I didn't have a lawyer. When Kirshner heard about the hang-up, we were back in the bungalow.

"Today's Friday," he said. "Monday we start shooting the pilot. But we got a problem. The problem is that we can't shoot the pilot till the contracts are signed, and they're telling me, Scardino, that you won't sign because you're a serious actor. This I can understand. This I can respect. You wanna be Redford. It's good to wanna be Redford. You wanna be Redford, I pick up a phone, Norman picks up a phone, you're Redford. You wanna be Redford, you're Redford. We don't got a problem, Scardino. But how about you, Paul? Why haven't you signed?"

"I don't have a lawyer," I said.

"That's not a problem. I pick up a phone, I get ten lawyers on the phone. Who do they represent? You heard of Paul McCartney? You heard of Sammy Davis? And how 'bout an Olivia Newton-John? You wanna talk big? I'll give you big lawyers. Choose one of them. Choose four. Choose ten. I don't care. It's not a problem. The only problem is if we don't get this contract signed we got a problem. We're friends, but if you don't sign, we got a problem. We're friends, but Norman says, 'Blow him off the deal,' we gotta blow you off the deal."

I picked a lawyer. He said a bunch of things that got me confused. I told him to call my father in Canada. Dad said, "I think it's all right, son. I made certain that the contract does not prohibit you from doing studio work. You'll be able to do as much extra work as you like."

Dad saved the day.

Meanwhile, Scardino struck the clause that gave Kirshner first call on his services. Kirshner caved. Scardino was Redford.

All was set.

Back to the bungalow to sign.

"Now we're friends," said Don. "Friends for life. I'm picking up a phone and calling Norman. Here's Norman Lear on the phone."

"Congratulations," Norman told us, not really knowing our names.

"Now Norman Lear is your friend," said Don. "Anytime you want, you pick up a phone and call Norman. It's a done deal."

But was it?

Chapter 20

A Black Cashmere Coat with a
Red Silk Lining

After the *Hereafter* pilot was shot, there was nothing to do in L.A. It would be months before we'd learn whether the show was picked up.

So back to New York.

Back to *The Magic Show*.

And, simultaneously, back to the beginnings of *SNL*. This was when Howard Shore was putting the band together and using me to rehearse the musical numbers.

Then came the strike by Broadway musicians.

Since age fifteen, I had been a loyal dues-paying member of the American Federation of Musicians. I accepted my duty and walked the picket lines with a sign outside the Cort Theater. I did so, however, with great reluctance, as did most of the other young working musicians. We wanted to keep working, but we had no choice. We also had no choice when it came to union meetings. They were mandatory.

The first meeting was called by our union leader, Lou "Russ" Russo. We were assembled in the union hall when Lou, who had wavy silver hair, made his entrance wearing a black cashmere overcoat. The coat resembled the luxuriously tailored overcoat worn by Lee J. Cobb in *On the Waterfront* when he played union boss Johnny Friendly. Lou Russo took off the coat and carefully folded it from the inside, neatly placing it on a chair so we all could see the red silk lining. As Lou "Russ" Russo spoke Brooklynese, also reminiscent of Cobb's movie role, I kept staring at the coat.

"I wanna report to the membership that this here strike will be over in no time because we got Mr. Frank Sinatra on our side," he said. "Mr. Sinatra, he comes from Hoboken. Mr. S, he loves musicians. He owes musicians his life and his livelihood. Now, he's got this show coming up at the Uris Theater, a Broadway house, and the Old Man don't like to cancel no shows."

The very thought that Frank Sinatra himself would be involved in our union dispute—that his intervention would soon end the strike—was nothing short of thrilling. The Chairman was coming to my aid.

A week passed without news. Then a second meeting was called. I arrived early. Lou Russo arrived late. He wore the same black cashmere overcoat. He went through the same routine of folding the coat inside out and placing it on a chair so that the red silk lining screamed at us. It screamed prosperity; it screamed power.

"I got good news to report to the membership, fellas," he said. "Two nights ago I went over to Jilly's and left word that I need to talk to Frank Sinatra. As you know, Mr. S frequents Jilly's on a regular basis, so I am most certain that I will be hearing back directly from Mr. Sinatra. Once I am able to sit down with him and explain what is happening with our union, I can guarantee you that we will have Frank Sinatra's complete support. That's the kind of guy he is. He will bring this strike to a speedy conclusion."

I thought to myself, *In order to get in touch with Sinatra, Russ is leaving word at Jilly's? Shouldn't he have a better way of arranging a meeting? Or is that what you did when you wanted to see Sinatra—you went to Jilly's?*

A week later, our third meeting.

Russ was early. When we arrived, his overcoat was already folded and placed on the chair. The red silk lining was already screaming.

"All right, fellas," said Russ, "I have news but it ain't the news I wanted to give you. Mr. Sinatra went over our heads. He went to the Federation in Jersey. Out of respect to his legend-hood, they are giving him special dispensation. He can play the Uris Theater, and his union musicians will be allowed to work. It's too bad, but the strike goes on."

* * *

Luckily for me, the strike did not impact TV, and I could work on *SNL* unencumbered. When it was settled, though, and *The Magic Show* resumed, the two jobs proved too taxing. I opted for *SNL*.

The casting of *SNL* had been a fascinating process. The guy who was destined to be the show's biggest star—John Belushi—almost didn't make it.

Gilda and Aykroyd had already been cast. Meanwhile, Gilda was dating one of the musicians in the *Magic Show* band. Boy, did Gilda have a musical soul! She was a Detroit soul sister. We talked about our mutual love for the Supremes. We commiserated over the tragic story of Florence Ballard, the Supreme who wound up on welfare and died so young. Poor Flo. After a stirring

Supremes skit in which Gilda starred, she passed by my piano and whispered in my ear, "That was for Flo."

Gilda was also the first friend of mine to get into Studio 54.

"Who do you see in there?" I asked. "Halston and Liza?"

"The only people I see in there," she said, "are my Aunt Zelda and Uncle Hymie. They come to town, I get them in, I leave, I go home to bed."

Before all that, though, as *SNL* was being cast, she came to the *Magic Show* theater to see her boyfriend, and Belushi was with her.

"We're sitting shiva," she said. (Shiva is the period when we Jews mourn our dead.)

"Who died?" I asked.

"John's career died," Gilda explained.

"I don't understand," I said.

"I don't either," Gilda continued. "I don't see how you could have blown the interview, John."

"It couldn't have gone worse," said John.

"What happened?" I wanted to know.

"Lorne Michaels asked me what I thought of television, and I told him I hated it."

"Why'd you say that?" I asked.

"Because I do," said John. "I hate it like the fuckin' plague. I told Michaels there's nothing good on TV and chances are there never will be. I told him that if he came to my house, he'd see spit all over my television screen."

"He must have loved hearing that," I said.

"I wasn't feeling any love from him," Belushi declared.

"We'll talk him into using you," said Gilda. "You gotta be in the cast."

Later Lorne said that he felt like John would be trouble.

Besides, Lorne was especially leery of people who put down tele-vision. Lorne loved television. But others—especially Chevy—campaigned for Belushi. Add to that the endorsement of Michael O'Donoghue, Lorne's ace writer, and John was in.

As history has recorded, the other cast members were Laraine Newman, who'd worked for Lorne in Hollywood, Jane Curtin, Chevy, Garrett Morris, and, of course, Gilda and Dan.

The first host of the first show was George Carlin. The first musical guests of the first show were Janis Ian and one of my idols, Billy Preston. That same year, other hosts included Richard Pryor, Dick Cavett, Lily Tomlin, Robert Klein, and Buck Henry. Musical guests included Esther Phillips, Gil-Scott Heron, Carly Simon, Bill Withers, and Al Jarreau.

I collaborated on a song with one of the writers, Marilyn Miller, who spoke to Lorne about giving me a weekly credit. Because I was doing some composing, the traditional acknowl-edgment might have been "special musical material by . . ." But the word at *SNL* was always "That's too Carol Burnett," mean-ing something smacked of an old-school variety show. "Special musical material" smacked of old school. Instead, I thought of those lounge lizard pianists who liked to say, "You've been lis-tening to the musical stylings of . . ." and, given *SNL*'s and my own fondness for kitsch, I suggested to Lorne that my credit read, "Musical stylings by Paul Shaffer."

When it appeared on the screen, though, my mother called from Canada and said, "It sounds like you're doing their hair."

So my credit became "Special musical material by Paul Shaffer."

Whatever the handle, it was all exhilarating stuff.

And what could be more exhilarating than being present when the Rolling Stones came on? I was in their first skit, appearing as

Don Kirshner, who wants to get backstage to see them. Belushi plays their bouncer and is determined to keep me out. "You're cut," he says. "You're not on the list." But the Kirshner character manages to sneak in and hang out with the bad boys of rock and roll. There I am, acting with Keith, Ronnie, and Charlie. Cool.

The problem, though, was that Lorne, overstimulated by the appearance of the Stones on his show, lost track of time. Something had to go.

I was in makeup, applying the final touches of the Palm Springs Kirshner tan, when Mick popped in and spoke to me—Paul Shaffer—for the first time in his life.

"You're cut," he said.

"Cut?" I asked.

"Lorne's shit-canned Kirshner. You're out."

I didn't care. Mick Jagger had spoken to me.

✦ ✦ ✦

Outside of Studio 8H, New York night life was jumping. I was surrounded by funky stuff. The funkiest soul band since James Brown was called Stuff. They played four nights a week at Mikell's, close to my little Upper West Side pad. I never missed a night. It was soul heaven. This was the group that consisted of pianist Richard Tee, guitarists Cornell Dupree and Eric Gale, and drummers Steve Gadd and Chris Parker. The leader was bassist Gordon Edwards. This was the same group that appeared on the second show of the second season of *SNL* backing up Joe Cocker. While doing "Feeling All Right," Joe was joined onstage by Belushi doing Joe. The Cocker-off was a classic. You couldn't tell if John was mocking Joe—or if it was Joe mocking John mocking Joe. Either way, it was a beautiful mockery and I was blessed to be there.

Who in their right minds would want to leave *SNL*?

* * *

"I think you should leave, Paul," said Norman Lear. "You'd be making a mistake if you didn't."

Lear had been the host of the second show of *SNL*'s second season. After the show, he came up to me and gave his pitch.

"We sold the pilot of *Hereafter* to CBS," he said. "We can't do it without you, Paul. We don't want to do it without you. What do you say?"

What does anyone say to Norman Lear?

Yes, Mr. Lear.

I had my doubts. I loved my New York life. I was playing dates in the studios with everyone from Barry Manilow to Burt Bacharach. I was in demand. I was developing special material with the kids on *SNL*, and I'd been put in some of the sketches. I was loving it.

But then I thought to myself: Wasn't it cosmic synchronicity that Norman Lear was hosting *SNL* that very week? Wasn't he there just to tell me that the time was right to tackle Hollywood? And when he said that I'd not only be in a hit TV sitcom, but I'd also be in a band destined to top the charts, who could resist that argument? Who could resist being bigger than the Monkees?

Scardino could; he was out. I couldn't; I was in.

I met with Lorne and told him about Lear.

"Paul," he said, "I think you should reconsider. We want you, we need you, we love you. We need to work something out. What will you be making in L.A.?"

"I start at fifteen hundred an episode."

"We're going to miss you."

Chapter 21

Hollywood Swinging

L.A. was a part of my mythological image of the United States. The Beach Boys had painted a picture of surf and sex under the hot Malibu sun, even as I was shivering on the ski slopes of frozen Ontario. L.A. played into my imagination as a musical paradise that housed *Shindig!* and the Whisky a Go Go featuring Johnny Rivers three shows a night.

L.A. was cool.

But unlike Las Vegas or New York, L.A. never became an obsession. I never dreamed of living in L.A. I went there because Norman Lear had beckoned me. I went there because my ego had been jacked up—a relatively common occurrence in my young life—and because I, like millions before me, bought into the notion of becoming a star.

L.A. is star central.

At the same time, I did not find L.A. especially alluring. I liked the weather and I liked the palm trees. I liked Fatburger on La Cienega and looking at the Walk of Stars on Hollywood Boulevard. I liked the nice ocean, and I liked the hills dotted with interesting houses. For the most part, though, to like L.A. you had to like driving. And I'm a lousy driver.

What I did like, of course, was listening to music in my car. "Hollywood Swinging" was the great L.A. anthem of the day. That was Kool and the Gang singing about wanting to get into a band and becoming a bad piano-playin' man. Me in a nutshell. The other anthem was recorded by a Southern California backup band turned into soul stars by writer/producer Norman Whitfield. Rose Royce's "Car Wash" provided the fuel that kept me tooling around in the smog, looking in vain for the center of a centerless city.

But how many car washes can you get in one week?

Shooting the show itself wasn't as exciting as I had hoped. The scripts were lackluster, and the chemistry among cast members never really kicked in. Let's face it: I'd gone from the hippest to the squarest. The highlight of my time in Hollywood was shopping for eyeglasses.

Lear's costume gal said I needed a hip pair of glasses. She thought it went with my character as a musician in the Hereafter band. I'd never looked at glasses as a fashion item, but when in Rome, baby. The costume gal took me to Optique Boutique.

"Elton John buys his frames here," said the optician, "and I have a pair we just made up for him."

"I gotta see 'em," I said.

The optician pulled out a pair of dramatic square frames done in pure-as-the-driven-snow white. I loved them. I also loved Elton's music—Elton's songs, Elton's sound, and Elton's soulful piano playing. Why not wear Elton's glasses?

"Will I look like a copycat?" I asked the costume gal.

"These frames look like they were made for you," she said.

"Even if they were made for Elton?"

"They were made for Elton with you in mind, Paul. Besides, Elton's off touring Australia. By the time he gets back to the U.S.A., he'll be sporting new frames."

"I'll take them," I told the optician.

For better or worse, that's how the Shaffer eyeglass frame obsession began: in blind tribute to Elton John. And I was fine with that.

* * *

The name *Hereafter* was changed to *A Year at the Top,* but it wasn't a year at the top. It was a year in the middle. It wasn't awful and it wasn't great. After shooting four shows, though, it became clear that it wasn't going to be the next *I Love Lucy.*

Nonetheless, I had to concentrate on the job at hand. *A Year at the Top* was shot on the KTTV lot where Lear's famous productions, like *All in the Family, Maude, One Day at a Time,* and *The Jeffersons,* were all taped.

If our show became famous it was only famous as Lear's first flop.

Flop or not, I'd wander over to the *One Day at a Time* set, where I met Valerie Bertinelli. She and I had a few fun dates. Enchanting personality. She was sixteen, I was twenty-seven, but, as R. Kelly would say, who's counting? I also met Valerie's friend and costar Mackenzie Phillips, whose dad was the Mamas and Papas' John Phillips, a man of great wit and musical talent whose trademark vocal arrangements—think of "California Dreamin'"—were exquisite.

One evening, after Mackenzie and I had helped out at a charity event, we went to Roy's on Sunset, an uber-hip hangout for Hollywood movers and shakers in the seventies. If you knew

Mackenzie well, by the way, you called her "Laura," her real name. Mackenzie, her middle name, was given to her in tribute to Scott Mackenzie, for whom Papa John wrote "San Francisco (Be Sure to Wear Some Flowers in Your Hair)."

Anyway, we get to Roy's, and Roy turns out to be a former music agent, Roy Silver. Given my fascination with fast-talking New York Jews, I'm pleased to meet Roy, and Roy is pleased to meet me because he knows about my connection to Lear and Kirshner. When I introduce Roy to Mackenzie, he's ecstatic.

"I held your father in my arms," he tells Mackenzie, "so people wouldn't see that he was vomiting all over himself."

Nice, Roy, I say to myself.

"Come to the bar, kid," he continues, "and I'll tell you more stories about your dad."

Mackenzie whispers to me, "Everywhere I go in this town, someone has another horror story about my father. I can't take it."

So we're at the bar. Mackenzie wants to get away—and I want to help her—but Roy's already deep into his next story.

"Funny story about your dad," he says. "We're in San Francisco. It's me, John, Scott Mackenzie, and Mama Cass. We're at the Fairmont, about to be served lunch, when the hotel manager comes up to us and says, 'I'm afraid you're going to have to leave.'

" 'What are you talking about!' I say. 'Who has to leave?'

" 'Your entire party.'

" 'Why?' I ask.

" 'Because we have discovered an inordinately large accumulation of chicken bones in Miss Cass's room. The bones are everywhere—in the bed, under the bed, on the couch, under the couch. The walls are smeared with mayonnaise and mustard. The sheets and towels are covered with ketchup. I'm asking your party to leave right now.

"I turn to John and say, 'John . . . where am I going to go with this?' "

Where am I going to go with this? I repeat to myself, thinking, *What a punch line!*

"Isn't that funny, Mackenzie," Roy now asks. "Isn't your father a scream?"

Mackenzie tries to smile but can't. Mercifully, Roy leaves us alone to enjoy our drinks, but ten minutes don't pass before he's back.

"This just happened last week," he says. "You know Giorgio Moroder, of course."

I nod. I don't know him, but I know of him. He's the Italian arranger who produced, among other smashes, Donna Summer's "Love to Love You Baby," complete with the sounds of confected orgasm.

Roy goes on: "So Giorgio's in here munching on barbecue spareribs—my recipe—and he waves me over and says, 'Roy. I have track. Hit track. But I need singer. You know singer?'

" 'Giorgio, baby,' I say, 'this is Hollywood. Every waitress in this place is an ASW (actress/singer/whatever).'

"So I wave the nearest waitress over to our table and say, 'Giorgio, meet Dora. Dora's a dynamite singer.'

" 'You be at studio tomorrow at 10 a.m.,' says Giorgio, 'we cut hit record.'

"Natch, Dora's smiling from ear to ear. The more I think about it, though, the more I can see Dora having a Donna Summer–sized hit, and all because of me. So before she quits for the night, I call Dora over and say, 'Look, honey, I put this deal together for you. I got you Giorgio. I gotta have ten percent.'

"Dora looks me in the eye, and immediately says, 'Five.' Even the waitresses are cutting my nuts off here in Hollywood, Paul, even the fuckin' waitresses."

✦ ✦ ✦

Hollywood is always merging the old and the new. It honors both, sometimes worships both, even as it simultaneously destroys both. By that I mean the old guys can come back when you least expect it, like Mickey Rooney coming back to appear on *A Year at the Top*. Mickey loved telling jokes: "Guy says, 'When I die, bury me in a copper coffin.' 'How come?' 'It'll help my arthritis.' " First time I heard it, I fell over. Eighth time it wasn't so funny. Mickey had big ideas. The Mickey Rooney Starbecue, for example, featuring the Judy Chili Burger and the Andy Hardy Sloppy Joe. Corny jokes and Starbecues aside, when Mickey appeared, everyone on the set was in awe: *We're working with the great Mickey Rooney.* When he didn't work out—hardly anyone did on that show—no one remembered that he had been there only the day before. Same thing with the new guys—me and Scardino and Greg Evigan, the three musicians who sold our souls to the devil/agent. Here one day, gone the next.

As you will soon see, the devil got his due; the show didn't last. Before my sitcom career was over, though, I had accumulated enough Hollywood stories to last me the rest of my life. That alone made the trip worthwhile.

My favorite Tinseltown story has a poignancy that touched my heart. I was there when it happened. A. J. Antoon, a Tony-winning Broadway director who had done a TV version of *Much Ado About Nothing*, was brought in by Norman Lear to direct the *Hereafter* pilot. A.J. wanted all of us, especially Norman, to see his Shakespeare. A screening was arranged.

When I arrived, I saw that the only others in attendance were two secretaries from the office and Woody Kling, an old-school writer for Milton Berle who had written our pilot. It was clear that Lear wasn't going to show.

Disappointed but undaunted, A.J. proudly introduced his version of Shakespeare, telling us to be on the lookout for certain key elements of his direction. The lights were dimmed, the film rolled, and we settled back to watch.

Five minutes into the ninety-minute production, Woody Kling jumped up, grabbed his suitcase, and leaned over to A.J.

"Beautiful, A.J.," said Woody. "I gotta run."

When I think of my time in the City of Angels, I think of that line. In that single moment, I saw it; I understood Hollywood and its cold-blooded warmth.

"Beautiful, A.J., I gotta run."

* * *

Hollywood could get you down. When I was especially down, when the smog of the city and the lack of sizzle coming off our show had us all convinced that we were going nowhere fast, I'd take a break. One day I was strolling around the lot, munching on a burrito and thinking to myself, *What the hell am I doing here? I could be cutting disco records in New York.* Then I saw it. Was it an apparition? Was it real? It couldn't be. But yes, it was. It passed me by like a parade. Four overweight stagehands were wheeling what I recognized to be the *Soul Train* mirror ball. They were transporting it to the stage where the show was taped. I chased after the ball like a Hollywood agent chases after his commission. *My God,* I thought, *Soul Train tapes here!*

Imagine the joy that washed over my heart when I learned that the guest for today's show was none other than the Love

Man, Mr. Barry White. I was inches away from the Maestro as host Don Cornelius began the interview. Barry had just released a new album, *Sheet Music.* The interview focused on the pun implicit in the title. Both men spoke so softly that I had to put my ear right up against the speaker to make out their words.

"We're here with the Man," said Don in his deep bottom baritone. "The Man, the Maestro."

"Well, thank you very much, Don," said Barry in a baritone several octaves deeper than Don's. Man, it was dueling baritones *sotto voce.*

"Why call it *Sheet Music,* BW?" asked Don, his honey-dripped voice plunging even lower.

"Well, Don, let me break it down to you, brother. You see there are two kinds of sheet music. There's the sheet music we use to write the songs that lead to romance. And then there's the sheet music we play when we feel love and share love and make love between the sheets. Talkin' 'bout the silken sheets of love."

"You're always talking 'bout love, aren't you, Maestro?"

"Don, I believe it's love that makes us and love that breaks us. Love, Don, is the magic we make when we dance and make romance. That's what Barry White is all about, Don. That's the thing that Barry White's heart never stops beating for—another song of love, another night between the sheets makin' sheet music."

"Well, no one understands love like Barry White," Don conceded, "and I'm hoping you can lay a little of that love thing on us later in the show."

"Don, nothing would make Barry White happier," said Barry, basso profondo.

And I'm thinking, *How low can these cats go?*

I was witness to Barry's preaching that day, and a week later

I returned to the *Soul Train* set to watch another minister of soul, Lamont Dozier of the great Motown songwriting team of Holland-Dozier-Holland. Lamont performed "Going Back to My Roots," a song he hoped would tie into Alex Haley's phenomenally successful *Roots* miniseries, which was currently tearing up the ratings.

The stage manager recognized me and afterward wanted to know if I was interested in going to the Commodores concert at the Forum. "You'll probably be the only white guy there, so I suggest taking a black woman. I have just the gal. She loves Jewish soul brothers, especially those like you who play funky piano."

My date was delightful. Together we climbed on our chairs and danced to "Brickhouse." Together we watched the spectacular show as the group exploded into Commodores hyperspace, where they performed their current hit, "Zoom."

Afterward we shared hot pastrami sandwiches at Canter's Deli. Turned out the sister had a thing for potato knishes. Go know.

Chapter 22

The Brady Bunch, The Ohio Players, and Mr. Chevy Chase

After shooting four episodes of *A Year at the Top*, everyone saw that the premise wasn't working. The episodes were so bad they never aired. Thus a major rewrite. The trio of musicians was slimmed down to a duo, me and Greg. We were no longer old guys reincarnated by the devil but simply a couple of young dudes who sell their souls to make it. Five new shows were ordered. The name of the act was changed to Greg and Paul, and every attempt was made to infuse the show with fresh energy. Unfortunately, every attempt failed.

Fortunately, I had lots of time on my hands. The producers paid me to stick around L.A. while these new scripts were being written. Meanwhile, Chevy Chase, who had also left *SNL* in its second season, had come to Hollywood to do an NBC special. When Chevy asked me to be his musical consultant, I was delighted. Two of his writers were Tom Leopold and Brian Doyle-Murray, two of my favorite people. Making matters even more enticing was the fact that we were working on the same soundstage as *The Brady Bunch Variety Hour*. This was the year that the Brady producers, Sid and Marty Kroft, were doing a series of shows with Donny and Marie Osmond. For those shows, the Krofts had built an ice-skating rink. For the Bradys, they had built a swimming pool in the middle of the set. The original Brady cast had been reassembled, including luminaries Ann B. Davis, Florence Henderson, Robert Reed, and Maureen McCormick. Brian and I were fixated on the show, largely because the above-ground swimming pool had windows beneath the water that allowed the cameras to shoot. We had access to those windows, allowing us to confirm the fact that swimming was indeed the ideal exercise for young women interested in getting in shape.

When Chevy called a staff meeting, he began by saying, "We need to make this short because Brian and Paul have to get back over to the Brady Bunch set as soon as possible."

Chevy was right. Who could resist the sight of Ann B. Davis singing and dancing poolside with a school of nubile young swimmers? As if that weren't enough, imagine my joy when musical guests the Ohio Players broke into their hit song "Fire" while the synchronized swimmers jumped into the pool with flaming torches.

I became so emotionally invested in the Brady Bunch production that I found myself crestfallen the day I saw that the show had been shut down.

"Why?" I asked.

"Maureen McCormick has contract issues. She won't leave her apartment in Westwood."

"I'll go see her," I said, volunteering my services. "I'll get her to be reasonable. On behalf of television fans everywhere, I'll do anything to keep this show going."

My valiant request was ignored, and I was sent back to the

set of Chevy's show, sadder but wiser in the ways of small-screen politics.

Another show, *The Liar's Club,* was also taping on this same lot. It was a panel/quiz show of small consequence where upcoming comics made appearances. Later I would learn that Letterman was one such comic. At the time, just to see the reaction it would elicit from the *Liar's Club* producers, Tom Leopold and I would tell them that Chevy loved their show and ask if they would consider having him on. The producers salivated. For weeks, we kept telling them that we were on the verge of delivering Chevy, and for weeks the producers treated us as though we were the Second Coming. Of course Chevy never came.

Tom had other schemes up his sleeve. At 5 p.m. sharp, the audience for *The Liar's Club* would line up, and at precisely 5:30 they would file onto the lot, marching past the closed door of the office where Chevy worked.

One day at 4:55 p.m., Tom, with nothing better to do, asked me, "Want to upset Chevy?"

"Of course," I answered.

"Watch this."

Tom approached the long line of audience members waiting to enter the studio and, in a booming voice, asked, "Who'd like to meet Chevy Chase?"

Everyone screamed, *"Me!"*

"Right this way," said Tom, leading the line right through the private office where Chevy sat behind his desk, looking over a script and smoking a cigar. The sight of these tourists traipsing through—in one door and out the other—was priceless. Chevy thought so too. He wasn't thrilled about shaking hands with a hundred and fifty people, but, ever the pro, he turned on the charm.

I was still in L.A. during the summer of 1977, when the first episode of *A Year at the Top* finally aired. By then Chevy had gone back east, where he and the other *SNL* kids were summering in the Hamptons.

A few seconds after that first episode had reached its painful conclusion, the phone rang. It was Chevy.

"I'm here with Gilda and Dan and John," he said. "We just watched your show and we want to say that we still love and respect you—hold on, Paul . . . What was that, guys? We don't? . . .

"Well, we still love you . . . What was that, guys? We don't? . . .

"Oh well, here, talk to Belushi."

"Paul," said John, "stop acting with your mouth open. Use your eyes."

I took his note and tried to follow his advice—advice from a man who went on to do the Blues Brothers movie with his eyes covered by shades.

* * *

I hung around L.A., shooting the remainder of my sitcom episodes. I wasn't happy. When I was asked to play and sing "The Antler Dance" on *SNL*'s special Sunday night show being shot at the Mardi Gras in New Orleans, I was eager to oblige. After all, I'd written the song with Marilyn Miller and Michael O'Donoghue. I had to do it. But I couldn't convince the *Year at the Top* producers that I'd be back in time for our next taping, so I went straight to the top. I went to Norman Lear, a frustrated performer himself, who said, "You have to go. Those are your compadres."

I flew to the Big Easy and arrived in time to sing . . .

A man in a mask walked into my room late last Saturday
  night
I said, "Hey Mr. Mask, what are you doing in here?"
He said, "There ain't no cause for fright.
I got a dance that's gonna beat the bump,
The hustle and the hoochie-coo."
And then he took off his pants and did the Antler Dance.
It's so easy you can do it too.

The camera then tilted up to a balcony in the fictional Antler Alley in the real French Quarter, where Michael O'Donoghue, wearing a black mask, raised his hands over his head and did the Antler Dance with wild abandon.

At this moment, I realized how deeply I yearned to get back to *SNL*.

Chapter 23

Paul at the Gramercy

"I am Eloise. I am a city child. I live in the Plaza."

Those words, written by Kay Thompson, were read to me by Mom when I was eight. Mom had the good taste to expose me to books about Eloise as well as Babar and Christopher Robin.

As my fashionable and loving mother—who herself dreamed of Manhattan penthouses and Parisian boulevards—slowly turned the pages, the fantasy drew me in: Imagine living in a sophisticated hotel in the most sophisticated city in the world and having the run of the place—room service; maid service; fascinating people continually checking in and checking out; banquets; weddings; parties on every floor. What could be better?

Nothing, I decided, when, at age twenty-eight, I moved back to New York from Los Angeles. I couldn't afford the Plaza, of course, but, at $1,500 a month, I could afford the Gramercy Park Hotel on Gramercy Park at 2 Lexington Avenue. These days the Gramercy has been reinvented as a five-star hipper-than-thou Ian Schrager production. But when I moved in—and stayed for eleven glorious years—the place was the essence of shabby gentility. The carpets were musty; the furniture was in disrepair; and a distinct funk hung in the air when you walked down the hallways. I loved it.

The Gramercy's clientele consisted of a devoted cadre of Europeans who had been coming for years, comforted to be served by the same receptionists and bellmen, many of whom were in their seventies. In addition, there was a noticeable constituency of elderly residents who had moved into the hotel back in the forties and clung to their rent-controlled rates. At about the time of my arrival, the Gramercy had been discovered by new wave and punk bands looking for a suitably disreputable alternative to the Chelsea. On any given day, you might see the Clash at the front desk or the English Beat in the bar.

I lived in two small rooms in the back with a nice view of the park. One room had two double beds, the other a sofa and two chairs covered in tattered velvet upholstery. There was a tiny kitchenette and a gas stove. I had the gas turned off because I had no intention of cooking. My television sat on a rickety metal stand, and my electric piano sat on the coffee table. I would practice while watching *American Bandstand.*

When I first moved in, I was told that the doorman had a key to nearby Gramercy Park itself, a charming enclosure of manicured greenery that was closed to the general public. Only residents of the immediate area had keys.

"I can open the gate," said the doorman, "but I can't leave you the key. I'll be back in a half hour to let you out. Enjoy yourself."

I took a quick walk around the park and then felt a wave of panic passing over me. I couldn't get out. I looked through the wrought-iron gate and saw people walking up and down the street. They were free. I wasn't. I was trapped inside like a hyena at the zoo. Twenty-five minutes were far too many to be alone with nature. You see one flower, you've seen 'em all. Somehow I managed to survive my imprisonment, but in my many years at the Gramercy, I never ventured into the park again.

Who needed to, when there was Ravi Shankar passing through the lobby? At breakfast I might see Taj Mahal eating an omelet. One evening in the dining room I looked up and there was Jaco Pastorius, the genius musician who had begun with Wayne Cochran and moved on to the avant-garde Weather Report. He was strolling around, playing his unplugged electric Fender bass guitar for the pleasure of the patrons. You couldn't hear what he was playing because the solid-body guitar, without amplification, had no resonance. But when he came to my table, I leaned in and could make out the brilliance of his improvisation. To this day I have no idea why Jaco had decided to serenade the diners with a free and inaudible concert, but that was the charm of life at the Gramercy.

Room service was superb. The hamburger was excellent, the fries crispy and salted to my exact taste. When I caught cold, the house doctor was there in a flash, happy to prescribe whatever antibiotics were needed. The doorman would fetch my medicine from the drugstore. I looked forward to getting sick.

Riding the elevator was always an adventure. One evening the door opened and there was Debbie Harry. She told me that she'd decided to live in the hotel. Passing through the lobby, I saw Paul Butterfield at the bar. I stopped to say hello. We struck up a friendship that resulted in my playing on his last album.

"Paul," he said to me, "I finally understand the blues. The blues puts a hurtin' on your heart. Man, I have an ulcer, so I eat nothing but sausage and peppers. I need eight hours of sleep a night, so I never get more than two. I should avoid stimulants of all kinds, so I seek out every stimulant I can find. Paul, I've got the blues."

No doubt, the Gramercy had a strong dose of the blues. But those blues could be chased away by the merriest and most unexpected circumstances. There was, for instance, the time that my queen Ronnie Spector and her husband Jonathan came to visit me in my room. We got happy on more than a few drinks and, on a mere whim, rushed down to the bar, where I sat at the out-of-tune upright piano and accompanied Ronnie as she sang every last one of her Spector-style hits. It was magic. People rushed into the bar, gathered around us, and, singing "Be My Baby" and "Baby, I Love You" with Ronnie, had the time of their lives.

My New York life would take strange turns. There would be ups and downs, changes I could never have anticipated, hits and flops, anxieties and ecstasies, but no matter the emotional weather, I could always find a modicum of peace in my little two-room suite in the back of the seedy Gramercy Park Hotel at the foot of Lexington Avenue in New York City.

Chapter 24

Catherine Vasapoli

At this juncture in my narrative, I'd like to introduce the love of my life, my wife-to-be. Our romance, which continues to this day, has been a circuitous but blessed journey. I must accept blame for those obstacles that blocked our path to the altar. You see, I was defiantly and passionately committed to the status of bachelorhood for at least another dozen years. Why would anyone marry before age forty? That was my point of view. Cathy saw it differently.

The Cathy/Paul saga starts in 1977 with a simple letter. Cathy, who was working as a receptionist at *Good Morning America*, wrote me a fan letter, saying that she'd seen me on *SNL* and thought I seemed like a nice guy and that she appreciated my talent. She didn't enclose a phone number, so there was no way to get in touch with her. Later, she pointed out that I could have called *GMA*. Perhaps.

Then Hugh Hefner came to New York. Inadvertently, Hef got me and Cathy together. Here's how it happened:

When Hef hosted *SNL*, he wanted to sing. I taught him

"Thank Heaven for Little Girls." Cute idea. During rehearsal, his assistant came running in every two minutes. "Have enough Pepsi, Hef? Is your Pepsi cold?" After downing a half dozen frosty Pepsis, Hef managed to learn the song and we were ready to go. But when he sang during the actual performance, he got two bars ahead of the band. No one seemed to mind. We were too busy thinking about the after-party, to be hosted by Hef at his New York Playboy Club.

It was at that very party that a gorgeous brunette walked up to me and said, "I'm Cathy Vasapoli. I'm the one who wrote you that letter."

"That was so sweet of you," I said.

We spoke briefly, but because I had been working nonstop for the past fourteen hours, my eyes were half closed. I wanted to talk to her more, but my concentration was waning. Someone else came up to me to say hello, and when I turned back to look for Cathy, she was gone.

Happily, she reappeared a few weeks later after an *SNL* show. She came with her friend Hal Wilner, who had been her classmate at NYU. Hal would later be hired by *SNL* to pick out the prerecorded music for the sketches. He turned it into an art form. I knew him from my work as a studio musician with his mentor, producer Joel Dorn.

After we all chatted, Hal went off, leaving me and Cathy alone. She invited me to her tiny studio apartment on Gay Street in the Village ("Gay Street that Fey Street," in the words of Tom Leopold). We spoke long into the night, but that was it. I was still a shy kinda guy. A week later I invited her to lunch. I was drawn to her upbeat personality and positive energy.

"I'm doing a studio session with Barry Manilow in an hour," I said. "Wanna come along?"

"I really can't," she said.

Later she told me that she adored Manilow and was dying to come to the session but didn't want to seem like a hanger-on.

Slowly but surely she became my girl. When she saw my two-room setup at the Gramercy Park Hotel, she exclaimed, "My God, I didn't think there was anyone in New York who had this kind of space! And it's all for you?"

My idea of a romantic weekend was to take Cathy up to the Concord Hotel to see Buddy Hackett, the bluest comic in the Catskills. His jokes were covered in excrement. Before checking out, I met the hotel's in-house rabbi.

"You'll come back next weekend," he said. "It's singles night. I guarantee, you'll get laid."

"Rabbi," I said, "I'm involved."

"*Boychik*," he said, "I've been involved with my wife for forty years, but that doesn't mean *I'm* getting laid."

* * *

Back at *SNL*, I was busy collaborating with the writers on special musical material. But I also had a comedic ace up my sleeve that I was ready to play.

While I was still in Hollywood, I had taken a call from Don Kirshner. "Paul," he said, "I've decided to go on camera on *Rock Concert*. The show needs an ID man. Maybe I'm stiff, I'm not stiff, whatever—Sullivan was stiff, but it was his show, he had the gig. I'm taping my first intros today, and you just gotta be there."

Next thing I knew, I was on the soundstage to witness an amazing transformation: This fast-talking Brooklyn record man went from his usual rat-a-tat machine-gun pitch—"forget-about-track-record-with-the-Sedakas-and-the-Carole

Kings-we-never-looked-at-a-contract"—to a scared-stiff discourse slowed down from 45 rpm to 33⅓ and delivered in a trembling voice, eyes wide open.

"I'm Don Kirshner and welcome to *Rock Concert*. It was only two years ago, in 1975, when Dee Anthony called me on a kid named Peter Frampton. This kid has the potential to be another Bobby Darin, another Bobby Rydell, another Bobby Vee. Today, thanks to the wonderful guidance of Abe Lastfogel and the fabulous William Morris Agency, Frampton has the biggest-selling album in rock history with a *Frampton Comes Alive*. I now present to you—and my wife Sheila loves him too—the fabulous Peter Frampton."

I was transfixed. This metamorphosis from slick to sludge was seared into my memory. So when I returned to *SNL*, I knew I was carrying a killer impersonation in my back pocket. But how to use it? One day it became clear.

Michael O'Donoghue had created his own on-camera persona named Mr. Mike, a morbid creep who told demented bedtime stories. Brian Doyle-Murray came up with an idea: The Mr. Mike and Tina Turner Revue, in which Mr. Mike, holding a guitar like Ike and echoing Tina's spoken introduction to "Proud Mary," starts telling his twisted tale, nice . . . and slow. Then Garrett Morris, in drag as Tina, picks up the tempo and sings "Proud Mary" at a ferocious pace.

The premise was great, but we needed a way to set it up and explain it to the audience.

"Kirshner!" I said. "I can do him. I can introduce the whole thing as Don Kirshner."

"Give me a taste," said Brian.

I froze appropriately, and with eyes wide open began to recite, "Mr. Mike and Tina Turner have been an exciting musical entity since they first appeared at the Crossroads Café in Clarksdale, Mississippi. Today, after having signed with Morty Shaffner and his fabulous staff at the IGF race-oriented agency, they continue to entertain audiences all over this great land of ours. Please welcome, and Sheila loves them too, the Mr. Mike and Tina Turner Revue."

"Paul," said Brian, "you're on."

My Kirshner on network television became bigger than his syndicated version of himself.

* * *

Meanwhile, Belushi was complaining about his bee costume. Belushi hated putting on the bee costume. It weighed a ton and made him sweat like a hornet in heat.

"I hate these bee sketches," said Belushi.

"Lorne loves them," said Aykroyd.

"Fuck Lorne," John exclaimed. "This is my last one."

"Wait a minute," Danny interjected. "I've got an idea. What if we get the band to put on bee costumes, and we all play Slim Harpo's 'I'm a King Bee.' I'll play harp and you'll sing the shit out of it."

"How's it go?" asked John.

Danny started singing the lyrics.

"Let's do it," said John.

Next thing I know I'm running around the *SNL* set in a bee costume. I understand why Belushi rails against this thing. It stings. It disorients me to the point that during rehearsal I wander into a Gilda/Garrett Morris sketch in my bee getup.

"What are you doing here?" asks Gilda.

"I don't know," I say.

When we do "I'm a King Bee" on the air, everyone loves it.

Belushi is sensational as a buzzed-up blues singer. In the middle of the song, he does a full flip and lands flat on his back. The audience licks it up like honey.

Now Danny and John are warming up the *SNL* audience as two blues singers, not bees but two guys dressed in dark hats, dark ties, dark suits, and dark glasses.

"Why the dark suits and dark glasses?" I ask.

"I was hipped to the look by Fred Kaz," says John, "the beatnik musical director at Second City in Chicago. He's the cat who told me that junkies always wore straight-looking outfits so they could pass. Check out William Burroughs."

Shortly thereafter, Lorne is featuring the singing duo, not as a warmup act, but as on-air performers. Not only that, I get to introduce them on camera in the guise of Don Kirshner. I give it the slowed-down, frozen-stiff, tanned, gold-chained, full-nasal Brooklyn brogue treatment of my show-biz friend and say . . .

"Today, thanks to the brilliant management of Myron S. Katz and the Katz Talent Agency, these two talented performers are no longer just a legitimate blues act. But with careful shaping and the fabulous production of Lee Solomon, who's a gentleman, and his wonderful organization, they have managed to become a viable commercial product. So now, let's hear it for these two brothers from Joliet, Illinois. Ladies and gentlemen, I give you . . ."

Chapter 25

The Blues Brothers!

The thing caught on.

Belushi and Aykroyd started showing up at local clubs to try out their act. They were a hit everywhere they appeared, especially at the Lone Star Café, where blues stars like Dr. John and Charles Brown often played. Before I knew it, they had a record deal. I figured they'd use a group like Roomful of Blues or Duke Robillard to back them.

"We want you," Belushi said to me one day at *SNL* rehearsals.

"To play piano on the record?" I asked.

"No, to be our band's musical director."

I was stunned. I was delighted. There was only one problem: we didn't have a band.

"We'll put one together," said John. "You and me."

A word on the great Belushi: I loved him. We called him "Bear Man" because he was big, hairy, and cuddly. John had a heart of gold. He grew up in Wheaton, Illinois, just outside Chicago, and had played drums in a rock band. His first love was rock. One of his favorite songs was "Kind of a Drag" by the Buckinghams.

Of course he could do Cocker, and his version of Ray Charles, channeled through Ludwig von Beethoven, wearing dark glasses and sniffing snuff, ranks with the greatest skits of Jackie Gleason and Sid Caesar. But John wasn't yet a blues fan. Danny was the blues maven and had a tremendous influence on John in that regard. He played records for Belushi and schooled him on the greats like Sonny Boy Williamson, Muddy Waters, and Howlin' Wolf.

When John went off to do *Animal House* in Eugene, Oregon, he met Curtis Salgado, a great harmonica player and blues singer who was the vocalist for Robert Cray's brilliant band. Curtis befriended John and became his next major blues mentor. They spent weeks together digging deep into the treasure chest of twelve-bar beauties.

Back in New York, John and I began discussing the personnel of the band. Steve Jordan, the *SNL* drummer, was an easy choice. Belushi and I both loved him. The big decision was the lead guitarist. If John was to be Mick, he needed a Keith. Belushi needed a killer guitarist to punctuate his vocals. Through John's rock-and-roll connections he learned about Mike Landau, a brilliant young musician. When we jammed with him, I was impressed but felt we needed someone absolutely drenched in the blues.

"Oh man," said John, "let's hire him. We need someone now."

"I'm hip, John," I said. "Mike's great, but I just don't think we can compromise when it comes to an authentic balls-out blues guitarist."

John thought long and hard. "Okay," he said, "we gotta go see Doc."

Doc was Doc Pomus, the ultimate blues guru. Once a blues singer himself, Doc was one of the great writers of blues and rhythm-and-blues and the reigning authority on all things blue. We caught up with Doc at Kenny's Castaways, a downtown club where the blues cats crawled. When we explained the situation, Doc had two words for us: "Matt Murphy."

I didn't know Murphy, but when the pope gives his blessing, you gotta eat the cracker.

"So Doc," I asked, "he's the real deal?"

"Real as rain."

We hired him on the spot. And Doc was right. Matt wailed.

"Now we need another guitarist," I told John. "A rhythm guitarist."

That's when Tom Malone, who had come aboard as trombonist/baritone saxist, mentioned that Steve Cropper, the fabulous guitarist of Stax fame—the guy who had backed Otis Redding and cowritten "Midnight Hour"—was available. What's more, Duck Dunn was part of the package. Duck was the bassist from that same Stax era and, along with Cropper, a member of Booker T. and the MG's. With Steve on guitar and Duck on bass, I knew we'd be grooving like mothers.

"We gotta get these guys," I told Belushi.

Belushi hadn't heard of them. I quickly filled him in on their pedigrees. Danny, who was a Stax fan, backed me up.

"This is a big break for us," he told John.

John concurred, and once we rounded out the horns with Lou Marini and Tom Scott on saxes and Alan Rubin on trumpet, we were set.

Atlantic Records had offered us the deal. The first record was to be culled from a nine-night stand we were set to play, opening for Steve Martin, then at the top of his stand-up game, at the Universal Amphitheater in L.A.

* * *

The next step was picking tunes: Danny, John, and I spent a week at John's house on Morton Street in the Village. Our goal was to listen to blues records and find songs that would work for us. But that didn't quite happen. *Animal House* had just opened, and John was getting calls and kudos from everywhere. This was, in fact, the week that John became a superstar. He couldn't be contained.

"We gotta stay here and listen to music," said Danny, doing his best to keep his pal focused.

"The Allman Brothers are playing Central Park," said John. "Let's go."

And with that, he was gone. Ultimately, though, we got Belushi's attention long enough for all of us to select killer material like "Hey, Bartender," "Shotgun Blues," and "Flip, Flop and Fly."

Then it was rehearsal time.

From the first second we hit the first groove, we felt the power. The combination of these musicians from disparate backgrounds worked in a way none of us had anticipated. We were stoked.

"The songs are good," said Steve Cropper, perhaps the greatest rhythm guitar in the history of rhythm, "but shouldn't we do more than old blues?"

"Yeah," said Duck Dunn. "Don't we want some hits?"

"What would you suggest?" I asked.

"Some straight-up soul," said Cropper.

" 'Soul Man' would work great," they both chimed.

"Soul Man" was the hit song that Isaac Hayes and David Porter had written for Sam and Dave. I agreed that it would be a perfect cover for the Blues Brothers. Steve and Duck, who had played on the original, taught Belushi how to sing it.

Next thing we knew we were winging our way to L.A. for the live recording gig. After our dress rehearsal, John's manager, the venerable Bernie Brillstein, approached me.

"Look, Paul," he said, "I hate to tell a client what to do with his act and I'd be the last one to say anything to John, but that intro number is all wrong."

The opening number was a blues shuffle.

"What do you suggest?" I asked, somewhat defensively.

"Something that won't put the audience to sleep."

As a result of the intervention of Bernie, a non-musician if there ever was one, we came up with a killer opening number: a heart-stopping lightning-fast "Can't Turn You Loose" while, in the wings, Danny made his dramatic announcement:

"Good evening, ladies and gentlemen and welcome to the Universal Amphitheater. Well, here it is the late 1970s going on 1985. You know, so much of the music we hear today is prepro-grammed electronic disco. We never get a chance to hear master bluesmen practicing their craft anymore. By the year 2006 the music known as the blues will exist only in the classical records department of your local public library. So tonight, ladies and gentlemen, while we still can, let us welcome from Rock Island, Illinois, the blues band of Joliet Jake and Elwood Blues—the Blues Brothers!"

Then here come Danny and John. John does a couple of cart-wheels before taking a key out of his pocket and unlocking the handcuffs linking Danny's wrist to a briefcase. Inside are

Danny's harmonicas. And from there, we're off and running. The crowd goes crazy. As Steve Martin's opening act, we almost outdo Steve. We're a bona fide sensation. Even the sainted Cathy Vasapoli, who has come to L.A. to hear us, is impressed.

"I love Linda Ronstadt and country music best," she says, "but you might really have something here, Paul."

The week is a blur of press conferences and interviews. Because of the heat from *Animal House*, Belushi has rocketed to outer space. His movie is a smash; his band is a smash. Danny is thrilled for his best friend. I'm thrilled. Brillstein is talking about a Blues Brothers movie deal. The Blues Brothers' album comes out. It's called *Briefcase Full of Blues* because Belushi, hearing my Elton John impression on the National Lampoon *Goodbye Pop* album, thinks I was singing "You got an English tailored suit and a briefcase full of blues" when, in fact, I was singing "briefcase full of *loot.*" No matter, on the strength of the hit single "Soul Man"—thank you, Steve Cropper; thank you, Duck Dunn—the album goes multi-platinum and starts making lots of loot. Any way you look at it, what once began as a comedy routine in bee costumes has turned into a show-biz phenomenon.

Before I continue the Blues Brothers saga, a quick word about the ethnomusicology of the matter. Blues purists started complaining we weren't playing pure blues. Cultural critics started carping on us as white boys ripping off black sounds. Some said Aykroyd and Belushi were inauthentic in their roles as bluesmen. Well, here was my attitude:

We were a tribute band. We played the music with unrestrained joy and sincerity. We loved the music. John wasn't a great singer—and he knew it. John was a good singer. Danny was a good harp player. They revered blues and R&B and, most importantly, through their comic genius, helped keep this stuff alive. The fact that, among others, Ray Charles, Aretha Franklin, and James Brown were only too happy to appear in the Blues Brothers movie testifies to the musical value of the project. Referring to Danny and John, Ray himself told me, "Those are some funny motherfuckers, and they're helping cats like me get work. God bless 'em."

Amen, Brother Ray.

Between my work on *SNL* and as musical director of the Blues Brothers, I was flying high—only to be shot down in a way that gave me, usually the happiest of piano players, a bad case of the blues.

Chapter 26

Divided Soul

I loved Belushi and wanted to help him.

I loved Gilda and wanted to help her.

I had a divided soul.

The Blues Brothers was about to be turned into a movie. In between creating *SNL* skits, Danny was writing a movie for Jake and Elwood. Elwood was named in honor of the man Danny and I considered the most boring personality ever to appear on Canadian television, Elwood Glover. Danny, knee deep in creating a Blues Brothers mythology, once came out of his office to ask a question.

"What's the most dramatic Catholic imagery imaginable?" he asked.

"The stigmata," I said.

Thus Sister Mother Stigmata became the nun in the film.

As the script started shaping up, it became clear that the band would play an important part. Reassembling the band would, in fact, provide the spine of the story. Danny wrote a scene for me where, appropriately enough, I was playing piano in a lounge in Chicago. The scene would climax with me, Danny, and John performing the Buckinghams' "Kind of a Drag." I looked forward to being in a big Hollywood movie.

Then, on the heels of the success of the Blues Brothers record, Gilda got her own record deal. She approached me to write songs with her and coproduce the album with Bob Tischler. Bob was producer of the *National Lampoon Radio Hour*. He and I had also worked on the live Blues Brothers record.

Figuring I could successfully shuffle among *SNL*, the Blues Brothers film, and Gilda, I agreed. I certainly had the energy. Plus, I'd known Gilda since our *Godspell* days and considered her the greatest female comic since Lucy. Even more important, she was a dear, dear friend.

The Gilda project began. Michael O'Donoghue wrote the hysterical "Let's Talk Dirty to the Animals." Gilda and I wrote, among others, "I Love to be Unhappy" and "Honey, Touch Me with My Clothes On," a look back at those days when extended foreplay was still the number-one indoor sport.

Meanwhile, when Belushi heard about the Gilda record, he pulled me and Tischler aside, whispering, "Don't do it. Just rest up for the movie. You guys are going to be coproducing the sound track of the film, and Gilda's going to be a distraction."

No doubt, John loved Gilda and Gilda loved John, but intense competition exists even among the most loving of comics. For all his sweet-hearted ways, Belushi was a killer competitor.

"Sorry, John," I said. "I gotta help Gilda. But I'll be there for you. Count on it."

What I didn't count on were the obstacles facing me on

Gilda's record. We cut it live in a studio with an audience. It was great, but needed heavy postproduction work, especially the music. Yet the more we worked on it, the worse it got. Meanwhile, Lorne Michaels, who was exec producing, wanted to hear it. The record wasn't ready, but nonetheless I had to fly to Lorne's house in Amagansett, Long Island. Gilda was there, and she and Lorne immediately heard that the album wasn't there yet. But I was out of time. I had to be in Chicago three days later to start working with Belushi and Danny on the film.

I was caught in between Gilda and Belushi.

Gilda smiled at me with those sweet eyes of hers. "Come on, Paul," she said. "I really need you on this."

I thought back to the band. It was a blast. The band was the bomb. But the experience had not been entirely positive. While John loved to heap praise on Duck and Steve and Matt, he ignored me, which was tough on my ego. Often he "forgot" to introduce me to the audience, and that was even tougher. He seldom used my title, "Musical Director." That was the toughest. Even though he gave me that job, he didn't think the audience needed to know that a rock band had a musical director. After all, the Stones didn't have a musical director; neither did Rod Stewart.

Meanwhile, Gilda had been nothing but wonderful to me throughout our long and warm friendship.

"Okay," I told her and Lorne, "I'll do it."

"Great," said Lorne. "I'll call Bernie and tell him."

Bernie Brillstein managed not only Gilda and Lorne, but John as well.

As soon as I got back to the city, I called my lawyer.

"I just pulled out of the Blues Brothers movie," I told him.

"You can't, Paul," he said. "I just did the deal."

"Well, undo it. I can't leave Gilda with a half-completed record. I gotta help her out."

"Why not do both? You go to Chicago for a week while Bob Tischler works with Gilda. Then the week after, you come back and work with Gilda while Bob goes to Chicago."

"Think that will work?" I asked.

"I know it will."

"Okay," I said. "Call Bernie."

Five minutes later, my lawyer was back on the phone. "Bernie said it's too late. You've already been replaced. Belushi told Bernie, 'Paul is no longer a Blues Brother. He'll never be a Blues Brother again.' "

The Blues Brothers went on and did the movie without me. I was crushed. The band I loved belonged to somebody else.

Meanwhile, things got worse. When Lorne played the record for my friend Jerry Wexler, the legendary producer, Wex said, "Hey, you're about to do *Gilda Live!* on Broadway anyway. Just record the fuckin' show and forget these tracks."

The tracks were forgotten. The tracks were shelved. Lorne produced *Gilda Live!* as a limited run at the Winter Garden Theater. I ran back and forth from the pit band to the stage, where I played numerous parts, including superschlep Arnie Schneckman to Gilda's supernerd Lisa Lupner. The highlight was Gilda doing the "Judy Miller Show" where, as a little girl, she's literally bouncing off the walls.

At one point Gilda said to Lorne, "Paul's great in the show, but he seems so sad."

"That's because Paul used to be in the Blues Brothers band," Lorne replied. "Now he's in the Judy Miller Show."

No matter, the crowds were large and enthusiastic. Lorne

was able to secure a film deal for *Gilda Live!* and I had the pleasure of working for director Mike Nichols. Mike graciously offered me a slot in his actor's workshop in Connecticut. I toyed with the idea, but it would have meant missing the fifth season of *SNL*. That was the season that began without Danny, John, and the musicians in the Blues Brothers band. Their movie had gone overtime, and they couldn't get back to New York. Meanwhile, Howard Shore put together a new *SNL* band that included soul saxist David Sanborn. Then, a big surprise:

It happened when I was out in Los Angeles for the weekend. I was at the Sunset Marquis Hotel, sunbathing on a Saturday afternoon, when Danny Aykroyd spotted me. He could not have been nicer. "Duck Dunn's having a barbecue for the band tomorrow," he said. "You've got to come."

"I'd love that," I said.

Danny hastened to add, "Belushi will be there."

I hesitated for an instant. Danny read my mind and said, "John will be glad to see you, man."

John was. He embraced me as soon as I arrived. And the first thing he wanted to do was to play me the sound track from the movie—the sound track, of course, I had had nothing to do with. As it played, the band did their choreography with John and Danny fronting. They were all so proud of the steps they had learned and wanted my approval. I was touched, but also conflicted and brokenhearted. After all, this was my band, but a band from which I was now excluded. The whole thing was bittersweet.

A few weeks later, though, the sweet overwhelmed the bitter when John asked me to return as musical director of the Blues Brothers for the big upcoming tour. Naturally I was happy to do so. Who doesn't want to be a Blues Brother?

We toured eight or nine cities and traveled on a twin-engine prop plane provided by Aspen Airlines. The plane was shaky, making all of us mindful of the late greats—Buddy Holly, Big Bopper, and Richie Valens. As we bounced through a ferocious lightning storm between Detroit and Memphis, I suggested that we write a song and give the publishing to our families. "If we crash," I said, "at least we'll leave behind an annuity for our loved ones." Naturally the song was called "Rock Tragedy," and we took turns writing verses:

Rock Tragedy
All they had to do was spend a couple more G's
Rock Tragedy
Involving several members of the MG's

Our bassist, Duck Dunn, who of course had been one of the MG's, contributed these lyrics:

Rock Tragedy
Insurance policies made out to Bernie Brillstein
Rock Tragedy
My man, he cleaned up good, but we got creamed

The tour had some rough spots. In Memphis, home of Booker T. and the MG's and Stax Records, our concert was attended by a crowd that was all white except for David Porter of the great Isaac Hayes/David Porter writing team. To add insult to injury, we didn't come close to selling out the venue.

The next day, we all went to the hotel pool to chill. Our group included two integrated couples. When the other guests saw a black man with a white woman and a white man with a black woman, they cleared the pool and went up to their rooms. We all got a bad case of the Memphis Blues.

* * *

I thought back to happier times with Belushi. One of those times involved an *SNL* skit in which—forgive my hubris—a certain semi-modest piano player made television history.

I was in a skit playing one of the "Minstrels of New Castle"; it was a medieval dramatization of a famous underground tape of a Troggs rehearsal. The Troggs were the group that my band had opened for back in Thunder Bay. The tape revealed them unsuccessfully trying to explain a simple beat to their drummer. The problem was that their only means of musical communication was to say "fuckin' " this and "fuckin' " that, as in "You had the *fuckin'* beat. Now you've *fuckin'* lost it." The *SNL* writers put us in old English costumes and had us re-create the scene. As the bandleader, I played recorder. James Taylor was on mandolin and Bill Murray was the hapless drummer. In place of *fuckin'*, TV standards required that we say *floggin'*.

I began by berating Bill. "It's so *floggin'* simple," I said. "We're in *floggin'* Gaunt Manor, *floggin'* Elizabeth of Gaunt is gonna come through the *floggin'* door any minute, listen to us play this *floggin'* song, and decide if she'll be our *floggin'* patron. Meanwhile, you can't play four *floggin'* notes."

Before the skit began, writer Al Franken told me, "That *floggin'* thing is hysterical. Put in as many *floggin'*s as you like."

So I piled it on. When Bill messed up the rhythm again, I said, *"Floggin'* listen to me for a *floggin'* minute. You just gotta *floggin'* pay attention."

I was deep into the character, brimming with confidence, when I said to Bill, "You threw the *fuckin'* thing off."

Oh fuck.

I realized what I did, but there was no going back. This was live. The skit went on. Belushi came out in drag, playing the part of Eleanor of Gaunt. John was anything but gaunt in the role. He was humongous. He took over Bill's drum spot and had the audience howling.

When the show was over, I saw Lorne and said, "I fucked up."

"You should have *flogged* up," he said.

"Sorry." I cringed.

"You just broke down the last barrier. Anyway, no one noticed."

Laraine Newman, who had also been in the sketch, added, "Thank *you*, Paul, for making television history."

Chapter 27

King of Hawaiian Entertainment

In late July, 1981, Cathy and I took a vacation to Hawaii. On our second day there, I almost lost my life in a car crash. I know, though, that there must be a God in heaven. Why? Because on our first day I got to see Don Ho.

Before I get to the scary part of the story, let me start with Mr. Ho.

I've always been intrigued by the "King of Hawaiian Entertainment." When Cathy and I took our seats in the beachside venue on Waikiki Beach and I looked up to see Don seated in his great wicker chair, I was filled with happiness. It didn't matter that the summer heat was sweltering. I loved how his Hammond home organ was covered with drawings of tiny bubbles rising from a champagne glass. "Tiny Bubbles" was Don's one big hit. As he sang it, I recalled the days when he had appeared on Johnny Carson or Ed Sullivan. His voice was soft and laconic. Ho was the lounge singer's lounge singer, the ultimate schmaltzmeister. This guy was Dean Martin on Valium.

With the moon shining above his shoulder, Don looked out

over the audience of admiring women. He had the visage of an aging prince with an aged Prince Valiant haircut. His voice had seen better days, but we didn't care. He was Don Ho, and that was all we needed. That's all he needed. After singing the first couple of lines of any given song, he didn't even bother to sing the rest. He didn't have to. A handsome young male background singer would take over where he left off. Don's message was *Hey, I'm Don Ho; I don't need to do an entire song. I'm so laid back I can't even be bothered singing a whole song.*

Every song was basically the same. It was "My Hawaiian Home" over and over again.

I didn't mind. I *wanted* every song to sound the same. I wanted to be lulled off to never-never land by this tranquilizing mood music. It gave me pause to reflect on my life. Maybe I didn't want to go back to New York. Maybe New York was too raw, too real, too crazy. I had heard that Jim Nabors had a show on the other side of the island and was doing quite well. Maybe *I* could have a show. Maybe I could cash in on my *Saturday Night Live* connection. I could call it "Paul Shaffer's Saturday Night Live Honolulu Luau." Carol Burnett, who had moved to Hawaii, could be a guest. Jack Lord would appear. I'd book young Hawaiian talent. Have a weekly limbo contest. Conduct surfing contests. Bring in the best singers from New York: Jerry Vale, Jimmy Roselli, Vic Damone, and, of course, Julie LaRosa. I'd form an all-ukulele band and never deal with winter again. Memories of my frozen Canadian childhood would melt under the island sun. I'd be happy for the rest of my life.

My sweet reverie was broken, though, when, right in the middle of the show, a woman from the audience got up and walked onstage. No one stopped her. I had never seen this before and couldn't help but be a little shocked. She was middle-aged, slightly portly, and obviously enchanted by Don. She stood before him for only a second or two when he stopped singing, grabbe'd her, and brought her face to his. Then he kissed her. I mean, *he kissed her*! From then on it was a free-for-all, one woman after another marching to the stage to place her mouth on the eagerly awaiting Don. Each kiss was caught on film by Don's photographer. And each woman was quick to buy the picture—at a premium price, of course.

At the end of the show, when the band exited, Don didn't move. He remained seated on his wicker throne, while the women who had kissed him lined up with their pictures for him to sign. To maximize Don's take, the photographer would snap still another picture of the female fan kissing Don once again. That print would be available the next day at the box office at 4:30 p.m.

Meanwhile, Cathy drifted over to the gift stand and bought a Don Ho bobble-head doll.

"Do you think he'd autograph it for me?" she asked.

"Are you kidding?" I said. "He'd autograph a thousand if you brought them to him."

Cathy got on line, her bobble-head doll in hand. As she approached the man, I leaned in to get a good look. True to form, Don kissed her passionately. I was happy for Cathy.

Don's photographer took the picture and gave us the pitch. We were willing to pay. I wanted to frame it and place it above the television set in my modest suite at the Gramercy Park Hotel.

"What was the kiss like?" I asked Cathy.

"Well, he felt clammy."

"Tongue?"

"Yes."

I was thrilled.

Overall, unfortunately, the vacation was anything *but* thrilling. July is the wrong month for Hawaii. The heat is deplorable; there are no ocean breezes; and the place is overrun by tourists—like us—looking for the cheapest packages possible. My mood was dark. I hadn't wanted to leave New York because Diana Ross was cutting a new album, the one with Michael Jackson's song "Muscles," and I was told I might be called for the sessions. My love for Cathy was strong, but I didn't see how it would be weakened if I hung around the city to record with Miss Ross. On the other hand, Cathy was strong on maintaining her vacation plans. We were going to Hawaii, and that was that.

The day after the Don Ho show, we decided to take our rental car up to Waimea Bay. The scenery was magnificent. The lush mountains and tropical waterfalls were breathtaking, if you like that sort of thing. Frankly, I'd rather be recording with Diana. Oh well, at least I could relate to Hawaii through rock and roll. Who could forget the Beach Boys' immortal anthem: "All over La Jolla and Waimea Bay, everybody's gone surfin', surfin' USA"? It was part of pop music history, and that had to be good enough for me. So let's visit Waimea Bay.

The waves were big, the sky was blue, and after ten minutes I got bored.

"Let's go back to the hotel," I told Cathy.

"You don't appreciate nature," she said.

"How can you say that? I'm looking at nature. I'm loving nature."

"You're not thinking about nature. You're thinking about the Diana Ross session you're missing," Cathy said.

"Nature is overrated," I said. "With all due respect to Springsteen, Miss Ross is the boss."

"Let's just go back to the hotel."

Like I said, it was a tough vacation.

On the way back to Honolulu, Cathy was driving when, on the left, she noticed the Dole Pineapple Plantation, an enormous expanse of manicured farmland.

"They give tours," said Cathy. "Let's take a tour."

Before I could argue, she took a sudden left turn to enter the plantation. A blind spot prevented her from seeing a car coming at us—speeding far above the legal limit—in the oncoming lane. The car struck the passenger side—my side—full on. Next thing I remember is waking up in an ambulance, the siren screaming, Cathy in there crying hysterically.

Cathy was virtually uninjured—minor hip pain—while my injuries were extensive: nine broken ribs, collapsed lung, fractured clavicle, cracked scapula.

I was in and out of consciousness, then I was out completely.

I woke up in an oxygen tent at St. Francis Medical Center in Honolulu with a priest in my face. "Son," he said, "we know that you are of the Jewish faith. Would you like us to call a rabbi? We can have a rabbi here within an hour."

Still out of it, I said, "Is it Yom Kippur?"

Misunderstanding, the priest said, "I don't know if that's your medical condition or not. I'm not a doctor."

"Yom Kippur is the Jewish Day of Atonement," I explained.

"So you do need a rabbi," said the priest.

"Is this a joke about a rabbi and a priest who go looking for pineapples?" I asked, still in a fog.

"I don't understand," said the priest.

"I don't either," I concurred.

Meanwhile, Cathy, the most organized of women, got an apartment in Honolulu so she could watch over me. After twelve days, though, I was released—or, to be blunt, kicked out. "You don't need the hospital anymore," they said. "You're cured." On my last day at St. Francis, I watched Prince Charles marry Lady Di on TV and thought to myself, *well, at least that's one marriage that will last.*

Next day Cathy wheeled me out of the hospital. I could barely walk.

"Where now?" she asked.

"I love you," I said, "but I need a break from New York. I'm going to L.A. I talked to Harry Shearer. He's back there now and wants to write some songs. I'll recuperate in L.A. Hollywood will heal me."

Chapter 28

The Healing Powers of Mr. Blackwell

I had the blues. The serious blues.

As you've seen, I'm not an unhappy man. I had loving parents who took me to see Sarah Vaughan in Vegas. In Jewish homes all over Canada, they're still talking about my version of "Exodus." Canada was good to me. I saw Jerry Lewis on cable and Ronnie Hawkins in Toronto. I wound up on American television playing piano and acting in comedy sketches. I performed on Broadway. I did record dates. I fell for a lovely gal named Cathy, and Cathy fell for me. So far, so good.

Then this accident nearly broke me in half. In truth, I hadn't realized the full extent of my injuries.

I checked into a hotel in Hollywood where I turned on the television and slept for three days. I was still too weak to walk. I had lost lots of blood. I had broken bones. My iron was down. My heart was heavy. What to do? Answer the ringing phone.

"You can't stay at that hotel." It was my friend Eugene Levy.

"Where should I go?"

"To my house. I'm coming by to get you. I'm bringing you home with me."

Eugene and his lovely wife Deb put me in their guest room and nursed me with loving care. There was some improvement, but I was still very sunk. There's a point where physical debilitation mixes in with some of those wicked B.B. King blues. I was at that point.

Then Harry Shearer showed up.

He came into my room. "Are you ready for Hesh?" he asked. "You haven't been out of the house for a week, Paul. It's time for a cultural excursion. If this doesn't help relieve your pain, nothing will. In all of Los Angeles—with its world-class art galleries, concert halls, universities, and museums—this is the one experience designed to lift the human heart. Get dressed, Paul. We've got a date with destiny."

It took me a long time to work around my injuries and get into my clothes. Harry helped me into the car. He drove me downtown. We parked and walked—I hobbled—to the corner of Fifth and Flower, site of the Arco Plaza, an area surrounded by skyscrapers and encircled by restaurants and stores.

"Here's why I brought you here," said Harry, pointing to a broadcast studio. The front of the studio was a large plate-glass window that allowed you to look in. The man sitting behind the microphone was dressed in a tailored three-piece suit of royal blue accented with chalk-white pinstripes. He wore a red silk tie, a pale blue shirt, and gold cuff links, each accented with a small diamond. His hair was perfect.

"Could it be?" I asked Harry.

"Yes, it is," Harry confirmed.

It was Mr. Blackwell, live and in person. A smile crossed my lips. Pain left my body. Along with a few other curious people, I stood before the window and, through the speakers placed out-side, heard the man broadcast Harry's favorite radio show.

Harry was—and is—the world's premier Blackwell maven. He does a frighteningly accurate imitation of this most man-nered of men. Harry had not only done Blackwell on *SNL*, but had performed his Blackwell act on countless occasions in front of his friends. When he spoke so lovingly of Blackwell's radio show, available only on the West Coast, I was always envious of those living in California.

Mr. Blackwell was most famous for his yearly worst-dressed women list. He liked to say that he never wanted to be known for a negative, yet he was. (On Streisand: "A masculine bride of Frankenstein." On Lindsay Lohan: "From adorable to deplorable.") With not quite bated breath, the world awaited his verdicts on which overfamous female stars had hideous taste. He loved nothing more than to run them down, and we loved nothing more than to relish his nasty pronouncements. His voice, like everything else about him, was a self-invented semicultivated patois that poorly covered up his native New Yorkese. He often spoke of his boyfriend, Spencer, and their sun-and-fun weekends in Palm Springs. He was, in fact, a fash-ionista's fashionista.

"What I'm about to tell you is shocking," he told his radio audience. "Bijan has closed his doors to the public. From now on, you can shop at his wondrous retail establishment by appointment only. But how will this history-altering move affect the Street?" he mused.

The Street, of course: Rodeo Drive.

For the rest of the broadcast, Blackwell asked other rhetori-cal questions: What will the woman be wearing this fall? Will her look be unstructured or have a tailored, tailored elegance?

Will restraint and subtlety finally be reintroduced to fashion or will we continue to slide down the slippery slope of crass commercialism from which there is no turning back?

Blackwell was quick to ask us not to confuse him with another gentleman named Blackwell who also moved in high circles. That Blackwell was famous for his celebrity registers. No, this Mr. Blackwell in the Arco Plaza, *our* Mr. Blackwell, was given his name by Howard Hughes, a fact that our Mr. Blackwell never tired of mentioning. His real name we dared not ask.

In short, those twenty minutes spent in front of the studio helped me in every way. The encounter added immeasurably to my understanding of Blackwell. Eventually I would do something of a Blackwell imitation myself, even if, as a brutally frank friend pointed out, I was imitating Harry Shearer imitating Blackwell. No matter, Harry proved to be a friend indeed on that summer afternoon in Los Angeles. He gave me the gift of Blackwellian rehab.

Unfortunately, the relief was short-lived. My pain returned with a vengeance. I did what most mature men would do in such a circumstance. I went home to Mother. I went home to Mother Shaffer and Mother Canada. I went home to Father. I returned to Thunder Bay, seeking the comfort of those who had loved me longest and loved me best. My childhood home. My childhood bed. There I would retreat for a month. I would be cared for by my parents' doctors. I would be served all my meals. I would consider my options in life. I would never touch a ukulele again.

Chapter 29

How Blue Can You Get?

Pretty goddamn blue.

Canada helped. Mom and Dad were great. But my body was still aching aplenty when I returned to New York at the end of summer. Cathy was there. Cathy was the best. Cathy wanted to get married, but I wasn't ready for anything close to that kind of commitment. I clung to the notion that a man shouldn't marry till he's forty. I clung to my perch at the gone-to-seed Gramercy Park Hotel.

I had no interest in going back to *SNL*. Lorne Michaels was gone and all the original cast members had quit. Jean Doumanian, Lorne's replacement, offered me the job of musical director, but with all my friends gone, it just didn't feel right. The thrill was gone.

I became a studio cat. Producers who knew me from *SNL* started calling. I was glad. Being a studio cat had great allure. As a kid, I'd read about the Muscle Shoals rhythm section who'd recorded with Aretha and thought, *Wow, that's cool. Maybe one day I'll get to do that.* Studio work was challenging because that meant sight-reading, and sight-reading music is not my strong suit. I persevered. I did an album with Desmond Child and Rouge. I was in a band with Patty Smyth called Scandal and played a Del Shannon–style synth solo on their hit, "Goodbye to You." I did a hundred jingles, everything from mouthwash to mayonnaise. Actually those sessions were pretty swinging because of my fellow musicians. You'd be playing with everyone from masters like pianist Richard Tee to bassist Marcus Miller to vocalist Patti Austin.

But even if the jingles raised my spirits, the pain in my body persisted. I did regular physical therapy and, on my doctor's orders, swam an hour a day at a health club pool. The healing, though, was slow in coming.

Back at the Gramercy, I was comforted by the Jerry Lewis Labor Day telethon. I had arranged my return to New York in time to see Tony Orlando host the local portion of the show. The split screen of Jerry in Vegas and Tony in Manhattan seemed to assuage my pain. When Tony looked into the camera, saying, "Now here's the song that made us friends," and then sang "Tie a Yellow Ribbon," hope returned to my heart.

Hope led me to remember happier days. I'd think back on those wonderful Celebrity Seders attended by the *SNL* cast members, Jew and gentile alike. Because I'm a seder pro, I often led the Passover ceremony. Lorne Michaels was so impressed with my expertise that he customized matchbooks with "Paul Shaffer's Celebrity Seder" written on the cover. Our first seder was held in a room at 30 Rock. We moved to other prime locations, including Wolf's Deli on Seventh Avenue and Sammy's Romanian Restaurant on the Lower East Side.

Naturally I'd do shtick. I'd open with "We welcome everyone here, our Christian friends as well as our Jewish brethren.

At Passover, we treat everyone as one. There is no delineation. So, before we get started, let's get the Jews on one side of the table and the gentiles on the other."

At the end of the seder, I'd give new meaning to the ritual of finding the hidden matzoh, the *afikomen*. I'd say, "Our esteemed producer Lorne Michaels has guaranteed the winner, whether Jewish or not, a special spot on 'Weekend Update.' Some of you may remember Stevie Wonder at last year's seder. When I gave him a piece of matzoh, he said 'Who wrote this crap?'"

Finally, I'd conclude, "Traditionally we say 'Next year in Jerusalem.' In other words, next year may we be celebrating our seder in the land of Israel. To that I would like to add, 'Next year real silverware for the seder instead of this plastic shit.' And I'd like to add my own personal benediction, 'Next year at Hef's mansion.' Good night, everybody. You've been beautiful."

The highlight was the Celebrity Seder attended by Paul Simon, his then girlfriend Carrie Fisher, and Carrie's dad, Eddie Fisher.

During the service, I said, "It's time for the salt-water-and-the-parsley blessing. We'll do it both in English and Hebrew. You know, I've always wanted to work with Paul Simon. Paul, if you would do me the honor of taking the English, I'll handle the Hebrew."

At the end, I invited Eddie Fisher to stand before the assembled multitude while, on yet another out-of-tune upright piano, I accompanied him as he sang his immortal "O, My Papa."

Alas, those days were gone. The fun and games were over. The best I could do was hope the phone would ring, with a booking on a jingle for women's sanitary napkins or men's underarm deodorant.

Then came the call.

Chapter 30

The Call That Changed It All

The story goes that when the great composer Billy Strayhorn was summoned uptown by Duke Ellington, Strayhorn heard that the A train was the quickest way to Harlem. He took that subway line and, on the way up to Duke's place, wrote a song about the trip that will live forever.

I have no comparable tale to tell about being summoned to a midtown office by Dave Letterman. I didn't write a great tune on the way over. I barely had a couple of bars of something in mind that might be a cool theme for Dave. I'd recently survived that near-fatal car accident. On that particular day my aches and pains were screaming from the top of my head to the bottom of my toes. I knew, though, that Letterman was a talented guy. I loved his morning show on NBC. It hadn't been big in the ratings, but it won two Emmys and critical raves. I saw Dave as the most brilliant comedy conceptualist around, and I knew that NBC was now giving him a show after Carson. *After* Carson! Naturally my lifelong tenet came to mind: *the later, the hipper.* Late-night TV was my milieu. My years on

SNL had reconfirmed that what I do best is play for a sort of edgy comedy.

When I walked in, Dave gave me a big smile. He couldn't have been more relaxed—dressed in a gray T-shirt, jeans, and Adidas wrestling shoes.

"Glad to see you, Paul," he said. "Thanks for coming in."

He made me feel welcome. That, of course, is his great gift. He said simply, "What are your ideas about a band?"

"R&B," I said.

"Would you feel restricted if it were just a four-piece band?" he asked.

"I'd love it. Four pieces is what I do best. We could turn on a dime. With four pieces, I could still do all the Motown and soul music covers I've been learning my whole life."

That's when Dave came back to me with, "I've always seen myself as Wayne Cochran anyway." And that's when I knew how much I wanted to work with this guy.

Later I learned that the director had wanted Leon Redbone to head the band. Dave also told me later that he remembered how I was not totally on my game during the interview.

"I knew something was off, Paul," Dave told me, "and I also knew you were the guy for the job."

Thanks to a benevolent God, Dave gave me the job of jobs.

My first job was to hire the other cats. Dave started calling us "The World's Most Dangerous Band." The name sounded like it came from the world of wrestling. I liked it. I thought it fit just fine. I also liked a group that played around town called the 24th Street Band. I had coproduced an album of theirs that hit in Japan. Their bassist, Will Lee, was fabulous. He's among the greatest bass players in the world. Will had played with every-one from Horace Silver to the Brecker Brothers to Bette Midler.

I had met him eight years earlier on my first New York session as an arranger. We now happened to belong to the same health club. In keeping with the Rat Pack tradition, we had our meeting in the steam room. I hired him on the spot.

The next day, in the same steam room, I met with my old friend, drummer Steve Jordan. What Will is to the bass, Steve is to drums. Outta sight. Steve and I sat in the steam, speaking of our undying love for the great mid-sixties *Temptations Live!* album, especially the band conducted by their musical director/guitarist Cornelius Grant. Steve was my first choice on drums.

Hiram Bullock was my first choice on guitar. He killed in all styles, from Wes Montgomery to Albert King to Jimi Hendrix. He also knew white rock and roll better than the white rockers themselves. Mention Crosby, Stills and Nash, he'd play their whole catalogue.

When I popped the question, Hiram's eyes lit up. "You kidding?" he said. "I'm in."

What I didn't know was that, due to mitigating circumstances, Hiram had hocked his guitar and had to steal it back to make the gig. But make it he did, and in NBC Studio 6A at 12:30 a.m. on February 1, 1982, in New York City, *Late Night* went on the air.

It was, from the outset, a beautiful thing, a cool combination of casual and off-the-wall, Dave in his chinos and Adidas footwear, me in my jeans, open-neck sports shirts, and Elton John frames, the band smokin' from the get-go.

The debut show was one of the best—also the scariest. Bill Murray was the guest. His idea was to sing "Let's Get Physical," the Olivia Newton-John hit, while actually doing an exercise routine. Bill showed up to discuss the bit, but the discussion was cut off when he said he had to go home to feed his dog. He never came back for rehearsal. Things got even more tense when, just a few minutes before air time, he still wasn't there. There was no substitute waiting in the wings. No Bill, no show. Finally he came running through the door and we kicked off the routine, totally unrehearsed. We hadn't even worked out the key. I figured it out as Bill, crooning lounge-lizard style, went from jumping jacks to pushups. At one point he grabbed our female stage manager and did the Shing-a-ling. Somehow, the thing came off—rough, but funny as hell.

Late Night was designed to be different. Unlike Johnny, there would be no second banana, no Ed sitting up there with the host. Later I read that it was Johnny's explicit intention that Dave not engage a big band. Johnny didn't want Letterman's show to echo his in any way. Thus we were free—and even obliged—to travel down new paths.

I admired Johnny's man, Doc Severinsen, who had played trumpet in the band led by Skitch Henderson, Steve Allen's conductor on the original *Tonight Show*. World-class musicians, including stars like Urbie Green, Clark Terry, Ernie Royal, Ed Shaughnessy, Shelly Manne, Pete Christlieb, Tommy Newsom, Grady Tate, Eddie Safranksi, Bucky Pizzarelli, and Lew Tabakin had passed through the ranks.

Now we were carving new wood; we were breaking from tradition with a quartet whose music, unlike Doc's swinging band, didn't harken back to the forties or fifties; at the start of the eighties, we looked back to the sixties and seventies for our inspiration.

After our first show, by the way, we got a compliment that still gives me shivers, a message from Tony Williams, Miles Davis's drummer and one of the swingingest jazz cats on the planet. "It's a fresh kick," he wrote in a telegram that we hung in the dressing room. "Keep it up."

Night after night, Dave kept it up with his wacky antics. Wearing an all-Velcro suit, he plastered himself against a wall; he leaped into a tank of water dressed as an Alka-Seltzer tablet, and into a gooey cheese dip dressed as a chip. Dave opened up the studio by going outside with remote cameras peering into all sorts of unlikely places. He liked to have slow-mo instant replays of the ripe watermelon falling from the roof and splattering on the pavement.

When I was hired, I was told Dave wanted someone to play off. Could I be his foil? Sure. But as those early weeks passed, the opportunity to kibitz never presented itself. I was frustrated.

My friend Harry Shearer, a supporter since *SNL*, urged me on. "You're a witty guy, Paul. Let your witticisms fly. Grab the mic."

But when I grabbed the mic, it was dead.

"What gives?" I asked the engineer in the audio booth. "I tried to speak, but my mic was off."

"Sorry, Paul," she said, "but I think they want it off."

I sought out the producer. "Is my mic supposed to be off?"

"No. On."

"Then tell the engineer."

The engineer was told and I was on.

Now what?

The next night when Dave said, "Say hello to my good friend Paul Shaffer," I was now positioned to take Harry's advice. "Well, thank you so much, David, and if I may say, it's such a nutty, mah-velous thrill to be with you this evening. In all of broadcasting, there's no finer a cat than Your Groovinence, my good sir."

Dave broke up. After the show, he said, "That was great, Paul. Give me more."

In time, I did. In time, I developed a kind of strange persona. I had spent my life studying the show-biz vets of past eras. Now was my chance to honor them by parodying them. I sincerely adored their insincerity. Their talent was inarguable. Their need to sound educated was my education in jive talk. I loved their language. I took it as my own, even as I illuminated its ludicrousness. I had fun.

For example, I'd tell Dave, "Forgive my hoarseness. I've developed a bad case of Vegas throat."

"What's that, Paul?"

"Well, man, when an entertainer performs two shows a night in an air-conditioned showroom and then goes out into the dry desert atmosphere, the reed can lose its resonance. Hence, Vegas throat. Can you dig it?"

"Paul, have you been anywhere near Las Vegas in the past year?"

"Not at all, man, but spiritually, like my mentor, Mr. Sammy Davis Jr., I suffer from a chronic case of Vegas throat."

Once I conspired with our director to set up a split screen—Dave on one side, me on the other.

"David," I said. "What time is it out there? Here in New York it's 12:45."

"Paul, I'm six feet away from you. What are you doing?"

"You know, Dave, I just love that split-screen telethon look with Frank in L.A. talking to Joey in Atlantic City."

"Talk to me after the show, Paul."

"Ouch, man."

It would take years to run out of show-biz clichés. But when I did, I had no choice but to give Dave what he really wanted—natural conversation.

Undoubtedly influenced by Steve Allen's off-the-wall bits, Dave took it further out and gave it stranger twists. One of my favorite early bits involved Bob Dylan's favorite character, Larry "Bud" Melman, whose real name was Calvert DeForest. Calvert was a pudgy older guy who wore thick horn-rimmed glasses and personified the lovable nebbish. On one Christmas show, he was set to read "The Night Before Christmas" with kids sitting around him. The prop book was in French because the prop people presumed Calvert would be reading off cue cards. But the cue card people presumed that he'd be reading out of the actual book, and that the book would be in English. So—no cards. The upshot was that Calvert was stuck reading a book to the kids in a language he didn't know. For several long minutes, he just died out there, fumbling and stalling and, in essence, saying nothing. He was confused, the kids were confused, and the audience most confused of all. When the camera came back to Dave, Dave's only comment was "It was magic, wasn't it?"

I howled.

I also participated in one of the most bizarre of the early routines. This one was suggested by producer and head writer Merrill Markoe. One day she asked me for the most esoteric information I could think of concerning pop music. I mentioned various guitarists who had played for Parliament-Funkadelic. That was the genesis of this skit:

Dave, Calvert, and I are taking a walk down the hallways of NBC into a deserted stairwell.

Dave says to Calvert, "Who played the guitar solo on 'Not Just Knee Deep?' "

"You mean the song that ran over fifteen minutes on side A of Funkadelic's *Uncle Jam Wants You* album from 1979?" asks Calvert while the audience thinks, *How the hell would he know?*

"That's the album," says Dave, "and the guitarist had to be Eddie Hazel."

"You're wrong," I break in. "It was Garry 'Starchild' Shider."

"You're both wrong," Calvert insists. "The guitarist was the great Michael 'Kidd Funkadelic' Hampton."

And so the conversation continues, each of us arguing over whose esoteric knowledge of Parliament-Funkadelic is more accurate, until Calvert pulls out a gun and points it at both of us.

"This is a stickup," he says. "Just shut up and give me your money."

At that point, the erudite discussion ends while Dave and I hand over our wallets to Calvert DeForest.

* * *

Dave also liked featuring stand-ups like Ellen DeGeneres, Jerry Seinfeld, and Jerry Lewis's friend Richard Belzer. Belzer has been *my* friend since the seventies when I was a recent New York arrival. I met him at a party given by Gilda. At the drop of a hat, the guy would break into his rooster-on-acid imitation of Mick Jagger doing "Satisfaction." I was impressed. He was, in fact, the first stand-up I'd met in the city. After we talked for a minute, he said, "I need to run over to Catch and do a late set. Be right back." "Catch" was code for Catch a Rising Star, the famous comedy club where everyone from Andy Kaufman to Larry David had appeared. I loved such show-biz talk. I loved being at a party where a comic could run off to a club, do his act, and return ninety minutes later and give you an in-person rundown of everything he'd just done on stage. I felt blessed.

Some years later, Belzer invited me and Tom Leopold to Catch. By this time, the Belz was the host. After introducing a stand-up, he'd head downstairs to hang out in the basement with an ultra-hip group of insiders. Soon Tom and I became regulars. I'd call Tom and say, "Shall we descend into Belzer's world?" Eventually the phrase would be truncated to simply, "Shall we descend?" That meant traipsing down to the basement and hanging with the Belz, who would have us in stitches. I'd be down there saying, "Isn't it great to be hip enough to know Belzer and avoid sitting upstairs in a comfortable air-conditioned nightclub where cute waitresses take your order and bring you whatever you want? Isn't it far better to be down here in the sweltering heat with the pipes dripping water on your head while Belzer gives you his unbiased nonstop critique of the comics whose acts you can't even hear?"

The Belz popped up again in my life when he was the warm-up comic on the very first *SNL*. That was an especially beautiful night because my parents had flown in from Canada. As testimony to their hipness, they went directly from the airport to Jilly's. When Dad, quick to characterize entertainers, heard Belzer, his comment was "Richard is an intellectual comedian." Many years later, I took my father to the Friars Club, where he had dinner with Belzer and Robert Klein. He again characterized the situation, saying to himself, "Young comics zinging each other."

My dad was capable of his own zingers. Once when he and Mom came out to catch me with the Blues Brothers in Hollywood, he was walking through the lobby of the Beverly Hills Hotel when he happened upon a nun in full habit.

"Going my way?" he asked her, referring to the Catholic-themed Bing Crosby film from 1944.

The sister looked at him and zinged him right back. "Everybody's in show business."

My mother could also zing. When I got on Letterman and started kibitzing with the boss, I once asked Dave on camera, "Have you ever had one of those Freudian slips when you mean to say one thing and something else comes out?"

"What do you mean by that, Paul?"

"Well, at dinner with Mom last night I meant to say, 'Pass the salt,' but what came out was 'You bitch, you ruined my fuckin' life.' "

Big reaction from the audience.

Dave picked up the phone and called my mother in Canada.

"Mrs. Shaffer," he said, "this is Dave Letterman, and we're doing the show right now. I just want you to be sure and watch us later tonight. You'll be especially proud of a certain conversation between Paul and I."

"Paul and *me,*" she said, correcting his grammar.

Dave put his hand over the receiver, looked over at me, and said, "I see what you mean now, Paul."

But of course he was only kidding.

I could never convince Mom of that, though. She was convinced that Dave never had her on the show again because of one thing alone: she had pointed up his grammatical mistake on national television.

And while I'm on zingers, allow me to document the recent roast of Richard Belzer. It was my debut as an official roastmaster. I took the role seriously. I was also heartened by the fact that it was not televised but was the first roast in history open to the general public at the prestigious Town Hall. It is my strong conviction that these roasts should not be televised. The presence of cameras diminishes the intimacy of the insults; and intimate insults are what roasts are all about.

This is how I opened:

"Town Hall—last time I was here I was eating Odetta. Seriously, though, my question tonight is 'What makes a man the Belz?' I begin with the notion of courage. When I approached Richard about this evening, he said, 'Paul, nothing is off limits. Do what you have to do. Say what you have to say.' So Belzer has no problem with my joking about the fact that his lovely wife, Harlee, is a former softcore porn actress. And the reason he has no problem is because there's such a big difference between softcore and hardcore pornography. In softcore, it just looks like she's rimming out the black guy's anus.

"But, I ask you again, what makes a man the Belz? We who are privileged to call ourselves Richard's close friends know that he endured a tough childhood. His own rabbi sucked his cock. This was right around the time of Richard's bar mitzvah. But that doesn't make him the Belz. It makes him a man who's gotta jerk off into a tallis, but it doesn't make him the Belz."

A tallis, of course, is the prayer shawl of the Jewish faith.

The Belz, Jewish to the bone, loved every minute.

Chapter 31

Blues, Brother

I loved John Belushi. Everyone who knew him loved him. You had to. John's craziness only made you love him more. That's because no matter what he was doing—even dancing on the graves of his fellow performers in that classic *SNL* film piece—you knew that he had a heart of gold. His energy was not normal. Neither was his love of life, on or off the stage. You wanted to be in his company. He wanted to make you laugh, and he did. He wanted to make you happy, and he did that too. His spirit was something to behold: Those close to him—coworkers, friends, and family alike—are fortunate to have known him.

When the news came of John's death, my reaction was disbelief, then shock, then unrelenting sadness. The magnitude of the tragedy took a long, long time to sink in. Cathy and I went to John and his wife Judy's house on Morton Street in the Village. Judy stayed downstairs, where she mourned alone. At one point I was asked to join her. "Paul," she said, "the memorial service is going to be held at St. John the Divine. John loved Jackson Browne's 'For a Dancer.' Please play it in his honor."

She also requested that saxophonist Tom Scott play a solo on the song. Tom had been in the Blues Brothers band, but he and John had had a falling out during the making of the movie *Neighbors*. It was important to Judy that this song serve as their reconciliation.

The service itself was quite amazing. I know John would have found it amusing, if only because it was the first church service I'd seen with a velvet rope and a bouncer with a list. It was like trying to get into Studio 54. I barely made it past the rope myself. Afterward, during the limo ride to the after-funeral, I heard a woman say, "I was thinking about how John's brother Jim said in his eulogy that so many people here had probably taken their first limo ride with John. I had my first Lear ride with John." For whatever reason, that struck me as so funny, I had to repeat the line. "Had my first Lear ride with John." My companion and former Blues Brother drummer Steve Jordan fell out laughing.

Years later, I was in Los Angeles. I had just flown in from New York and was at the car rental office near the airport. The clerk recognized me and said, "I know you played with John Belushi. He was a great star. You know, he was in one of our cars when he had his little thing."

Dear God, I thought to myself, *the man is describing John's death as "his little thing."* Then I asked myself, *Was he really in the car when he died? Well, no, not literally. Contractually.*

The more I considered the "had his little thing" phrase and the unapologetic pride with which it was uttered, the more I was convinced that John would have appreciated such a description of his demise. Irony—deep, rich, and always a little twisted—was at the heart of John's comedy.

Chapter 32

I'm No Homophobe, or How I Came to Co-write "It's Raining Men"

Even after I was hired by Letterman, I continued to play recording sessions. I did so because I liked the work, the challenge, and the camaraderie. When the phone rang in the morning, the caller might be anyone from Yoko Ono to the ad man/mad man in charge of the new Speed Stick campaign. I was always ready to run out to a studio gig.

Enter my good friend Ron Dante. Ron was an early supporter of mine, a lovely guy and Barry Manilow's producing partner. Barry was on top of the world and Ron was right there with him. I'd played on some of Barry's early hits, such as "Somewhere in the Night," "Jump, Shout, Boogie" and "Ready to Take a Chance Again." Ron was ready to take a chance on me again when he came looking for an arranger for his new artist Paul Jabara.

Paul would win an Oscar for writing the disco hit "Last Dance" by Donna Summer. But back in the seventies, he was just a new artist with a few hot ideas. Would I write arrangements for him? Sure.

By the way, to say that Paul was gay would be like saying *Ben-Hur* was a movie with a small chariot race. Paul had a strong sense of how to speak to the gay club audience.

I arranged a few early disco tracks for Paul, including a song called "One Man Ain't Enough." Apparently it wasn't, because the song never went anywhere. But Paul was definitely working toward a groovy thing.

A few years later he called me, very excited. "Donna Summer's been cold for a little while, and I got the title that's gonna bring her back. You were so great arranging 'One Man Ain't Enough,' I want you to help me compose this one."

"What's the title?" I asked.

" 'It's Raining Men.' "

"I'll be right over."

When I got to Paul's place, he elaborated. "The boys will love it. They're the ones who are gonna bring Donna back, but we gotta hit 'em where they live."

He had the whole lyric concept; he really just needed someone to put music to it. I hammered out a tune and cut a demo. By the time we were done, I thought, *Gee, this is pretty good.*

But fate moved against us. Between the conception and execution of this song, Miss Summer had been born again. Needless to say, she wasn't keen on recording a ditty that had her howling "Rip off the roof and stay in bed." That was bad enough. But she really took exception to the chorus with its "Hallelujah, it's raining men, amen!" Thus she passed on the song, calling it blasphemous, condemning Paul to eternal hellfire, and sending him a Gideon Bible. True story.

Paul knew he had a hit and recorded it anyway. He even planned to debut the song live in Central Park on Gay Pride

Day. Now usually I wouldn't play any of my work for my girl-friend Cathy, who was my toughest critic. She was also unaware that the ego of the artiste is extremely fragile. But this song was different. Maybe it was because Paul was an Oscar winner, maybe it was because the demo was great, but I decided to take a chance and play it for her anyway.

As soon as Cathy heard the chorus, she rolled her eyes and said, "Eccch! What were you guys thinking? This sucks!"

I was crushed, but Paul Jabara was indomitable. He called me up and exclaimed, "You simply *must* come hear 'It's Raining Men!' in the park. He went on to explain the scenario. "I've got this killer gal named Zenobia to sing lead and a bunch of girls from Studio 54 who will be wearing yellow rain slickers with red bathing suits underneath. I got a whole stage production. Gay Pride Day won't know what hit it."

"Paul," I said, "I could be wrong, but isn't Gay Pride Day normally a bunch of militant lesbians standing around shouting that they're here, they're queer, and everybody better get used to it? I don't know if it's the right crowd."

"Nonsense," Paul replied. "It'll be huge."

Cathy was incredulous. "Not only did you ignore what I said about that lousy song," she told me, "but now you wanna go to a gay rally in Central Park? Let me tell you something: if anyone takes a picture of you at Gay Pride Day and it appears in a magazine, you'll be sorry."

Now I'm no homophobe. Neither is Cathy. But back then, things weren't as they are today. Maybe she had a point. So it was with a heavy heart that I told Paul I couldn't make it. I wished him luck.

Several weeks later, Gay Pride Day rolled around. Cathy and

I had been sore at each other that morning. What else was new? We weren't speaking, but we had a reservation for bike rentals in Central Park. We went anyway.

There we were. Riding bikes, not talking, and having a miserable time. Toward the end of the day, I looked at my watch and remembered Jabara's thing. Hey, it was about to start. Begrudgingly, Cathy agreed to ride over to the bluffs, where we could see the festivities taking place on the Great Lawn. We had a panoramic view.

Sure enough, there was a big butch lesbian onstage chanting, "We are everywhere ... we will BE everywhere," all to thundering applause.

I had been right.

"And now ladies and gentlemen," the lady concluded, "Paul Jabara with a song you're all going to be loving this summer."

Zenobia came out and started the opening verse:

Humidity is rising ... barometer's gettin' low ...

That was the cue for the backup dancers. Except the number hadn't been rehearsed and the girls were out of step. One of 'em couldn't wait to get out of her yellow rain slicker to show off her tiny red bikini. Another slipped and fell on her booty. The whole thing was a giant mess.

But Zenobia kept singing:

For the first time in history, it's gonna start raining men ...

Then the big build to the chorus:

It's raining men! Hallelujah! It's raining men! Amen!

On cue, a giant tanned-and-greased muscleman came out in a black speedo, grinding his pelvis to beat the band.

By then, the crowd had started to boo and hiss. No one was amused.

God bless Paul Jabara; he'd completely misread his own audience.

And there I was, astride my rented bike, next to my angry girlfriend, up on the bluffs, watching the whole sordid affair.

This was the only song I'd ever written!

People were booing!

I turned to Cathy and said, "This is the most bizarre thing that's ever happened to me."

She turned to me and exclaimed, "Well, I TOLD you the song sucked when you wrote it!"

With that, she rode off without another word, leaving me to shout after her:

"Why do you have to hurt me on Gay Pride Day?!"

* * *

"It's Raining Men" went on to be a huge hit, recorded and rerecorded by the likes of the Weather Girls, Geri Halliwell, the London Gay Men's Chorus, and my main *whatever*, the unambiguously talented RuPaul.

Cathy has since softened her attitude toward the song . . . especially since it continues to pay our phone bill.

During our dating days back in the eighties, Cathy loved to surprise me. One day she said, "Paul, how'd you like to have dinner with Chas Chandler?"

"Chas Chandler? The bass player for the Animals! This guy discovered Jimi Hendrix! I'm there."

I don't know how Cathy did it, but two days later I'm sitting across from Chas over spaghetti carbonara at La Strada East. This cat had stories to tell. Me, I had nothing but questions.

"How'd you come up with that bass line on 'We Gotta Get Out of This Place'?" I asked.

"Actually, Paul," said Chas, a portly Brit from Newcastle, "me bass was out of tune. What sounds intentional was nuthin' but a bloody accident."

"Who did you listen to growing up?" I wanted to know.

"I loved the Shirelles, man, and that bird with the Chantels that sang 'Maybe.' "

"That's Arlene Smith. I've got a video of her that would kill you. She's on *The History of Girl Groups*. It's filled with those Brill Building stories that always end the same—'And then the British Invasion wiped us out. We couldn't compete.' "

"Hey, mate, I've got to see that fockin' show."

That's all I needed to hear. We went back to my suite at the Gramercy, where I slipped in the tape. Chas was especially fixated by Don Kirshner's interview on Spector.

"Phily was an artist," said Don. "We'd cut three sides for $1,500—no problem. Phily would go in the studio—one song, four grand."

"Stop the bloomin' tape," Chas exclaimed. "That's why those Brill Building blokes lost their way. Do you know how much it cost us to make 'House of the Rising Son'?"

"How much?"

"Fifteen fockin' dollars. With enough left for pints all around. British Invasion, my arse."

Chapter 33

The Gig of Gigs

Being Letterman's bandleader *is* the gig of gigs, especially for a piano player who once survived by working topless bars. Every night's different. Every night's a challenge. And of course every night means working with Dave, whose pitch-perfect wit keeps us all in tune. I'm forever grateful for such wonderful work.

But if any gig could rival the excitement of being on nightly TV with Dave, it might be the annual Rock and Roll Hall of Fame induction.

It all began when Ahmet Ertegun thought I'd be the right musical director for the induction function. Ahmet had taken a shine to me when I first worked for him on Robert Plant's Honeydrippers' record. He appreciated my adaptability.

"You and your band can back up anyone and everyone, Paul," said Ahmet. "You have the right flexibility and the right feel. The gig is yours."

The problem was that the first Rock and Roll Hall of Fame dinner, to be held at the Waldorf Astoria in New York, was scheduled for the same day as a Letterman anniversary special.

If the special had been slated for our normal taping time—mid-afternoon—I'd have no problem running across town and making the dinner. But Dave's idea was to have the entire show taped on an airplane heading for Miami. Then, always the most generous of bosses, Dave would treat everyone to a weekend of sun and fun in Miami Beach.

The only solution was for me and the band to turn around and fly back to New York the second we landed in Miami. Because Dave was supportive of my participation with the Hall, he offered to pay half the cost of a private jet. When Ahmet's co-chair of the Hall, *Rolling Stone* founder and publisher Jann Wenner, said they'd pay the other half, we were set. All this sounds cool except for one thing: I was convinced that the little jet carrying us back to New York would crash and burn. In my fevered imagination, it seemed inevitable. Ours would be the next big rock and roll air disaster. A private plane heading for the Rock and Roll Hall of Fame? Please, you couldn't ask for a hipper disaster. I thought I was destined to be remembered with the Big Bopper, Buddy Holly, and Ritchie Valens. Otis Redding and the Bar-Kays had been on such a flight. So had Jim Croce.

In an act of musical perversity, every time we went to commercial on that Letterman anniversary broadcast, my band and I played a song by an artist who had gone down in flames. Commercial one: "Chantilly Lace." Commercial two: "That'll Be the Day." Commercial three: "La Bamba." Station break: "Dock of the Bay." Commercial four: "Soul Finger." Commercial five: "Bad Bad Leroy Brown." I was petrified during both flights, but the music saw us through. We returned safely to New York and made it to the Waldorf on time.

From then on, I'm happy to say that my band has performed

at virtually every induction dinner. The gig has been a blessing and a blast. The Hall got me even further inside the secret life of rock and roll. It also added to my repertoire of rock and roll stories.

Many of the stories came out of the jams. As years went on, I'd become famous—or infamous—for arranging legendary jams.

That first year all of us were hesitant to ask the legends we were inducting—including Chuck Berry, Ray Charles, Jerry Lee Lewis, James Brown, and Fats Domino—to perform. After all, they were there to be honored, not to sing for their supper. However, at evening's end a monstrous totally spontaneous jam session exploded out of a photo op, and the cats ran for their instruments. Before we knew it, Chuck Berry was on the floor, his neck resting on the audio monitor, doing a reverse hump as he banged out "Roll Over, Beethoven," while Jerry Lee bashed the high keyboard counterpoint. That gave me the courage to ask John Fogerty to roll out "Proud Mary" and Steve Winwood to give up "Gimme Some Lovin'," two tunes by two singers who had not sung those songs in years.

That jam was a dream, others near nightmares. One such occasion resulted in my getting on Eric Clapton's shit list. This, as you can imagine, is a source of considerable pain for me.

Let me begin the Shaffer/Clapton saga in the eighties, when Eric sat in with my band on Letterman. He was the first major musician to do so. This was important because it opened the door for other stars to do the same. In other words, if God thinks Shaffer's band is good enough, God's disciples will follow.

Next time Clapton was in New York, he invited me to hang out with him and his pal Phil Collins, another lovely chap. Suddenly I was tight with the Brits and loving every minute of it.

Eric was even giving me etiquette advice about an upcoming state dinner in Canada where I was to meet Prince Charles and Princess Diana.

"The Royals are very strict about protocol," said Clapton. "Whatever you do, don't speak to the Prince and Princess until they speak to you."

The big moment arrived. I was in a reception line with a number of dignitaries. Brian Mulroney, Prime Minister of Canada, was slowly making his way down the line with the Prince and Princess at his side, introducing each of the guests to the Royals. When they finally got to me, things did not go well. I saw a blank stare on Mulroney's face; he had no idea who I was. I thought of Clapton's instruction—*don't speak till you're spoken to*—but no one was saying anything. Time stopped. At that moment, I bravely decided to break with royal protocol. I said to Prince Charles, "Hello, Your Highness. My name is Paul Shaffer, and I'm the bandleader of *Late Night with David Letterman* in New York."

"Really?" the Prince intoned. "How late?"

"Well," I answered, almost apologetically, "we start at half past midnight."

"Oh," the Prince said with a chuckle, "count me out." He then continued on his princely way. Meanwhile, the poor Princess looked so sad, I let her pass without saying a word. I think she was grateful.

Then in 1999, Clapton and I were both participants in the Save the Music Concert on the White House lawn. I was musical director, and a host of stars, including Al Green, Garth Brooks, and B.B. King, were on the bill. Bill and Hillary were in attendance.

During rehearsal, I tried to set up some format for the song that Eric and B.B. would be playing together. I did that because, left to their own devices, neither one of them would take the first solo. They had too much respect for one another. The result would be an uncomfortable silence.

I suggested that B.B. sing the first verse and that Eric take the first solo.

"Paul," said Eric, "this is the blues. We don't need to plan things out. Just let it develop."

"I understand, and you're absolutely right," I said. But as James Brown had told me, I had the pressure of the time.

"We need some kind of road map, Eric," I suggested.

He looked at me like I was an enemy of the blues.

"Have it your way," he said, but he wasn't happy.

Nonetheless, the performance was stellar.

The president was especially pleased. He's a blues lover to the core. After the concert, he came over to have his picture taken with the horn section. He was standing right next to me when, for some reason, I felt obligated to let loose with a wisecrack.

"Mr. President," I said, "if you had come on Letterman instead of Arsenio Hall's show to play your sax, I'm sure you would have won anyway."

Clinton's face fell and he said, in dead earnest, "I wish I had been asked."

Oh shit, I thought to myself, *I've pissed off the leader of the free world!*

To compensate for my blunder, I mailed the president a box of Rico reeds for his sax. "Pres," I wrote, "check these out." When he sent me a handwritten letter of appreciation, I realized that the leader of the free world probably had more important things on his mind than a misplaced quip from a piano player.

Meanwhile, my tenuous relationship with Clapton wasn't

getting any better. Our next encounter came at the Concert for New York, the benefit after 9/11, for which I also served as musical director. Paul McCartney organized the event, which included everyone from Bon Jovi to Jay-Z to the Who and Mick and Keith. There was also the comic relief of Billy Crystal, Jimmy Fallon, and Adam Sandler as Opera Man bashing Osama bin Laden. Meanwhile, in an attempt to keep the show moving and the stars happy, I was operating on overdrive.

David Bowie opened. I'm a fan. I also believe, having heard both their voices, that Bowie and Anthony Newley are the same person. As Belzer says, "Did you ever see them together?" Just saying.

For his opening song, Bowie planned to sing live to a prerecorded instrumental backing. My tech had been instructed to hit "play" on the playback machine when Bowie gave the cue. When he did so, the machine stuttered, and Bowie was out there without the music he needed. It wasn't pretty. Pro that he is, Bowie covered up admirably and afterward, feeling sick—he had food poisoning—went straight to his dressing room.

I followed him to offer my sincere apologies. But as I was rushing to Bowie's room, Eric Clapton popped out of another room. Superstars were popping out everywhere.

"Paul," said Eric, "I must talk to you right away about the song I'm to play."

"Sorry, Eric," I said, "I can't talk right now. I need to see Bowie."

"Bowie's already played," said Eric. "I haven't."

I felt the pressure of the time.

"Eric," I said, "just give me a sec."

I found a sick Bowie in his dressing room, and I apologized profusely. Ever the gentleman, Bowie graciously let it slide.

Speaking of apologies, I once had to make a colossal one to Bowie's twin, Newley. This happened on Letterman when Anthony had agreed to sing with my band. As the song progressed, I inadvertently modulated way higher than I was supposed to. To reach his final note, poor Anthony nearly busted a gut, but made it. As he went offstage, I heard this horrific howl: "FUUUUUCK!"

I had to apologize, and I did. "You always hurt the one you love," I wrote in a deeply contrite letter. Newley wrote back: "My final note was so stratospheric, dear Mr. Shaffer, that dogs in Alaska are still holding their ears in pain."

Back at the Concert for New York, Eric and I had our meeting. He then went onstage and killed with Buddy Guy. But alas, I don't think the evening brought Eric Clapton and myself any closer together.

Some years later I would play for Eric in another context. This was the Rock and Roll Hall of Fame dinner during which Clapton and B.B. King were inducting the same Buddy Guy. This time I knew not to interfere with Eric's flow. But when Joel Gallen, the producer/director of the show, took me aside, I got a little sidetracked. "Paul," he said, "this may be one of the last times that these three giants play together. It's got to be classic. Make sure that B.B. sings one chorus, just like Eric and Buddy."

The rehearsal was slated for mid-afternoon. It was a typically crowded schedule. In addition to Buddy, the other inductees were U2, Percy Sledge, the O'Jays, and the Pretenders. Many acts, many songs. I was harried. When it was time for B.B., Eric, and Buddy to play, against my better judgment I began to explain how I thought it should go.

"Please, Paul," said Eric, "this is the blues. Just let it develop."

Oh, God, I realized, *I've alienated "God" again.* I backed off. But as the song "developed," B.B. didn't sing. Remembering the producer's edict, I stopped the band and said to the three guitarists, "Guys, I think we need to get the format straight. I'd love for B.B. to sing the first chorus."

"You're prescribing a format," said Eric, "and killing the spontaneity."

"I just want to make sure that B.B. sings," I explained.

Eric wasn't happy. Eric didn't think I understood the blues.

During the actual performance that evening, the song came off brilliantly. Turned out Eric was right. The guys did what they wanted, regardless of the rehearsal. I guess you'd have to say that Eric's blues are deeper than mine. But I had the pressure of the time.

That same pressure impacted another major musical meeting involving another hero of mine: the immortal Mr. Sammy Davis Jr.

Let me preface my Sammy story by saying that on the wall of my study, among many mementos, my prized possession is a plaque in the shape of the state of Israel. It reads, "An artistic and cultural award presented to Sammy Davis Jr. in Washington, D.C., July 13, 1965, from the Ambassador of Israel." The plaque was purchased at an auction authorized by Sammy's estate. I look at it often. It takes me back to that night at the Apollo when I first met the man. He and I participated in the "Motown at the Apollo" television special. Everyone was there—Wilson Pickett, the Four Tops, Smokey Robinson, Luther Vandross—and I was in soul heaven. When Sammy showed up, I introduced myself. "Paul Shaffer," I said. "I work on the Letterman show."

Sammy smiled his crooked smile and said, "Groovy, man, I know who you are."

My heart skipped a beat.

My next experience with Sammy happened on the Letterman show. In the eighties, Dave decided to do a week in Las Vegas. At that time, Cathy—with whom I was still breaking up to make up (and making up to break up)—was working as a talent coordinator for Letterman. That meant she booked the acts. Cathy was great at her job because she'd never take "no" for an answer. Her tenacity was legendary.

Cathy pulled a coup when she got Sammy to agree to fly all night to Vegas right after his performance with the Boston Pops. But there'd be no time for rehearsal, which meant we'd have to play something he already knew well. Cathy gave me Sammy's hotel number and within minutes I was calling. When he picked up the phone, I said, "Schmuel, it's Paul Shaffer."

Schmuel is "Sam" in Yiddish. It's the way the Rat Pack referred to him, and I was delighted to be using their term of endearment.

"Paul, what's shaking, baby?"

"I know you're coming in to Vegas to perform on the show, Schmuel, and I can't tell you what an honor it is. Just calling to ask what you'd like to sing."

"You figure it out," said Schmuel. "I can do anything at all with that band of crooks of yours. Just pick something nutty-mahvelous, baby. And tell all the cats hello."

"I'll get back to you with the song," I said.

"Take your time, baby, it's all about taking your time."

But of course I was feeling the pressure of the time. What to play?

Will Lee had two great ideas: "On Broadway" George Benson–style or "For Once in My Life" Stevie Wonder–style.

I called back to see which song Schmuel preferred, but this

time a woman answered the phone. "This is Altovise Davis," she said.

"Alto!" I boldly exclaimed. That's how the Rat Pack referred to her on Carson. "This is Paul Shaffer from Letterman. Is Schmuel there?"

"Schmuel is sleeping, sweetheart," she said without missing a beat.

"Will you have him call me?"

"Of course."

But he never did. And every time I called, he was either working or sleeping.

The morning of the show I was feeling some panic. Schmuel was flying in, and we still didn't know what he wanted to sing. At 10 a.m., the floor manager said I had a backstage call. It was Sammy calling from the plane.

" 'Once in My Life' will be fine, Paul," he said. "Key of E going into F."

"Great!" I was relieved.

I was also eager to work out an arrangement. For our week in Vegas, I was supplementing our four-piece rhythm section with saxist David Sanborn and the Uptown Horns. We whipped up a chart, nursed it, rehearsed it, and put it on tape. That way when Sammy arrived, he could hear it.

Then another backstage call. Sammy's plane had landed early, and he was on his way over. When I greeted him at the backstage door with a big "Schmuel! We're thrilled you're here," I was a little taken aback. He looked extremely tired and frail. He walked with a cane.

"We have an arrangement, Sam. You can rehearse it with the band."

"No need, baby. Gotta conserve my energy. I'm just gonna go to my room and shower."

"I wanna make it easy for you, Schmuel. So I'll just play you a tape of the arrangement on the boom box. That way you'll hear what we've done and tell me if it's okay."

"Man, I know the song."

"I know, Sam," I said, "but what if you don't like the chart?"

"I'll like it, I'll like it."

"But what if the key's not right?"

"Okay, if you insist."

I slipped the cassette in the boom box and hit "play." To my ears, the chart sounded great. Sammy closed his eyes and, in Sammy style, nodded his head up and down to the groove. He smiled.

"It's swinging, man," he said, "but think of how much more fun we could have had if I hadn't heard this tape."

His words still resonate in my ears; the notion still haunts me. Sammy swung that night, but as he was performing, I couldn't help thinking that his carefree feeling about time—as opposed to my lifelong notion of the pressure of the time—was coming from a higher spiritual plane. As a musician, I've always thought I rushed. I still think I rush. The great players never rush.

It reminds me of that moment when I watched Ray Charles turn to his guitarist, just as the young guy was about to solo, and say, "Take your time, son. Take your time."

Chapter 34

My Elvis

I place Phil Spector in the highest category of musical icons. His productions are to rock and roll what Wagner is to opera. He does it bigger than anyone. On a list of my cultural idols, Phil is number one. I have enormous and genuine admiration for his genius as a songwriter, producer, and musical visionary. He's my Elvis.

I even like Spector's musical idiosyncrasies. For example, he has great passion for recording in mono. For years he gave away lapel buttons that said, "Back to Mono." His commitment to mono and opposition to stereo was understandable: he didn't want his famous Wall of Sound deconstructed. He didn't want the listener to be able to hear any of the individual elements in the Wall. He wanted the mix heard as he himself had designed it. He didn't want the listener to be able to shift over to the right speaker or the left speaker and hear any details. In short, he wanted to retain the integrity of the Wall. He wanted the Wall to stand as he originally built it.

Not only did I love Spector's Wall, but I loved the singers and songs he developed. I've mentioned my fanatical devotion to Ronnie Spector and the Ronettes. I also loved the Righteous Brothers singing "You've Lost That Lovin' Feelin'," loved Tina Turner singing "River Deep–Mountain High." I loved the whole smorgasbord of superb Spector schmaltz.

In fact, in 1984 when Ellie Greenwich mounted her musical *Leader of the Pack* at the Bottom Line, she asked me to play the part of Phil, who produced many of Ellie's songs.

"I've never met Phil," I said. "I don't know what he sounds like."

"Yes, you do," Ellie reassured me. "Phil is one of those guys who based his hipster lingo on Ahmet Ertegun. Just do Ahmet and you'll be doing Phil."

That was easy. I knew Ahmet and loved his hipster lingo. Once, for example, Ahmet had used me on a Laura Branigan session. He was convinced that if Laura covered the Exciters' "Tell Him," it would be a hit all over again. The session went well. Marcus Miller was on bass and I played synthesizer. The track was smoking, but Laura never quite found her way through the smoke. Undaunted, Ahmet took us all to Gallagher's, the midtown steakhouse, for a postsession dinner. We were joined by another producer who, in order to protect the guilty, shall remain nameless. With absolute abandon, the producer pulled out his vial of cocaine and indulged right there at the table. Ahmet was faintly amused. "If you do this in public with such blatancy," said Ahmet, "you must be a good producer."

When Laura ordered oysters, the topic turned to food.

"I love oysters," I said, "but I can't eat them anymore. I had a bad one not long ago and got so sick I had to promise God I'd never eat another one again."

"Shall I tell you something?" said Ahmet. "I recently promised God that I would never do heroin and angel dust together. But it's such a great high, don't you think?"

Of course he was fabricating this pose. At the time Ahmet said this, he must have been sixty. Sixty seemed extremely old to me, and I was convinced that his tongue-and-cheek tidbit was the hippest thing I'd ever heard—until I heard Ahmet say something even hipper.

We were backstage at a concert when Ahmet ran into a woman who knew him from the sixties.

"Oh, my dear Ahmet," said the lady, "last time I saw you, you were seated in a folding chair in the wings of a Led Zeppelin show, fast asleep and snoring quite loudly."

"What used to make me snore," said Ahmet, "I don't do no more."

No wonder Phil was so enamored of Ahmet.

The first time I saw Phil in person was 1989, the year he was inducted into the Rock and Roll Hall of Fame. He attended the ceremony with power attorney Marvin Mitchelson. Phil favors the company of power attorneys. I played Phil "Be My Baby," approximating the Wall as best I could. I didn't think I'd ever see him again.

A few days later, I was in the studio working on my album *Coast to Coast*. That album is a story in itself—my compilation of rock/pop/soul songs performed by everyone from Will Smith to Bobby Womack to Dion. I wanted to pay tribute to the key music centers, so every weekend I'd fly off and cut a tune in New Orleans or Chicago, Minneapolis or L.A.

Coast to Coast didn't rival Michael Jackson's *Thriller* in sales, but it did express my musical heart. One song I cowrote with

Steve Cropper and Don Covay called "What Is Soul" contained this rhyming couplet:

Soul is Jerry Wexler and Ahmet
The funkier you are, the bigger Cadillac you get

At this particular *Coast to Coast* session, I was working with Brian Wilson. I had bonded with Brian and his boys when they invited me to the Beach Boys' 20th Anniversary Concert in Honolulu. It was my first trip back to Hawaii since my near-fatal accident. At first I wasn't going to go. But then I remembered Jan and Dean's top-ten hit that Brian had cowritten, "Dead Man's Curve." One of the unwritten laws of rock and roll is that every surfer must return to confront Dead Man's Curve. My Dead Man's Curve was that highway in Honolulu at the turnoff to the Dole Plantation. I had to go back. The power and pull of surf rock drew me back. The kick of playing with the Beach Boys helped me confront my fear. I was asked to introduce my number.

"As a young lad growing up in the frozen north of Canada," I told the bikini-clad crowd, "I dreamed of a day such as this. I was a shy and retiring teenager when God suddenly gifted me in a way that brought summer sunlight to my dark winter mood. I learned that the Beach Boys were coming to my hometown of Thunder Bay. I bought my ticket weeks in advance. A good two hours before showtime, I was seated in the front row. These were the original five Beach Boys, no sidemen, no keyboards. When it came time for 'Surfin' U.S.A.,' I was on my feet. But because there were no keyboards, the organ solo went to Carl on guitar. I thought to myself—*Paul Shaffer, you could play that organ solo. You know it note for note. Paul Shaffer, you could be a Beach Boy.* But, alas, I was not called to the stage that night long ago in Thunder Bay. I couldn't be a Beach Boy. But on this sun-kissed beach on this sun-kissed island, today I am happy to say that I *will* play that organ solo. Ladies and gentlemen, today Paul Shaffer is a Beach Boy."

It was a nice moment. From then on, Brian and I were friends. At this *Coast to Coast* recording session, though, I encountered a bit of a problem with Dr. Eugene Landy, the clinical psychologist who had attached himself to Brian as his groovy guru/Svengali. Landy also fancied himself a songwriter and had been writing lyrics for Brian's recent songs. He really wanted a piece of the mixed-genre number for my record called "Metal Beach." It was a helluva production, with Joe Walsh, Joe Satriani, and Dick Dale on guitars.

"Got these amazing lyrics, Paul," the good doctor said to me. "And Brian loves them."

I looked over the words with quiet suspicion. They hinted at psychological subtexts that were beyond me. They didn't come close to fitting the groove. At the same time, though, Brian was under Dr. Landy's spell. Brian was following the doctor's orders.

I needed an idea.

An idea came.

"Sorry, Doc," I said, "but 'Metal Beach' is going to be a surf instrumental. No lyrics."

Landy looked at me with a certain artistic longing in his eyes.

"Are you sure?" he asked.

"Positive," I answered.

It was at this session that the engineer's assistant told me I had a call.

"You know who it is?" I asked.

"Phil Spector's assistant."

I was amazed but skeptical. Was this a joke?

"Mr. Shaffer, I'm calling for Mr. Spector. He would like you to meet him at the Plaza Hotel this evening and wonders if you have any suggestions about going to hear jazz."

I couldn't believe it. Phil Spector wanted to hang out.

That night, bonding over big-band jazz, we became friends. That's when I learned that, as far as raconteurs go, Phil is in a class with Kirshner and Ertegun. He had endless stories about the mono days. He also has great knowledge of music of all kinds, and I was thrilled to go along for the ride.

The ride went on for years. Whenever Phil came to town, we were off to another evening of conversation and music. Sometimes he got music mogul Allen Klein to take us to a Knicks game at Madison Square Garden. Other times were quieter. Once I invited Cathy along when we went to hear the impeccable Peggy Lee.

Peggy was in her twilight years. As she sat on a piano bench in front of the band, she cut quite a figure. Quite a large figure. Her hair was platinum, and her face was framed with severe black glasses. Her voice, though, was as sensitive and lovely as ever. As she performed the sensuous "Fever," you had to lean in to listen. That's how quietly she sang.

Unfortunately, Phil, although a devout Peggy Lee fan himself, held a large newfangled mobile phone in the palm of his hand. He couldn't restrain himself from playing with the keys. The tones from the keys made loud sounds, so loud, in fact, that a gentleman at the next table over gently tapped Cathy on the shoulder. Pointing to Phil, he whispered, "Please tell him to stop making that noise."

Always the world's most sensitive and polite person, Cathy thought about the request. She thought about the man's justifiable irritation; then she thought about Phil's quirky personality. While she weighed the two conflicting notions, the man repeated his request, "Tell him to stop."

Cathy had two words for the man:

"I can't."

On another occasion, Phil took me to the Rainbow Room to see Keely Smith, the former straight-faced foil for Louis Prima. That's when we ran into Liza Minnelli. Liza and Phil greeted each other warmly, so warmly that I detected perhaps a history between them. Keely sang beautifully and came to our table after the show, regaling us with Vegas lounge stories, my favorite literary genre. Naturally Liza had stories of her own—of Mother Judy, Dad Vincent, and assorted ex-husbands. But these tales were merely warm-ups for Phil, who kept us all in stitches with his accounts of the rough-and-tumble Brill Building days when rock was young and the world innocent. By then it was 2 a.m. I had to excuse myself and head home.

"Oh no," said Phil. "It's early. We're all heading over to P.J. Clarke's for drinks. The fun's just begun. You can't leave."

I was insistent, but Phil was even more insistent.

"Look," I finally said, winning the argument with humor, "you're Phil Spector. You can wake up tomorrow at noon, pick up the phone, learn you've made a million dollars on a Crystals' reissue in England and go back to sleep. That's your day's work, Phil. I've gotta get up and play the piano."

He smiled and relented.

Of all the fresh kicks I've enjoyed as a musician, the highlight has got to be playing on a Spector session. It happened when Phil wanted to test the waters to see if he could once again make his mark on popular music. He had left his suite at the Waldorf Towers and flown back to his L.A. home. He was ready to record and even recruited his original engineer from the glory days, Larry Levine, and as many of his original wrecking crew of musicians as he could find.

"Paul," said Phil, "the Wall is going up again. I want you on the session."

My manager said he was paying everyone triple scale and, except for me, they were all L.A.–based musicians.

"I'll try and get you travel expenses," my manager said.

The next day I learned Phil had refused.

"Fuck it. I'll be there anyway," I told my manager. "I'd pay *him*."

When I got to L.A., I went directly to the studio.

Phil had a plan: he had written a song and was going to fine-tune an arrangement, cut a master, and hire a singer like Linda Ronstadt to put her voice on it. It was Old School thinking: own everything. But the music world had changed radically since the days when Phil, in the role of a Roman emperor, looked over his stable of singers and declared, "You, Darlene Love, sing this one," or "You, Bob B. Soxx, sing that one." I'm not sure whether Phil understood that singers had been liberated. I had heard, however, that there had been a time when every Spector session began with the singing of "We Shall Overcome."

The notion of getting a Linda Ronstadt or a Bette Midler to turn over all power to Phil was a pipe dream, but I didn't care. The Wall was all.

There were no fewer than thirty musicians in the studio, including six guitarists and six keyboardists. I was one of two synthesizer players; the other was Alan Pasqua, a great jazz pianist. Phil was renowned for including jazz masters on his sessions. In fact, he had vibist Terry Gibbs playing shaker.

His overall strategy was this: to achieve the perfect balance, to create the perfect sound. Then and only then would he go for a live take.

Because I was Phil's pal, I had an all-access pass to this heavy-duty sonic construction project. I could pass freely from the studio to the booth and watch him work. Phil wanted leakage. He said leakage was the mortar that joined the bricks that built the Wall.

"Leakage," he explained, "is what creates the room sound. I want that sound to wash over everything."

Leakage meant that the sound of the drum could leak into the guitar mic, and the sound of the guitar could leak into the drum mic. Getting maximum leakage meant taking down the sound booth walls separating the musicians. Leakage meant opening up the sonic floodgates and letting go of traditional engineering restraints. Larry Levine knew about leakage.

But in this modern studio, Larry Levine couldn't duplicate Phil's original methodology. The Back to Mono Rail was a little off track. The arrangement, hastily crafted by Jack Nitzsche, had several empty bars. Everything needed fixing and everything took time.

The Wall went up slowly. Phil mixed down the acoustic guitars to an infectious chug-a-chug-chug shaker beat. Then he folded in four acoustic pianos, then three percussionists. Next he had me and Pasqua looking for synth sounds. I didn't really know the instrument, so Alan helped me find a classical guitar patch that Phil liked. Phil put a deep reverb on the sound and mixed it in with everything else. The next thing I knew, I was standing in the control booth, listening to myself as part of the Spector sound. Holy shit!

The horns came next. Everything was being layered and relayered. Everything was getting bigger and bigger. The Wall was getting higher and higher.

But unfortunately the Wall had cracks, and Phil couldn't get what he wanted. He kept running from the control room, where he was entertaining celebrity friends like O.J. attorney Robert Shapiro, to the floor of the studio, trying to make it all happen. By midnight, the Wall was up, but wobbly. The drummers had yet to play.

"Guys, we're not going to get it tonight," Phil finally said.

We hadn't even played the whole thing through. There was never a live take.

The musicians were crestfallen. They would have played all night for Phil. One by one, though, they packed up and filed out. I stayed for the postmortem.

"Too bad about those missing bars," Phil said.

"I wish they'd had the right tape delay," I added.

"But I'll tell you something, Paul. Thirty guys sure sounded warm in there."

At that point it hit me: Warmth. That's what I loved about the Spector sound. *Warmth.*

We went out for drinks afterward.

"The nerve of you, asking for expense money," Phil said over a Cointreau straight up.

I blamed it on my manager.

"You know, Paul," Phil started to needle me, "some of the cats thought you were just here for comic relief."

"Which ones?" I asked, panicking.

"Never mind," he said.

With that, we toasted the memory of Richie Valens.

The project was abandoned, but many months later I received a beautifully written letter from Phil saying that I had played skillfully on the session and had earned the right to consider myself a brick in the Wall of Sound.

On another occasion in L.A., Phil presented me with my very own "Back to Mono" button. That night we went to the Vine Street Bar and Grill, a jazz club where Anita O'Day was appearing. I told Phil how my dad loved Anita and considered her, along with Sarah, Ella, and Billie, one of the greats. "Your dad has good taste," Phil told me. Anita had survived a long and difficult life, which she had documented in *Hard Times High Times*, her candid autobiography.

Anita's set was stunning: "Wave," "Tenderly," "Tea for Two," "I Cover the Waterfront," "Sweet Georgia Brown." Despite her advanced age—or perhaps because of it—she swung with percussive ease. At seventy-five, she was free as a bird.

We went to meet her in her dressing room. She was polite to Phil, though it wasn't clear whether she knew who he was. When she saw me, though, she greeted me with a hug. "I love the Letterman show," she said. "I watch it every night. I dig the band." And with that, she reached into a Saks Fifth Avenue shopping bag, fished out a copy of her autobiography, and said, "Paul, this is for thou."

Hip, I thought. Phil forced a smile.

Later that night we went to the Polo Lounge where, lo and behold, we encountered our idol, Ahmet Ertegun. Ahmet was at a table with a young couple from the Midwest who were honeymooning in Beverly Hills. Ahmet had given them a bottle of Dom Perignon and, if I read the situation correctly, was also angling to give the bride a private toast in his suite. In his ultra-suave manner, he was arguing that, beginning with the honey-moon, an open attitude toward marriage is the only way to ensure a long-term relationship between a man and woman.

Phil and I were intrigued by Ahmet's romantic maneuvers. Who else but the great Ertegun would hit on a newlywed in the presence of her husband?

The couple recognized me from Letterman, but they hadn't heard of Phil.

"Phil Spector is a genius," said Ahmet. "In the dark and dreary music business, he is one of our bright lights. I respect him tremendously. There is, however, a major and irreconcil-able difference between Phil and myself."

"What is that difference?" asked the extremely impression-able young bride.

"Well, I am a proponent," Ahmet said drolly, "of stereo."

＊ ＊ ＊

Years later, Phil was in New York and asked that I join him on another jazz jaunt. Richard Belzer was also along for the ride. Phil explained that a reporter profiling him for a national mag-azine would be part of the entourage, but not to worry, the jour-nalist would be without his pad. I assumed that meant that the evening would be "off the record."

We started out at the Plaza. Then it was on to Elaine's for dinner. The reporter was silent and, as Phil had promised, was not taking notes. No one took pictures. The second stop was Fez, a downtown downstairs jazz club where Phil wanted to hear the Mingus Big Band, an edgy orchestra dedicated to the music of the immortal Charles Mingus. The band was a groove, and before long I was asked to join them onstage.

"You can't play this stuff," said Phil. "It's too far out."

Nevertheless, I got onstage, sat at the piano, and had a ball. Calling upon the illuminating spirit of my mentor Tisziji Munoz, I managed to dance my way through the avant-garde arrangement and add some improvisational touches of my own. The band was pleased and so was the audience.

Phil wasn't.

"You cheated," said Phil. "You rehearsed it. I'd bet a million bucks you rehearsed the fuckin' thing before we got here."

"Make the check out to cash, Phil. I don't cheat. I just play."

Several months later, the profile of Phil appeared. Off the record indeed! The evening was recounted in detail!

Belzer and I were described derisively as friends of Phil who were not on the A-list. In the words of the reporter, we were on the "J-list . . . Jews of middle vintage whose show-biz lives let them hang out and on for eons without having to smile in the middle box of 'Hollywood Squares.' " I thought the remarks had a somewhat anti-Semitic tinge. Besides, the characterization was inaccurate. Both Belzer and I had proudly appeared on that classic game show loved by millions. So there.

Chapter 35

Loving Gilda

When Gilda went off to marry Gene Wilder in 1984, it left a hole in the soul of the *SNL* crowd. We thought of her as *our* Gilda. We were convinced that we loved and understood her more deeply than anyone in the world. So when, five years later, we heard she had contracted ovarian cancer, we were devastated. It couldn't be happening, not to someone with the life force and love-giving spirit of Gilda Radner.

By then she and Gene were living in Connecticut and, understandably, not answering anyone's calls. They were contending with Gilda's debilitating condition.

When I heard, though, that her days were few, I had to call. Miraculously, Gene answered.

"It's Paul Shaffer," I said.

"Oh, Paul," said Gene. "Gilda's right here. I know she'd love to talk to you."

"Paul?" It was Gilda's distinctly sweet voice, but a voice that had grown terribly weak.

I quoted the Stevie Wonder song from *The Woman in Red,* the film she did with Gene. "I just called to say I love you."

"I love you too, Paul."

"You know, Gilda, I still feel awful that your record didn't turn out better. I really messed that one up."

"Oh, for God's sake, Paul, forget about it. That's old news. Let yourself off the hook."

"Thanks, Gilda. I will. Hey, I'm thinking about that moment I played piano while you auditioned for *Godspell* with 'Zip-a-Dee-Doo-Dah.' I fell hopelessly in love with you. We all did."

"And Paul, how 'bout back in Toronto when I walked into one of our little parties with Peter Boyle on my arm and your jaw dropped to the floor."

"You told us you'd picked him up on a plane trip. We were so in love with show business back then, any star would have knocked us out."

"Paul, you're the most show business person I know," said Gilda with that laugh we all cherished.

"Baby, you're a star," I said. "Your light will never dim."

Gilda passed on May 20, 1989. Her light shines even brighter today.

* * *

When Lorne Michaels decided to "produce" a private memorial for Gilda, he did so in typical Lorne style. He decided it would be held in Studio 8H, the *SNL* home, the most appropriate stage imaginable. In our world, when someone dies, all we know how to do is put on a show. So we put on a show for Gilda.

As was his MO, Lorne called it for 4 p.m. but didn't make his grand entrance until 6. None of us objected. After all, we were all there because of Lorne.

I started off the evening by announcing that the Harlem Boys' Choir would sing a song. I have no idea why the Harlem Boys' Choir had been chosen by Lorne, but so it was. They sang splendidly. I also performed "Honey, Touch Me with My Clothes On," one of the songs Gilda and I wrote for her one-woman show. The three ladies of Rouge sang it, the same three who had accompanied Gilda on Broadway.

Then the comedians. Laraine and Jane were touching. They really missed Gilda. Danny Aykroyd told of his getaway weekend with Gilda when, in his words, "I finally had this irresistible lady all to myself." There were other such loving remembrances on the part of Gilda's male cohorts. It became a Gilda love-off: who loved her more, who loved her longest, who loved her best.

But the entertainer who caught the dark-and-light comic moment with greatest clarity and humor was Bill Murray. Bill got up in front of the audience of Gilda's *SNL* peers and said what we were all thinking but were too afraid to put into words. "Of course we all loved her," said Bill. "She was our Carol Burnett, our Lucille Ball. She was our own special genius. The more vulnerable she became, the more we adored her. And then one day—beyond the control of any of us—she met her Prince Charming. Suddenly she was out of our sphere. She was in Connecticut—with *him.*" Here Bill paused for effect before uttering the words "Gene Wilder killed Gilda."

What may now appear harsh in print was just the comic antidote we needed. It was the biggest laugh I'd ever heard. We laughed uproariously. We laughed until it hurt. We cried until it hurt. We're still laughing. We're still crying.

Chapter 36

"Kick My Ass—Please!"

Among the immortal lines we remember from the movies—
Clark Gable's "Frankly, my dear, I don't give a damn," Marlon
Brando's "I could've been a contender," Robert De Niro's "You
talkin' to me?"—are these words spoken by Artie Fufkin the
promo man, played by yours truly in the great rockumentary
This Is Spinal Tap:

"Kick my ass—please!"

I am referring, of course, to my brief movie career during
those wild and crazy eighties when, perhaps because of the buzz
from my sitcom *A Year at the Top,* I was in great demand. While
I didn't have a starring role in *Spinal Tap,* there was some talk
about a supporting actor Oscar nod—mainly from my mother
who saw a nuanced interpretation that others may have missed.

This Is Spinal Tap was written by Harry Shearer, Michael
McKean, Christopher Guest, and Rob Reiner. It's a mockumen-
tary about a make-believe rock band. The original idea was for
all four screenwriters to portray the band members. Three of
them did, but legend has it that Rob couldn't fit into the spandex.

That's how he got to play the part of the doc film director. Reiner was, in fact, the real-life director of *Spinal Tap*.

The filming technique employed the use of scene outlines rather than an actual script. The overall plot was planned, but the dialogue was a kind of free-for-all improvisation. Some of the actors might cook up their comic lines in advance, but they wouldn't reveal them until the cameras rolled. People were breaking up right and left. On playback, though, Rob would say, "That's okay. You *would* break up if someone said something like that. We're leaving it in."

There are some who say my role as Artie Fufkin was type-casting. Of course, I have known a gang of brilliant promoters over the years, the greatest of whom is Donny Kirshner. Certainly I had Kirshner in mind as I developed the character.

In my key scene, Artie has arranged a record signing for the band's new release, *Smell the Glove,* at a retail store. He arrives wearing a silver satin tour jacket. When not a single fan shows up, though, Artie is humiliated. He tries to blame the store manager, berating him unmercifully. To express his disappointment, Artie tells him, "We're talking about a relationship here."

"Artie, don't take it so personal," the manager says.

"Forget about personal, what about a relationship?" asks Artie, invoking the spirit of the great Don Kirshner.

Ultimately, though, Artie assumes the blame for the fiasco. In a moment of mea culpa passion, he bends over and tells the band, "Kick my ass! Enjoy! Kick an ass for a man! I'm not asking, I'm telling with this! Kick my ass—please!"

By the way, the movie did kick ass.

* * *

In 1843, Charles Dickens wrote a timeless fable called *A Christmas Carol*. Its two lead characters are Tiny Tim and Ebenezer Scrooge. One hundred and forty-five years later, my good friend Bill Murray used the story as a launching pad for the film *Scrooged*.

I was asked to participate.

My screen time in *Spinal Tap* might have spanned six minutes. My screen time in *Scrooged* was considerably shorter—six seconds. It was memorable nonetheless, mainly because of the presence of one Miles Davis.

The setup was this: Miles, a true jazz icon, would be leading a group of street musicians during a Christmastime outdoor scene as Bill Murray walked by. I was in the band along with Larry Carlton and David Sanborn. I couldn't believe my good fortune. In wide-screen Technicolor, I was Miles Davis's keyboardist.

During the musical prerecord, Miles said, "Where's the drummer?"

"It's a street band, Miles," said the music director.

"So what?" said Miles. "Even the Salvation Army got drums."

That's when I pulled in Marcus Miller to play drums on a machine.

Miles began sketching out the way he wanted us to play "We Three Kings of Orient Are."

"We'll do it in three," said Miles, "then go to a funk section."

Carlton whispered in my ear, "Why is Miles directing this thing? Why do we have to do it the way Miles wants it?"

"Maybe because, um, he's Miles?" I said.

The result was a major music lesson for me. I was playing synth bass. Instructing me, Miles said, "Paul, don't play the root. Don't land on the root. Ever. Play around it, but never hit it." In doing so, I realized this rootless technique floated the whole thing. It immediately sounded like Miles.

The six seconds on camera were extended to six full minutes on the album sound track.

Miles was also a wonderful artist and illustrator. I had the great honor of having him sketch me as I appeared to him on Letterman. He then gave me the sketch. As if that wasn't enough, he pointed to his sketch pad and said, "Paul, pick out another one. Pick out whatever you like."

I liked a sketch of Miles being serviced by a lovely Asian babe.

"You have good taste," he said.

"Thank you, Miles. So do you."

"Hey, Paul," he added. "Let's do this Christmas song on Letterman."

"Groovy."

The very next Friday, Miles came on the show and played "We Three Kings" with my band.

During rehearsal, listening to us vamp on a Sly song, he came over and said, "If it ain't funky, you can't use it. Ain't that right, Paul?" I smiled in agreement as I absorbed one of the great compliments of my career. Then, in that same rehearsal while we were playing "We Three Kings," Miles brought our level down to a whisper. "This is how you get guys in a rock band to listen to each other," he said. On the show itself, the World's Most Dangerous Band never played with greater subtlety. Miles was magic.

Picture this:

We're on the set in Seinfeld's apartment. Jerry, Elaine, and Kramer watch TV.

Downstairs buzzer sounds.

"Who is it?"

"It's George."

"Oh hi," Elaine says. "Come on up."

A beat.

The front door opens.

And there, ladies and gentlemen, instead of the irascible Jason Alexander, stands the irascible Paul Shaffer.

Kramer does a double take.

It could have happened. It was the late eighties. The Letterman show was going strong, and I was frantic with activity. At that point I was winging it without an assistant. I wasn't answering mail or returning phone calls. Who had time? Which might have been why I hardly noticed a call from Castle Rock Productions, Rob Reiner's company. I thought to myself, *Castle Rock . . . that sounds familiar*, but I didn't make the connection, which was funny, considering that I'd done *This Is Spinal Tap* for Rob. But that's what happens when you're burning the candle at both ends.

In any case, I read the message, which said that Jerry Seinfeld was getting his own TV series and he wanted me to be his sidekick. "You don't have to read for it. You got the part. Just call us back."

An offer and I don't have to read? Hmm, tell me more . . .

But then I got to thinking: Jerry Seinfeld was just one of so many comics who passed through our studio night after night. Jerry's great, but what kind of show could he possibly have?

So I never returned the call. *Schmuck.*

In an alternate reality somewhere, I can't walk down the street without being identified as George Costanza, and Jason Alexander is playing keyboards on late-night TV.

Chapter 37

Take My Limo, Please

My relationship with the one-named diva Cher began in the seventies. That's when producer Ron Dante flew me to Hollywood. I was excited when she came to Ron's bungalow at the Beverly Hills Hotel dressed in white fur and heels higher than I'd ever seen on a white woman. She was extremely cordial and got right to work.

"Paul will be writing some of the arrangements for your record," Ron said.

"Which ones?" she asked.

"I thought I'd give him 'Bound To Please,' " said Ron.

"Great," said Cher. "That's an S&M number."

"Then I'm bound to get it right," I said.

Cher smiled. "Please do."

I started to play, she started to sing, and there was that voice.

Ron gave me some tunes to arrange. One of them, "My Song (Too Far Gone)," co-composed by Cher, was a lament on the end of her relationship with Gregg Allman. I made the guitars weep.

"My Song" made the album, but my other arrangements for

the rock numbers didn't. Cher's label, Casablanca, was deep into disco and consequently loaded the record, *Take Me Home*, with dance ditties.

I cherished the chance to work with Cher, though, and, in secret, developed what I considered to be a highly respectable imitation of the singer's vocal style. I found the right time on Letterman to publicly perform it: late December.

'Twas the night before Christmas when, on the air, I began what would become my annual Cher tribute. "You know, Dave," I said, "around this time of year I can't help but reminisce about my favorite episode of the *Sonny and Cher Comedy Hour*. As a lad back in Canada, I remember watching their Christmas episode, the one where William Conrad, of the popular detective series *Cannon*, guest starred. After the comedy sketches, they moved into an extended Christmas medley. Mr. Conrad did "We Wish You a Merry Christmas" in his rotund, jovial manner. Everyone had a lot of fun. Then it was time to get serious. The lights came down. A street lamp appeared and snow started to fall. Cher made her entrance wearing a gorgeous Victorian overcoat. Her hands were in a muff. The pianist played lovely arpeggios, and Cher began to sing 'O Holy Night.' "

It was at this point that I broke into song, my voice crying in Cher-like cadences, "Woah hol-eh niiiigh, the liiiighs so briiidl-eh shiiiine-oh . . ."

Years later, I was happy to learn that Cher herself would be appearing on Letterman—largely due to the efforts of one Cathy Vasapoli, booker extraordinaire. Not only was Cher coming on the show to sing her new single, "I Found Someone," she had requested that my band back her up the week before on *Saturday Night Live* as well. So there we were, in Studio 8H with Cher, waiting to go on the air. During the commercial break just before the performance, someone in the audience yelled out, "Shaffer, do 'O Holy Night'!" I sang only a few notes, much to Cher's delight.

"You sound more like Sonny," she said.

I took that as a great compliment because I always felt it was Sonny who had taught Cher to sing. I always heard Cher as Sonny, only with a better instrument. I was also aware of Sonny's seminal influences.

"Sonny sounds more like Louie Prima than Sonny," I told Cher.

"And Louie Prima," said Cher, "sounds more like Louie Armstrong than Louie Prima."

A week later, I was preparing for Cher's appearance on Letterman. In what amounted to another coup, Cathy had also booked Sonny, but only to converse. Cher had made it clear that she wanted no duet.

I was in the booth with Cher, listening to a rehearsal playback of "I Found Someone," when I happened to see Sonny walk by. Remembering all his great Sonny and Cher productions, I invited him to listen to the arrangement. There was a wistful look in his eye when he said, "Paul, that's great."

Showtime. Cher looked like a million bucks and sang the hell out of "I Found Someone." She did great panel with Dave. Then Sonny came out and joined them. They spoke of the old days with obvious nostalgia. Sensing the mood, Dave bravely popped the question: "Cher, how about singing something with Sonny?"

The audience went crazy, and I immediately started vamping on harpsichord the opening chords of "I Got You, Babe." The tremendous energy released by Dave's request was too much for Cher to resist. She and Sonny got up and performed their immortal hit. When he sang the line "Put your little hand in mine," he actually grabbed her hand. As Doc Pomus would say, it was a "Magic Moment." As LaVerne Baker would say, "I Cried a Tear."

Their triumph electrified all of us. After the show, we were glowing. I was rushing. My band and I had to speed to the airport to catch the last flight to L.A., where, the next morning, we were due onstage at 9 a.m. to rehearse our stint on *Comic Relief 2*.

Then calamity struck. Our limo was nowhere to be found. There we were, on the curb, waiting in vain. Frantic calls did no good. It looked like we'd miss our flight.

"What's wrong, Paul?" asked Sonny.

"Our limo's gone missing."

"Take my limo, please."

"I couldn't do that, Sonny."

"I insist," he said, and with that he practically pushed me and my band members into his limo.

"You're a prince, Sonny," I said, "but what will you do?"

"Oh, don't worry about me, Paul. I'll catch a ride with Cher."

As we pulled away, I glanced back to see the scene at Cher's limo. First Cher got in, then her wardrobe gal, then her makeup artist, then her manager, her agent, then her press agent, then daughter Chastity, and then, finally, squeezing in where there could not have been an inch of extra room, was her former husband, mentor, and producer—the gallant Mr. Sonny Bono.

Chapter 38

Viva Shaf Vegas

I admire Federico Fellini. Who doesn't? I admire his film *8½*. As is widely known, the movie is deeply autobiographical, a reflection of both the artistic and romantic confusion that surrounded his hectic life.

I am not saying that my life in the late eighties was as hectic as Maestro Fellini's. Nor would I ever compare my meager creative talents to his. But I do admit to considerable romantic confusion in my early life, and following in Fellini's footsteps, I did attempt to chronicle this confusion in a TV special.

My tack was humor. To unearth that humor I needed to be comfortable. I needed a creatively stimulating environment. Fellini liked Rome. I liked Vegas. Rome reflected the decadent culture that intrigued Fellini. Vegas reflected the decadent culture that intrigued me. Fellini liked to escape into the wild images that fed his imagination. I would do the same. Through this somewhat bizarre TV special, I would work out the problems of my life.

What were those problems?

I loved Cathy. Cathy loved me. Cathy wanted commitment. I was not ready to commit. Cathy wanted marriage. I was not ready to marry.

"When will you be ready?" she asked.

"I don't know."

"Your fear of commitment is what keeps us fighting," she said. "Then when we fight, you begin to question whether the relationship will last."

"I need time," I said.

"How much time?" Cathy had to know.

"I don't know."

"When will you know?"

"I can't say," I said.

"Then maybe we should break up."

"Maybe we should," I halfheartedly agreed.

It was our breakup, and my new freedom to play the field, that prompted the idea for *Viva Shaf Vegas*. Cathy had become a booker for the Letterman show, and suddenly Cathy was everywhere. I felt the pressure of the time. I had to make a decision: marriage or no marriage?

I remember Dave Letterman giving me advice. "You know, Paul, it's hard to find someone you can relate to at all. So if you do find that someone, maybe you shouldn't let her go."

* * *

Dave, of course, was right, but I just wasn't ready. I decided not to marry, at least not now. So Cathy and I broke up and both decided to date other people.

On the heels of this new and somewhat uncomfortable freedom came a fascinating offer: Cinemax asked me to do a television special. They wanted an hour-long program of my own design. Harry Shearer would direct and cowrite a script with me and Tom Leopold. I would star and work out my inner demons through the medium of film.

"Make it as edgy as you want," said Cinemax. "Put in all the 'inside' show-biz humor at your command."

Creative freedom was ours.

Of course Fellini had Marcello Mastroianni as his alter ego. I suppose I could have asked Woody Allen to play me. After all, Ronnie Spector had once called me "the Woody Allen of rock and roll." But Woody, whose dedication is to Dixieland jazz, hates rock and roll. And besides, my one meeting with Mr. Allen wasn't exactly encouraging.

I was at a restaurant when I bumped into Jean Doumanian, former *SNL* producer. "I'm having dinner with Woody," she said, "and he'd love to meet you." I followed Jean to a corner table. There was the great comic auteur himself. "What a great pleasure to meet you," I said, reaching out my hand. He offered his, limp as a dishrag. That was it. He gave me a quick glance and not a single utterance. My expectation of being asked to join his party and discuss the nature of American comedy was dashed. I turned around, went back to my table, and finished my oxtail soup alone.

No, Mr. Allen was not a likely candidate to play the part of Mr. Shaffer. For better or worse, Mr. Shaffer would have to play Mr. Shaffer.

It was Mr. Shaffer Goes to Vegas—that's the idea that Tom, Harry, and I brainstormed. Here's how it would go:

Mr. Shaffer is having trouble with Hope Crosby, his love interest, as he navigates the single life in New York City. "I don't know whether to date you or do a road picture with you," he tells her. She wants commitment. He doesn't. He can't resist fleeing to Vegas, where he's offered a headliner's show in the main room of the Tropicana. Obviously it's a fantasy. There are topless showgirls. There's the acrobatic duo of Carlo and Carlos, whose bodies are spray-painted in gold. My pal Tom plays himself, a screenwriter who sees my existential dilemma—to commit or not to commit—and directs me toward a Vegas guru, Sam Butera of Sam Butera and the Witnesses, the original Louis Prima backup band and a legendary lounge act. Sam asks a probing question—"Paul, are you regular?"—but leaves me to search for my own answers. My Odyssean journey takes me into the loneliest of lounges, where I'm invited to sit in with a Blues Brothers tribute band. That doesn't thrill me, but seeing the Checkmates does. The Checkmates are playing at a downtown dive, the Mint, and ask me to play on their hit "Black Pearl."

My dive into the deep sea of Vegas sleaze doesn't uncover a black pearl, but it does get me a white one. Her name is Donna and she's ready to rock. The morning after, she tells me that her mother was once *Gallery* magazine's Gatefold of the Month. Donna takes me to the trailer park run by her dad, who turns out to be rock and roll royalty. He was the sax man for the Rockin' Rebels. Suddenly we all break into a video-style romp, doing the Rebels' 1962 smash, "Wild Weekend," and everyone in the trailer park is dancing up a storm.

Donna is cool, but Donna's boyfriend, who plays in the Blues Brothers clone act, isn't happy about her dalliance with me. Donna disappears. I find another female friend and take her back to a suite for a tumble in the hot tub, only to find out that, underneath, she isn't a female at all. I send her packing, "Sir," I say, "take your leave."

Hope comes in from New York and finds me nursing my wounds at the Mint. She says she still loves me. I still love her.

But what to do?

As I'm hesitating, Hope takes off with the Belushi guy from the tribute band, and I get jealous.

Has the fantasy of flying my freak flag in the freakiest of entertainment frontiers run its course?

I appear that night in my show at the Tropicana. I play, I sing, I dance. My topless gals surround me with love. I incorporate Robert Goulet and Redd Foxx into my act. But finally, in Fellini-esque fashion, I find myself doing what the Italian director did at the end of *8½*. I join all the elements of my life and fantasies in a circle of love. I make them all dance. I bring Hope onstage. Harry, as a bearded rabbi, runs out to marry us. There is a chuppah, a canopy symbolizing the home that Hope and I will share. The topless gals gather around us; Tom is best man; and the fabulous duo of Carlo and Carlos are our head ushers. A unicyclist rides in with our rings. Vows are exchanged. With my right foot, I smash the glass that has been placed on the floor, the traditional ritual that reminds us of our responsibility to help repair the world. Here in Vegas, my own life has been repaired. All the disparate elements—the Blues Brothers cover band, the Checkmates, Sam Butera and the Witnesses—are now aligned.

In my fantasy film, I have embraced Hope.

In my real life, Hope is Cathy.

Cinemax says that the film is too "inside." This after they urged us to make it as "inside" as possible. It doesn't matter. The show airs at 1:15 a.m. People like it.

In my fictional life, Hope and I are married onstage.

In my real life, Cathy and I are married in *shul*. It is a small, family wedding.

Before the wedding, Dave Letterman throws me a bachelor party at 21.

After the wedding, my bachelor days are but bittersweet memories.

This happens in 1990. I am forty years old.

Chapter 39

Mel Gibson and the Jews

A Pop Culture Analysis

Back at the University of Toronto, I majored in sociology. You might remember that I wrote my thesis on the subculture of avant-garde musicians. I got an A on the paper along with my professor's remark that I had a knack for analysis. The aforementioned topless bars drew me away from academia, but academia left its impact on me.

As someone who, for more than a quarter century, has been in the privileged position of watching celebrities up close, I have made a study of this group. They are a funny lot. Many are sincere. Some are not. Most are sensitive. Most are ambitious. Most crave love and approval. Some are cautious, some reckless, some caring, some quite insane. Many overreact—to a less-than-flattering review or an innocent remark that they may take as an insult. You can never tell what will trigger a celebrity or what the result will be.

I know.

I was involved in such an incident.

And I have reason to believe that my behavior may well have

changed the landscape of our pop culture and, in a vastly more important way, even changed the always-sensitive dynamic between Christians and Jews in the United States of America.

Mr. Mel Gibson, one of our most enduring movie stars, is Mad Max, Lethal Weapon, and Braveheart all rolled into one. Before he became the Christ, however, he came on Letterman to publicize one of his many splendid films. During that particular show, we had a funny bit going called "May we turn your pants into shorts?" Members of the crew and staff would come onstage, only to have Dave and me, with scissors in hand, cut off their trouser legs at the knees. Dave would snip the left leg while I snipped the right.

After Mel had charmed his way through Dave's graceful interview, Dave asked him, "May we turn your pants into shorts?"

"Sure," said the amiable actor. "Why not?"

I was called over to help circumcise Gibson's trousers. That's when my hand slipped and the state of Judeo-Christian relations changed forever.

Believe me when I say that the slip was unintentional. I merely placed the scissors too close to Mel's skin. In doing so, I cut him. The skin broke. He bled. Drops of Gibson's blood fell to the floor. Mel looked at me murderously. He was enraged. He had been bloodied by a Jewish piano player.

Because of my Hebrew heritage, I couldn't help but feel great guilt when I started hearing about Gibson's bloody movie, *The Passion of the Christ.* I couldn't help but wonder whether the slip of my hand had caused what some reviewers were calling a blatantly anti-Jewish version of the Crucifixion story. In observing some of the actors whom Gibson had selected to play the Pharisees, the group urging Christ's death, I couldn't help but notice that one of them seemed to resemble me.

For a moment or two, I considered sending Mel a Christmas or Hanukkah gift—a pair of fine woolen Brooks Brothers trousers or perhaps madras Bermuda shorts. I wanted to let him know that the shedding of his blood had no sacrificial symbolism on my part. But I never sent the pants and I never sent the shorts. I wondered, though, if I should invite Mel over to the house for Passover dinner. Instead I took Cathy's suggestion and sent him a first-aid kit. I never heard back.

The coda to this story took place in the exclusive celebrity-hangout restaurant Nobu in the downtown Tribeca district of New York City. I was dining with Harry Shearer when who should walk in but Mr. Gibson himself. As he walked by our table, he stopped, regarded me, and said, "Ah, the Slasher."

"Hi, Mel," I said. "I hope the first-aid kit helped."

"Very funny," he replied with a hearty laugh.

✳ ✳ ✳

Another bizarre cross-cultural phenomenon took place between me and the honorable senator from Idaho, Larry Craig, he of the wide stance. This occurred before Craig's unfortunate arrest in an airport bathroom. Strangely enough, we were involved in a musical collaboration.

Cathy's brother Joe had arranged a fund-raiser at his home in Washington, D.C., for a worthy children's adoption organization. He asked me to play at the event and requested that, as part of the program, I include Senator Craig, a supporter of the cause. Apparently the senator had a broad knowledge of Broadway musical tunes. In some circles, such knowledge would be viewed suspiciously, but I cared not. I was delighted to go to the Capitol and meet with the senator. We chose a song to perform together. In retrospect, the choice seems unfortunate—"Anything You Can Do I Can Do Better"—but at the time it seemed right, especially sung with a set of special lyrics. We performed it in my brother-in-law's home. The Shaffer/Craig duo was received warmly, and a great deal of money was raised. The benefit was a success. After that, I never saw the senator again on either a personal or professional basis to the best of my recollection. I swear.

* * *

Returning to the subject of Shaffer slipups, I am obliged to include an incident involving that fabulous star of the silver screen, Miss Julia Roberts. Millions of men, myself included, have secret and not-so-secret crushes on this delightful actress. But few are actually designated to ask her questions about her love life. Alas, that was my mandate.

When Miss Roberts appeared on Letterman, Dave was understandably nervous asking about her personal life. She had just ended a relationship. Because she is so genuinely sweet, one does not want to invade her privacy. During the opening segment, Dave danced around the issue. He was afraid to ask her whether she was dating again and, if so, who the lucky guy might be. His reluctance added to the humor of the interview.

In the second segment, there was a discussion of whether the delicate question should be asked by me. Always a good sport, Julia asked the audience to vote—"Should we allow Paul to question me or not?" The yea's had it, and the camera turned in my direction.

"So Julia," I said, pausing for comic effect, "are you getting laid these days?"

The audience went crazy as Dave jumped out of his chair, screaming, "Paul, are you nuts!" He came over to the band area in a mock assault on me, but Julia, putting her arms around Dave from behind, held him back.

When Julia and Dave returned to the desk, Dave continued the charade, saying, "Paul, Julia may be very sensitive about the topic. This isn't a bachelor party, my friend."

Julia continued the chastisement, adding, "That was wrong on so many levels, Paul."

Then Dave, a master of timing, allowed a beat or two to go by before turning to the gorgeous movie star and saying, "But what about it, Julia?"

Julia loved the whole thing and, as we went to commercial, came over to plant a kiss on my forehead. Eugene Levy saw it and said, "She kissed you like Snow White kissing one of the seven dwarves." I'll take it.

* * *

Before getting off the subject of ladies, let me mention one of pop culture's favorite creatures, Miss Britney Spears.

My Britney incident coincides with the period when she had just presented her husband, Kevin Federline (K-Fed, as he's known among the *Us Weekly* crowd), with divorce papers. It was all over the news. As it turned out, Britney was in New York and had called our show, saying she'd like to come on.

Well, if Miss Spears excels at anything, it's proving that there's no such thing as bad publicity. Her request to appear on Letterman was her way of saying, "Yes, I might be going through a divorce, but I'm slim and I look terrific." (At the time, she was still sporting undergarments.)

Be that as it may, Britney had become somewhat of a regular on Letterman in that she had developed the habit of dropping by to say hello unannounced, much like Bob Hope used to do with Johnny Carson.

Realizing this, one of our producers set about orchestrating a gag. For musical accompaniment, I was to play "Thanks for the Memories," a wink and a nod to the Hope/Carson connection. The song, of course, was Bob's theme.

Cut to me, riding the elevator, with none other than the luminous Miss Spears.

She looked fantastic.

After exchanging cursory greetings and pleasantries, I wanted to explain why, when she came out later that evening, she'd hear this old-fashioned song, so I said, "You know, you're a regular Bob Hope, dropping in on our show all the time."

And she said, "Who's Bob Hope?"

"Well, dear, before your time, there was a beloved comedian named Bob Hope."

Nada.

"He was wildly popular during the golden age of television."

Zilch.

"He went all over the world with the USO, entertaining the troops for morale."

Still no reaction.

"There's a street named after him in Burbank," I said.

"Oh yeah! Right!"

We rode for the next several seconds in silence. I heard her thinking. Then a lightbulb lit above her adorable head. She broke into a smile and, pointing right at me, said, "Oh, you're Dave's deejay, aren't you? That's who you are!"

Let me say that I respect the art form of the deejay. And though Ms. Spears's characterization of me may have been somewhat unorthodox, I began to think, *In the Spears universe, deejays are what's happening. Deejays are cool.*

Thus, I took the handle of deejay as a compliment.

But then I thought even further. *Perhaps there was some merit to actually becoming a deejay. Why, the deejay Grandmaster Flash was inducted into the Rock and Roll Hall of Fame! Wouldn't I like to be inducted into the Rock and Roll Hall of Fame? What's more, celebrities dated deejays. Deejay AM dated Nicole Richie and recently was seen with Mandy Moore. Deejay Samantha Ronson dated Lindsay Lohan. I'd like to date Lindsay Lohan. Maybe the deejay life was just what I needed. I'd call myself deejay PM because I only work a few hours in the afternoon taping Letterman.*

Ms. Spears has since moved on with her career. I, meanwhile, have begun to study turntablism. I'm making progress. I'm getting pretty good.

Chapter 40

On the Night Shift

Whole books have been written about what have come to be known as the Late-Night Wars. They were waged in the early nineties when the glorious reign of Johnny Carson was coming to an end. As Dave's friend and loyal soldier, I was close to the action but not really part of it. My position was clear: whatever was good for Dave was good for me.

When rumors first started flying, Dave called me into his office and said it plainly: "They're thinking about giving us the 11:30 spot, Paul. What do you think?"

"That'd be great. But I'm also loving this late spot. I've been having a ball."

"Well, let's just see how it plays out."

Ultimately it played out in Dave's favor. CBS gave him an offer he couldn't refuse—the 11:30 spot, creative freedom, and a beautiful midtown theater on Broadway. The network was willing to renovate the Ed Sullivan Theater, historically one of the most important venues in American entertainment, for our exclusive use.

At the time, I had started my second album, this one with the band. Naturally I wanted to call it *The World's Most Dangerous Band*. The musical concept was my group playing Booker T.–style numbers like "Green Onions" and "Hip-Hug-Her." The entertainment concept was to do it like a party. Guests would pop in between songs to greet me. I especially liked Lou Reed's line: "Sorry I'm late, Paul, but I had to come all the way over from the Wild Side." Marty Short showed up as old-time songwriter Irving Cohen: "Give me a C, a bouncy C."

Ringo dropped by.

"I'm knocked out that a Beatle is here," I told him. "Will you sit in, Ringo?"

"Sure," he said.

"Great, man," I said, "will you play 'Love Me Do'?"

"Absolutely," Ringo agreed, "but that's the one Beatles song I didn't play on."

Phil Spector's appearance was a coup. When we had our brief party chitchat at the start of one song, I put his voice in a booming reverb, as if he traveled everywhere with his own echo chamber.

I regret all the tragedy that has surrounded Phil in recent years. We're not as in touch, but the mad genius will always be my friend. I will continue to praise his work and honor his exalted place in the history of our musical culture.

I was thrilled when Eartha Kitt agreed to say hello on the record. I ran over to the Carlyle, where she was appearing. In between shows she was totally in character—an impatient, mysterious goddess. She purred her answers to my questions, but, alas, I was so nervous I messed up the tape recorder and came up blank. But Eartha had pity on me. She dropped the goddess bit and invited me back the next night. More relaxed, I explained that Letterman would soon be moving to the Ed Sullivan Theater, where she had appeared countless times.

"Yes, my dear," she said. "Ed was so devoted to me he built me a special dressing room above his on the third floor."

"Why, Miss Kitt," I said, "that's the very dressing room that's been assigned to me. What an honor!"

The sultry singer purred her approval and gave me fabulous party chatter for my record. From that moment on, I have never undressed in my dressing room without invoking the image of the eternally seductive Miss Eartha Kitt. When she recently passed, I lit a candle and placed it atop the dresser that had once been hers.

The final guest at the record party was my pal Richard Belzer, playing his iconic character Detective Munch. Munch came in at the end to bust us all. It was a blast.

The problem, though, was that I couldn't call the record *The World's Most Dangerous Band.* Apparently that name belonged to NBC as "intellectual property."

"Maybe so," said my father, who had come to New York for a visit. "Legally they may have you, Paul, but as I recall you're on excellent terms with NBC president Robert C. Wright."

Dad was right; Wright and his wife, Suzanne, had always been especially cordial to me.

"Call the man," my father suggested. "With one wave of his wand he can make the legal problems disappear."

When I called, Wright's secretary put me right through.

"Happy to hear from you, Paul," said the network exec. "Sorry to see you go."

I explained my situation. It seemed a most modest request. Just let me keep my band's name.

"It is certainly reasonable," said Wright, "but I'm afraid that matters of intellectual property go beyond the jurisdiction of this office. There's nothing I can do."

Oh well, I lost an old name but gained a new network.

The record, produced by Todd Rundgren, was mainly cut in Woodstock. Woodstock, in rural New York state, has a distinguished musical history, but as previously noted, I don't like woods. Who needs fresh air and clear country skies? I would have preferred to work in polluted Manhattan where the fumes from Tin Pan Alley are too powerful to ever die. I nonetheless put up with the beauteous bucolic setting, made the double-CD record, and was forced to call it *Paul Shaffer and the Party Boys of Rock 'n' Roll: The World's Most Dangerous Party.*

The World's Most Dangerous Band, as both a name and an entity, had to be retired. A new birth was required. The powers that be wanted a larger configuration than the quartet of Shaffer, bassist Will Lee, drummer Anton Fig—one of the giants of his instrument, who can play with Kiss one day and Dylan the next—and master guitarist Sid McGinnis, renowned for, among other things, his work for Peter Gabriel and Paul Simon. For this new band, Dave suggested a name along the lines of Paul Shaffer and the CBS Orchestra. I bought his suggestion immediately. I liked it because of its historical resonance; I thought of Skitch Henderson and the NBC Orchestra. Skitch had been the *Tonight Show*'s first musical director, followed by Milton Delugg and Doc Severinsen. I was happy to carry a name that referenced such a noble tradition.

But how to augment the band?

My first picks were Bernie Worrell—the keyboardist and "Flashlight" behind George Clinton's unending funk—and the wonderfully versatile and inventive guitarist Felicia Collins, whom I stole from Cyndi Lauper's band. Turned out that Bernie was covering some of the same territory as I. The redundancy didn't quite work, and I realized I needed to add horns. Horns meant arrangements and more complex voicings. A horn band can never be as flexible as a simple rhythm section. But the players I chose are masters of flexibility: Tom Malone, whom I knew from *SNL* and the Blues Brothers, plays every ax from piccolo to tuba; Bruce Kapler knows more tunes than I do; and Al Chez is the Maynard Ferguson of rock and roll.

With this new band, I've had any number of occasions to back hip-hoppers. The show insists on a more musical presentation than just a turntable and a rapper. The show insists on all-the-way live. It got all-the-way live when we jammed with Jam-Master Jay and Run-D.M.C., Snoop Dogg, The Game, and 50 Cent. Live Hip-Hop—What A Concept!

In moving from a quartet to an octet, our new band mirrored Dave's move from NBC to CBS. Things got bigger and better. Whereas before I let the guests come out to bare applause, now I was asked to create what we in our industry—and by our industry I mean, of course, our business—call "play-ons."

My band and I would get together before the show and, for ten minutes or so, it'd be free-association time. Everyone would throw out ideas for songs that seemed to match the guests. I'd pick the one that made me laugh hardest and use it for the play-on.

Examples:

Ellen DeGeneres: "I'm a Girl Watcher."

Marv Albert, who famously insisted that his hairpiece was a weave, not a wig: "Dream Weaver."

Tom Snyder and Craig Ferguson, who at different times

had been tapped for a talk show after Letterman: "I Will Follow Him."

Nicole Kidman: "Skin Tight."

John McCain: "Beautiful Loser."

Kyra Sedgwick, star of *The Closer:* "The Closer I Get to You."

Politicians could be especially sensitive. When we chose "Soul Man" to play Bob Dole on—only because it rhymed with "Dole Man"—Senator Dole was surprisingly pleased, so much so that he used the song for the remainder of his presidential campaign, much to the dismay of its composers.

When Al Gore came on, I ran into one of his Secret Service guys backstage. "Hey, Paul," the armed gentleman said, "whatever you do, please don't play 'You Can Call Me Al.' It's way too obvious."

"Oh," I said. "What would you suggest?"

" 'Tennessee' by Arrested Development."

Wow. A hipster in the Secret Service.

Chapter 41

Bad Taste

Taste in comedy is a tricky issue. I leave it to the metaphysicians to clarify that thin line between wildly funny and wildly inappropriate. The problem is that wildly inappropriate often equals wildly funny. Sometimes the most hysterical joke is the most tasteless. The very absence of taste is what makes a lot of stuff funny.

Case in point: A Chevy Chase roast I was asked to emcee.

This happened years *after* Chevy was the biggest comedy star in the country.

I was fond of kidding Chevy, just as Chevy was fond of kidding everyone else. It's what we did.

When the Friars Club wanted to roast Chevy, it would be for the second time. Chevy was reluctant, and for good reason. There are three prerequisites for making a good roast:

First, *roast the star when the star's on top.* When a star's up, it's okay to knock him down. But when he's down, knocking him further down isn't necessarily funny.

Second, *recruit friends of the star.* Make sure that the roasting is done by people who love the star so genuinely that their vitriol is born of affection, not real rancor.

Third, *don't televise.* TV kills the intimacy and murderous fellowship that are the hallmarks of a memorable roast.

Unfortunately, Chevy's second roast failed on all three counts. Chevy only accepted because the sponsor offered to donate $100,000 to his wife's charity. He may have also accepted because he had fond memories of his first roast. That's when Robert De Niro, Al Pacino, and a slew of studio heads flew in to sit on the dais. This was different, however. De Niro and Pacino were nowhere in sight, and, in fact, the only people on the dais who actually knew Chevy were myself, Laraine Newman, Beverly D'Angelo, and Al Franken. Al, by the way, may not have loved Chevy like the rest of us did.

The dais was so bereft of A-list celebs that I began the roast with a song called "We Couldn't Get Anybody Good." The lyrics went like this:

Tonight is Chevy's big night
We called his friends to invite them all to join us
And roast him
But nobody would.
[Chorus girl one]: Does he have a career?
[Chorus girl two]: I think he died last year.
[All]: We couldn't get anybody good.

Toward the end of the song, I was handed a fedora and a raincoat that I threw over my shoulder. In Sinatra style, I sang, "How sad the dais! You call this a show? How can you roast a man when no one will go and sit on the dais? Jack shit for a dais. How sad the dais! It blows!"

My monologue was pretty rough and, naturally, in bad taste. At the same time, I realized that some taste was required. That's why I decided not to use this line: "I don't really recognize anyone on the dais. Well, that looks like John McEnroe over there. But if you're here, John, who's beating up Tatum O'Neal?" Horrible taste.

Instead I said, "Many people asked what went wrong with Chevy's career. True, he's burned lots of bridges. He was abusive to people. I think it was the acting. If you really want to know, though, what happened to Chevy's career, I can explain it in three grams."

Al Franken took over where I left off. Al was much rougher. He really ripped into Chevy. He talked about how he respected Chevy's public revelation that he was hooked on pain pills for his back. That took character. That took courage. Al remembered how Chevy ground up those pills and applied them directly to his back. He talked about the time Chevy and Laraine went in on a kilo of back pills. The harder Al hit, the funnier he was.

Even I got hit. Lisa Lampanelli, an insult comic who makes Don Rickles look like Mary Poppins, got up and said, "Paul, I love you. Every time I look at you it reminds me I gotta clean my dildo."

Another comic, Todd Barry, said, "I see Paul's band is here but they're not gonna play. They're absolutely wiped. They had to learn four bars of a Blink-182 song." The band fell out.

After the dinner, I found Todd.

"You nailed us with that Blink-182 line," I said.

He replied, "I wanted to say Matchbox 20, but I thought Blink-182 was just a little more insulting."

Back to boiling Chevy in hot water, Richard Belzer said,

"The only funny bone Chevy has in his body is when I'm fucking him in the ass."

When it was time for Chevy to speak, we were rooting for a great rebuttal, but Chevy was genuinely hurt and could only say, "Wow, that was rough." He turned to Franken and said, "Jesus, Al . . . my daughters will never see this." Then he sat down.

I felt terrible. After the dinner, Tom Leopold, who had written many of my scathers, said, "Let's make sure Chevy's okay." So Tom and I, along with Lew Soloff, went up to Chevy's hotel room. Lew has a big heart and, like me, was hurting for Chevy. Lew is all about sincerity. He sincerely loves everybody. I'll drop by Lew's place, for instance, while he's finishing up a phone call with "I love you, I love you, I love you."

"Who was that, Lew?" I'll ask.

"Wrong number," he'll say.

Up in Chevy's room, we were sympathetic. "Sorry it was so hurtful, Chevy," I said.

"You're kind to come up here, Paul."

"I feel terrible about that three-gram joke I told," I said. "I'm going to tell the show to edit it out before it airs."

"Don't."

"Why?"

"It was funny."

* * *

Another roast in which I participated was one I'd been waiting for my whole life. I'd get to roast Jerry Lewis.

In my personal equation, Jerry is to show-biz comedy what Phil Spector is to pop music production. As Cole Porter would put it, Jerry is the top. And in order to roast him, I was determined to top everyone who came before and after me.

I had a head start because Belzer was roastmaster. Richard was the one who had gotten Jerry to agree to fly to New York from Vegas for the affair. Jerry would do anything for Belzer, especially after Belzer had gotten Jerry on an episode of *Law and Order: SVU*, playing his uncle.

The roast was private—which made it that much more special for me—and Belzer gave me an extra-good spot. I had a monologue that led to a song with special lyrics. I hired the best comedy writers I knew, Tom Leopold and Bill Scheft, to help me develop material. I wasn't going to be just good; I was going to be phenomenal. I had to do it for Jerry, just as Jerry did it for his kids.

I worked my *tuchus* off. I rewrote and rehearsed, I practiced until my timing was perfect. Not since my bar mitzvah had I approached a public performance with such a passion to please. And in this case, the one person I wanted to please more than anyone was Mr. Jerry Lewis.

The big day arrived. Jerry arrived. He was seated down the dais not far from me. When called to stand before the podium and do my thing, I took a deep breath, relished the moment, and went into it. The preamble to the song was long, too long. The account of my personal fondness for Jerry's telethons was too detailed. The explanations of my love of Jerry's talent were too complicated. The jokes were too hip for the room. In short, I died. Even worse, in the midst of my horrible death, even before I got to the song, Jerry got up from the dais and left!

I had to chase after the poor man and bring him back.

"Jerry," I said, "you can't leave now."

"I thought you were finished," he said.

"Please, Jerry, just listen to the song."

He heard the song and tried to smile. But the smile didn't

work and neither did the song. The song died. And that very evening, on the plane back to Vegas, Jerry Lewis suffered a heart attack.

* * *

Thank God, Jerry survived the song and the attack. Our relationship survived as well. On Jerry's next trip to New York, he brought his young daughter. Belzer suggested that Tom Leopold and I join them for lunch and bring our kids as well. We all met at Café Fiorello across from Lincoln Center—Jerry, Belzer, Tom, and me at one table, the kids at another.

This was when my daughter, Victoria, was twelve and my son, Will, was six. The occasion was merry and went without incident. Jerry was delighted to be surrounded by a group of devotees. We were delighted to hear his stories about the glory days of *The Nutty Professor* and *The Bellboy*. Toward the end of the lunch, Will came over to my table and said, "Daddy, can we get the check?"

"Sure, son," I said.

Jerry looked over at Will, who has extremely attractive Asian facial features.

"Does he know any Chinese words?" asked Jerry, after Will had gone back to the children's table. Before I could explain, Jerry went on: "Sometimes it's valuable to teach a child a few words in his mother tongue to give him a connection with his past."

"Actually, Jerry, my kids aren't adopted. My wife, Cathy, is Italian-*Korean*. That's why my children have that exotic look."

Jerry tuned me out. Instead he leaned over to whisper in Belzer's ear, "Well, I guess the kid does good laundry."

In a perverse way, I loved the story and couldn't wait to tell my friends that my child was the object of Jerry's dated ethnic humor. That Jerry—what a nut!

Later that same year I took my family to see Harry Shearer's annual Christmas show that he puts on with his lovely wife, Judith Owen. Cathy wanted Harry to meet our kids; he hadn't seen Victoria since she was an infant and hadn't met Will at all. This evening, though, Harry's Christmas spirit was interminable. He never left the stage. The show went on for so long the kids couldn't take any more holiday cheer.

"Let's just bring them to the side of the stage," said Cathy, "so Harry can at least get a glimpse of them."

While playing bass, Harry sidled over to stage right.

"Harry," I said, "we gotta split. You remember Victoria, of course."

"Darling," said Harry, "you've grown up."

"And this is my son, Will."

"Does he know any Chinese words?" Harry asked out of the side of his mouth. That Harry—what a nut!

I can't conclude my examination of bad taste in humor without revisiting the memorial service for comic Sam Kinison. Poor Sam was killed in a car accident in 1992 at the tragically young age of thirty-eight. I liked his wild humor and admired his extreme antics. And though I had met Sam, I really didn't know him and wouldn't have attended the service were it not for Richard Belzer. Sam and the Belz were so close that Belzer had been asked to emcee Kinison's memorial. Richard insisted I attend. "It'll be hysterical," he said.

I noticed that, driving to the church in L.A., Belzer seemed to be taking a strangely circuitous route through streets lined with strip clubs.

"Why are we going this way, Richard?" I asked.

"Just take a look at the signs. These are the people who loved Sam best."

It was then I noticed one tribute after another:

"Totally Nude! Sam, we'll miss you."

"Naked from Top to Bottom! R.I.P. Sam Kinison."

"Stripped from the Hip! Big, Busty and Topless! Sam, you were the best."

"Split beaver! Shaved! Goodbye, Sam."

Chapter 42

Family Is Everything

On April 8, 1993, my wife, Cathy, gave birth to our precious daughter, Victoria Lily. The day after the birth I was on the air, accepting Dave's congratulations and commenting on his remark that "Victoria Lily is a lovely name."

"Thank you, Dave," I said. " 'Lily' was my maternal grandmother's name, and Victoria . . . well, she's a stripper I once dated."

Naturally I was jesting, but now I wonder whether, even as an infant, Victoria was ingesting her father's humor just as I ingested my parents' humor. Some fifteen years later, as a beautiful and bright teenager, Victoria was walking with me on Central Park South, when we happened upon an art gallery that seemed to call us inside. We focused on a small bronze sculpture of an elephant. We noticed that its surface had the texture of a hide.

"It was crafted in Africa," explained the proprietor. "That coating is taken from the actual mud in which the elephant bathed. The artist used the mud as the final surface treatment."

"How much is it?" I asked.

"Ten thousand," was the answer.

I thought about it, but passed.

Once we were back on the street, the lovely Victoria asked, "Why would anyone pay ten thousand dollars for an elephant coated in its own shit?"

* * *

My beloved son Will was born January 21, 1999. He is a young chess master as well as a budding musical talent—on trumpet, on the shofar at High Holy Day services, and, along with sister Victoria, on the Rock Band video game. Will is our second exceptional child.

The other day, my children and I were discussing their first words.

"Mine were, 'I want this,' " said Victoria.

Will looked up from his Game Boy and slyly quipped, "Mine was 'photosynthesis.' "

One household, three comics, and all under the capable command of the sainted Cathy, who steers the Shaffer ship with frightening efficiency and undying love.

"Family is everything," I once said to my daughter Victoria.

"Oh, Dad," she said, "you're such a bullshitter. You know you'd rather be laughing with Belzer, playing with John Mayer, or staying up late with Marty Short than driving me and Will to school."

"No, Victoria," I said, doing my best Tony Soprano imitation, "family is everything."

* * *

Between the birth of Victoria and Will, I got a great gig—musical director of the closing ceremony of the 1996 Summer Olympics in Atlanta. I look back on the event as a career highlight. The only problem was that during the opening segment of the evening's program I was nearly crushed to death.

Dig:

It happened when Gloria Estefan, Tito Puente, Sheila E., and I were on a float riding around the inside perimeter of the stadium. Gloria was wailing away, singing out her fabulous "Conga" hit. The crowd was going wild. I was relishing the moment, when suddenly hordes of people broke through the barricades, rushed our float, and tried to climb aboard, tilting the thing precariously to one side. I had no idea what was happening. My mind started racing: *Could it be a gang of red-neck Southerners going after the Jew leading the Latin band?* Whatever it was, I found myself throwing these strangers off the float, using my hands and feet to beat back the invaders. As the float started to tip over, I envisioned the end of my young life. I saw the obit in tomorrow's *New York Times:* "Mob Kills Gloria Estefan, Tito Puente, Sheila E. and Accompanist."

Thanks to a gracious God, though, the float stabilized and the eager assailants were beaten back. Turned out they were Olympic athletes who rushed the field too early and, overly excited, decided they needed to join us on the float. By pushing them off I averted the first of several near disasters.

The second involved the architect of rock and roll, Little Richard. One of the great aspects of this event was the free rein given me by the producers. I could book anyone. Richard was high on my list. We decided to prerecord his vocal the Friday afternoon before the ceremony.

"There's only one thing, Paul," Richard said. "I need to be out of here by 5 p.m. It's *Shabbos,* and I'm an Orthodox Jew. Have been for years. After sundown, I do no work."

As it turned out, the session went long. It took Richard a

while to get into his normal manic mode. When he did find his groove and was ready to prerecord his vocal, it was already 5.

"Sorry, sweetheart," he told me, "but I'm out of here."

I was prepared. I had looked up the official sunset time in the Atlanta almanac. I brought out the book and pointed to that day's date. "Sunset will occur at 5:21," it read.

Richard couldn't help but smile. "Baby, you're a better Jew than me."

In those next twenty-one minutes, we captured a brilliant Little Richard vocal.

The excitement built when the producers said that Stevie Wonder wanted to participate and would soon be calling. A little while later, I was called to the phone. On the other end I heard a voice that resembled a news anchor, in, say, Des Moines, Iowa. The intonation was white as rice. The voice started talking about special lyrics to Stevie's birthday song written for Martin Luther King.

"Are you representing Stevie Wonder?" I asked the voice.

"Man, I am Stevie Wonder," said Stevie Wonder.

The next day Stevie showed up with this new set of lyrics. He thought we should do it "We Are the World" style, with the full cast taking turns. I liked the idea.

"Steveland," I said, using his real name, "there's a line here that I'm not sure I understand."

"Which one, Paul?" he wanted to know.

"The one where you wrote, 'Before Olympiads become an illusion.' I'm not sure I know what that means."

"Give me a break, man," said Steveland, "I just wrote the shit this afternoon."

Ambiguous lyrics or not, Wonder was a huge success. The concert was tremendous—B.B. King, Richard, Gloria, Sheila, the Pointer Sisters, and Faith Hill. Faith wanted to do "Will the Circle Be Unbroken."

"Great idea," I said, "but let's do it with a white gospel group and go for a Jordanaires sound," referencing the vocalists who often backed Elvis.

"I don't care if they're Martians," said Faith, "as long as they sing their asses off."

Everyone sang his or her respective ass off.

But how to conclude such an evening of spectacular singing?

Al Green testifying about "Love and Happiness."

The post-concert was nearly as much fun as the concert itself. Stevie asked me to dinner, where, for our own entertainment, we played what he called the Song Game.

Stevie started a song, and I had to continue with another, thematically linked to the first one. It got tricky, but it also got funky. At one point I picked up a Melodica—a wind instrument that has a keyboard—and accompanied Steveland as he sang Ray Charles's "What'd I Say." At the conclusion, every diner in the establishment rose and gave us a thunderous reception.

If I might borrow Sammy Davis's 1984 description of *Late Night with David Letterman*, the entire Olympics affair was "a gas and a giggle."

Chapter 43

What Kind of Host Am I?

I've been given the opportunity to host Letterman a few times when Dave couldn't make it. The most memorable was the first in 2003. The writers worked overtime to cook up material, and so did I. I put on my pinstriped suit and hit the ground running.

"This is fabulous," I said. "What were the odds of *me* being available tonight? I usually spend this part of the show staring at Dave's ass. But this is a new angle. Now I can cut *myself* off. Seriously though, did you see the Academy Awards last night? Joan Rivers showed up in a bulletproof face. Hey, I hear Monica Lewinsky is getting her own reality show. The twist is that every week a guy is voted off *her*. It's going to be called *Joe Blow*. As you know, I'm Dave's sidekick or, as some prefer, Dave's whipping boy. And even though I am a celebrity—whatever the hell that means—and even though I am treated royally, it really doesn't matter how many people I hire to say that I'm terrific. Tonight I stand alone. Yes, it's lonely in this spotlight. The pressure's on and it's time to dig down deep and ask myself the toughest of questions . . ."

At this moment, the band broke in with "What Kind of Fool Am I?" and I sang, Sinatra-style, a set of special lyrics:

What kind of host am I?
Do I have what it takes?
Up till now all I've done is play songs during commercial
　breaks
What kind of host am I?
Will I pass this test?
Or will the viewers flip to Leno during my first guest?
Will I rock the Top Ten List
Like David Letterman?
Stay tuned cause tonight I'll boast of the kind of host I am!

Another treat that evening was the presence of the great Mike Smith, my substitute on keyboards. He had been lead singer and organist for the Dave Clark Five, the band that rivaled the Beatles during the British Invasion and a group I loved dearly. When they appeared on Sullivan—as they had dozens of times—and I saw Mike standing at the Vox Continental organ, I vowed to never sit again. To this day I play standing proud—all because of Mike Smith. That night Mike did a terrific version of "Because," a ballad Cathy and I consider *our* song. It was a beautiful experience and may have even gotten Mike to reexamine the possibility of touring the United States. He saw that we, his true fans, had not forgotten him.

Then tragedy struck. Repairing a fence outside his home in Spain, Mike suffered a freak accident: he took a fall and landed on his head. His spinal cord was damaged. Mike was paralyzed from the waist down. He was flown to England and admitted to a hospital specializing in spinal injuries.

I knew I had to do something for Mike because musically Mike had done so much for me. When I learned that the Zombies were touring North America, an idea came to me: Why not a British Invasion tribute to Mike Smith? I booked B.B. King's club on Forty-second Street and started pursuing other acts. Miraculously, Peter and Gordon, who hadn't appeared together in thirty-seven years, agreed to perform. So did Denny Laine from the Moody Blues and Billy J. Kramer. Will Lee's Fab Faux, the most spot-on Beatles band on either side of the Pond, signed on as the opening act. And then we were set.

And then we were sunk. A plane accident at the Toronto airport grounded all flights, including the one for the Zombies. Five hours before the show, they were stuck in Canada with no way out. I was in a panic, and when I mentioned this to Letterman, Dave felt my pain. "Give me a minute," he said. "I have an idea." Next thing I knew, Dave had arranged for the group to fly in from a private airport on a private jet. As hard as I tried to pay for it myself, my boss wouldn't take a dime.

The show was halfway over at B.B. King's when I was able to tell the audience, "The Zombies have landed! They *will* be here!"

And, boy, were they ever! Rock and roll fanatics are still talking about the evening, especially the grand finale when we did an all-star version of Mike Smith's great classic "Glad All Over."

After all this, I wanted to see Mike. I wanted to hand him a copy of the DVD of the concert. I decided to fly over to England and present it to him personally. I did it because I figured that, after putting on that benefit, I'd earned the right to a trip overseas and a visit with my hero.

I landed in London and took the train to the hospital an hour north of the city. Mike was in good spirits. Miami Steve Van Zandt had given him an electric wheelchair. He had enough motion in his hand to manipulate the controls. His breathing was labored—he was on a ventilator during the evening hours—but he could make himself understood. He greeted me warmly. I said I had come to give him a copy of the DVD.

"Can we watch it together, Paul?" he asked.

"Of course."

We sat and watched the entire show, which had begun at 11 p.m. and didn't conclude till 4 in the morning.

Tears streamed down Mike's face.

"I don't know how to thank you," he said.

"You don't have to."

"Would you mind coming back tomorrow so we can watch it again?"

"I'd love to."

Turned out that Mike and I, seated side by side, watched the DVD three days in a row.

Two years passed.

By now it was 2008, and the Dave Clark Five were going to be inducted into the Rock and Roll Hall of Fame. I was especially touched that I would get to play Mike's greatest hits. Mike was set to attend.

Ten days before the induction dinner, though, Mike Smith died. That evening, when we sang "Glad All Over," we felt his beautiful spirit all over us. I felt grateful to have known him as a friend.

✦ ✦ ✦

Dave Letterman, of course, has also been a great friend. When I learned that he required a quintuple bypass, I immediately called the chief rabbi of the state of Israel to make a *m'shabeirach*, a special prayer for the sick.

"Is he Jewish?" asked the rabbi.

"No," I said, "but he's in show business."

"Close enough," said the rabbi. "I'm praying as we speak."

The prayer worked, and Dave came through like a champ.

During this same period, another prayer of mine was answered. I got a street named after me in Thunder Bay. I felt like, as Jesse Jackson would say, "I *am* somebody." I even went as far as to announce the honor on the air.

"Dave," I said one night, "at this very moment, you can move on up to Thunder Bay and boogaloo down Paul Shaffer Drive."

"What? They named a street after you? I'm outraged! *I* don't even have an alleyway in Indianapolis."

"Dave, you deserve a boulevard."

"A boulevard, hell . . . I want the entire interstate beltway around Indianapolis."

"What would they call it?"

"Well, they could call it 'The Dave,' as in 'take the Dave, it'll cut your time in half.' "

"I like it."

"Or, how about the 'Letterman Bypass'?"

"That's it," I said. "I'm calling the governor."

Chapter 44

The Grinch Who Ruined Christmas

This happened only a few years ago. I relate the story now not only to give you a glimpse of what a day in my Letterman life is like, but to document what is musically, year in and year out, my most satisfying moment—the holiday show when I get to conduct the great Darlene Love singing "Christmas (Baby Please Come Home)."

On this particular December morning, a snowstorm has hit the suburbs where I start off my day. My car's stuck and requires pushing by me and three of my neighbors. I feel like I'm back in the frozen hell of my Canadian childhood. It's murder getting it out, and when we finally do I find myself slipping and sliding all over the road. Miraculously, I make it to Manhattan in one piece, but I'm distressed because, due to the delay, I've been unable to call Ellie Greenwich. Every year I must speak to Ellie on this day of days. I must do so not only because she wrote the song with Jeff Barry and the song's producer, Phil Spector, but because Ellie *is* the song. Her musical spirit is what the song is all about. Our conversation never varies.

"Ellie," I begin. "The time has come. I'm so excited."

"Me too, but I have an idea of how to do it."

"How?"

"Start off the opening chorus a capella."

"Great idea," I always say. "Then we can bring the band in at the first verse."

"That sounds good."

"But come to think of it, Ellie, I better just do it like the record. There's no improving on perfection."

"Good luck, Paul, and thanks for keeping the song alive."

This is a conversation I absolutely need to have—it's my good luck touchstone—but as I arrive at the Ed Sullivan Theater, I realize I'm late. Now I have the pressure of the time.

The nine background singers have already arrived for the massive production number. Before I deal with them, though, I close myself off and, one more time, listen to Darlene Love's record from 1963. I remember its unfortunate history: Released just weeks before Kennedy's assassination, it was the only original song on Spector's Christmas album. Along with the rest of the record, the tune faded in the wake of the national tragedy. Nonetheless, "Christmas (Baby Please Come Home)" has remained a favorite of singers and musicians and, for my money, is *the* definitive yuletide anthem.

After I listen to the record and renew my inspiration, my long-suffering assistant, Daniel Fetter, appears with a report from the production meeting.

"We don't know what's going to happen in the first act after the monologue," says Daniel.

"*Mah nishtanoh,* babe," I tell him, quoting the section of the Passover seder that asks, "Why should this night be different than any other?"

Daniel only half laughs. He's only half Jewish. If I had time, I'd tell him the joke my father never tired of telling me—how Barry Goldwater was turned away from a restricted golf course. "No Jews allowed," he was told. "I'm only half Jewish," said the senator. "Can I play nine holes?"

Daniel runs down the rest of the show. Little by little, we get a general idea of what will happen. In the second act, I'll do Cher singing "O Holy Night," and actor Jay Thomas will tell his getting-saved-by-the-Lone-Ranger tale, a story that never varies year to year. Dave loves it, and so does the audience. After that, Jay and Dave will throw footballs at our Christmas tree in an attempt to dislodge the meatball on top, another hallowed tradition.

Acts 3 and 4 will be devoted to Paris Hilton. We'll play her on with "I Love Paris." She'll be deadpan hysterical. She always is. Act 5 is announcer Alan Kalter's voice-over jokes. And act 6, my big act, will be Darlene.

At 4 p.m. it's time to rehearse. There are strings and extra horns, a percussionist, chimes and bells, and, as always, Tom Malone's brilliant arrangement. There are three guitars to approximate the six on Spector's original. There's an upright bass to augment Will Lee's electric bass. There's a carefully engineered mix to be balanced by Harvey Goldberg so that, if we can't build a wall of sound, at least we can put up a fence. There's also the challenge of how to present Bruce Kapler's baritone sax solo. Every year Bruce, dressed in a custom-made Superfly Santa suit, makes an unorthodox appearance. Last year he flew in on cables. This year he'll emerge from a giant gift box pushed onstage by two leggy ladies in slinky Ms. Claus costumes. We run the song down a couple of times before the lovely Darlene herself appears. She sings it twice with full orchestra. In the final chorus, fake snow starts to fall. Beautiful.

At 5 p.m. sharp, I run upstairs to dress: red silk Versace suit; glitter-green Dolce and Gabbana tie, Ferragamo alligator lace-ups. Jew be stylin'.

In makeup I see Dave for the first time all day.

"How's your holiday season going, Paul?" he asks.

"Boring," I say. "How's yours, Dave?"

"Boring," he says.

Fired up, we're ready to go.

The audience has been loaded in. At 5:25 I hit the stage. At 5:30 we blast off.

We fire on all cylinders. The show hums. Darlene tears it up. After the big number, Dave comes out and says, "Beautiful job, everybody. Good night. We'll see you next year."

My band's especially relieved because they have other gigs to get to. They're halfway off the stage when director Jerry Foley says we need to redo our closing theme because, with all the scattered mics, the stage looked messy.

"Fine, Jerry," I say, "but can we hold the audience? My band needs to get out of here, so let's do it now."

I say this because we can't play while the audience loads out—a seven- to ten-minute process. The band has got to go! I have the pressure of the time.

"No problem, Paul. We'll hold the audience."

It takes a minute for us to get ready. But just as I'm about to count off the theme, I see the audience standing up and filing out. I explode. I start screaming at the stage manager, "Who the fuck told you to let the audience go? Who do you think you are, the director? The director and I had it all worked out, and you've fucking ruined the whole goddamn plan. What the fuck is going on here?"

My mic is hot, and the audience hears my every word. Making matters worse, it isn't the stage manager's fault. He hadn't gotten the word to hold the audience. Any way you look at it, I've blown it.

The next day the *New York Post* prints a letter from an audience member reporting on being at the Letterman Christmas show. She writes that the show was beautiful, even meaningful. Everything was simply perfect and in keeping with the holiday spirit. Then suddenly Paul Shaffer threw a fit and started cursing like a sailor. He ruined everything. The world might see him as a nice guy. But now the world must be warned: he's the grinch who ruined Christmas.

The *Post* is good enough to let me respond. I offer my humblest apologies to all concerned. I explain that I had the pressure of the time.

Chapter 45

Patriotism and Religion

I love my country of birth, the great nation that has recently awarded me the Order of Canada, the highest civilian honor the country bestows.

For what? Cutting off a guy's pant leg?

No, seriously, I'm humbled.

At the same time, I now love my adopted United States of America, the land that gave me the music that changed my life, a career that has exceeded my wildest expectations, and a family I adore. Having lived in the United States my entire adult life, I've become a naturalized citizen.

I am not much of a political maven. I am certainly not an ideologue. I tend to listen to—rather than participate in— political disputes. Like everyone else, though, I was shaken to the core by the tragedy of 9/11. Those of us living and working in New York City experienced the nightmare on a frighteningly visceral level.

Dave Letterman's response was especially moving. I call Dave a patriot because of his instinctual love of country. Out of that instinct, he called me after the United States had gone to war against the Taliban.

"How'd you like to go to Afghanistan, Paul?"

While my patriotism doesn't exist at the high level on which Dave's operates, my response was immediate: "What an opportunity! Let's go."

"Great. I want to take you and Biff. We'll go for Christmas Eve and spread some good cheer."

Biff, our stage manager, is a Vietnam vet and all-around great guy.

Dave was too modest to bring over what other entertainers might call "a show." He was also insistent upon keeping our trip low key. No TV cameras. No footage for *Late Show*. He just wanted to hang out with the soldiers. Which is what we did. It turned out to be one of the deepest experiences of my life. It was scary, nerve-racking, and incredibly rewarding.

We flew through the night to the Sultanate of Oman in the United Arab Emirates, where we transferred to a C-130 military cargo plane that took us into Afghanistan. Dave and I were in the cockpit kibitzing with the pilots. Suddenly the humor ended when we were told we were about to make one of those wartime landings. That's when, at high altitude, the plane lunges into a downward spiral, releasing flares so that heat-seeking missiles might seek the flares instead of the plane. Just when it felt like we were about to crash, the plane pulled out of the spiral and eased down.

On the ground at Kandahar airport, we were greeted by an officer. "Don't wander off," he said. "Land mines are everywhere." The airport had been captured from the Taliban, who had used it as their headquarters. The hangar was now riddled with bullet holes.

We climbed into two old Humvees and started greeting the divisions one by one. First the army, then the air force, then the marines. Dave was wonderful. "We're just here to say that everyone back home is thinking about you," he told the soldiers. "We want to thank you for everything you're doing." He had time and a good word for everyone.

Everyone wanted his or her picture taken with Dave. Dave made everyone smile. When it came to the marines, though, as we were posing their commander barked, "I don't want to see *no* smiles!"

A group of soldiers gathered in the hangar, where I led them in carols. We sang "Silent Night." Outside the hangar, the night was silent, eerily so. The sky was astoundingly clear. It was Christmas Eve. I noticed one star shining brighter than all the others. "I feel like something's happening in Bethlehem," I told Dave. "Let's rent three camels and get the hell over there."

A female sergeant approached me to thank us for coming.

"We're here to thank you," I said.

"I have two kids back home," she told me.

"Wow," I replied, "what a sacrifice!"

"Are you kidding?" she said. "I gotta help clean up this world for them."

A male officer wished us a Merry Christmas. "I'm worried," he said.

"Why?" I asked.

"Because it's just a matter of time before we go into Iraq. And no one wants to go."

Our plan was to get into another C-130 and head up into the mountains to the Bagram base. We got on the plane only to be told that the trip was canceled for the evening. There was trouble at Bagram.

That night Biff and I shared a room in the airport with a sergeant. At about 3 a.m. I used a flashlight to make my way to the latrine.

The next morning the sergeant said, "Was that you fumbling around last night?"

"Yes," I said.

"Christ," he said. "I almost went for my gun."

I imagined the headline in the *New York Post*: CHRISTMAS EVE TRAGEDY: FRIENDLY FIRE FINISHES OFF LETTERMAN'S JEW SIDEKICK.

It was still too dangerous to approach Bagram, so we were forced to fly back to Oman, where we entertained our troops at the Seeb base. The soldiers hipped me to the lingo. The C-130 was a "Hercules." Greenwich Mean Time was "Zulu Time." The frozen military dinners were MREs—Meals Ready to Eat. They were hungry for a little lighthearted humor. Dave had them laughing. I sang, "I'll have a Seeb Christmas without you." During the show, I was so tired I began hallucinating. On the plane home, I realized that these men and women had shown us what bravery in time of war is all about.

A year later at Christmas, Dave, Biff, and I were off again, this time to Baghdad. Dave chartered a private jet that flew to Kuwait. The stewardess couldn't wait to tell us that Jennifer Lopez and Ben Affleck had recently chartered this same plane. According to the attendant, they had asked the entire crew to squeeze into the cockpit so that the famous couple could couple in private.

We flew from Kuwait to Baghdad in another C-130. We visited some of Saddam's palaces that had been taken over by our military. The mood was up because Saddam had just been captured.

We performed a little in each palace. Dave spoke beautifully, of course, and then introduced me. This trip I had my own lyrics to the tune of "White Christmas":

"I'm dreaming of an Iraq Christmas . . . had Christmas Eve dinner on a C-130 Hercules . . . at 0800 Zulu a big chick named Lulu . . . passed out the MRE's . . ."

Then I said, "Now here's some old Bob Hope jokes. Hey, I gotta tell ya, I'm a little nervous being over here in Iraq. This morning my toaster popped, and I surrendered to the maid. But General Sanchez reassured me. He promised to have my blood type available, even if he had to kill the chicken himself. Hey, seriously, there are no psychiatrists in Iraq. They know you're nuts or you wouldn't be here."

I wrapped up singing:

Now that you got that bastard Saddam
Our Christmas stateside will be safe and warm

The cheers were deafening.

Then we were loaded into a convoy that left the protected Green Zone. There were gunners at the front and gunners at the rear. All of a sudden, the convoy took a sharp turn off the road and followed a circuitous path. We later heard that a decoy convoy had been sent ahead of ours. Intelligence suspected that the enemy was interested in taking out our group of VIPs. In fact, the decoy convoy had been attacked, but fortunately suffered no casualties.

Dave never blinked an eye. I blinked both eyes. Over and over again.

Our third Christmas trip also took us to Iraq. This time Dave figured we should bring along a comic. Always loyal, he chose his friend Tom Dreesen. Tom had been a longtime friend of Sinatra's. In fact, he was the opening act for many of Frank's appearances. Like many of us, Tom's obsessed with all things Sinatra. Unfortunately, I don't have any Sinatra stories. If I did, I'd be telling them night and day. Tom Dreesen has loads of Sinatra stories. He tells them night and day.

In fact, Dreesen told an endless stream of Sinatra stories on our endless plane ride to Iraq. In long and hilarious disquisitions, Tom delineated those situations when one was required to address Sinatra as Mr. S; when one called him Mr. Sinatra; and when one was free to refer to him as Frank or simply the Old Man. Tom offered up delicious descriptions of Frank's compound in Palm Springs; he told us that each guest bungalow was named after a Sinatra hit and let it be known that he always stayed in the Tender Trap.

Naturally these stories charmed me entirely, even if—or especially because—they stood in such vivid contrast to our goodwill mission. Our show was a simple affair. Dave welcomed everyone and expressed his gratitude to the troops. Military personnel, most of whom were excellent, performed. Tom told a few hilarious jokes, followed by a few tunes played by yours truly. Then came two novelty chick acts from the *Late Show*. The first was the Hula Hoop Girl, whose name describes her routine. Next came the Grinder Girl. The Grinder Girl was something to behold. This frisky lassie placed a grinder—a revolving drill bit—right on her crotch and bent over, and when the grinder began grinding, sparks flew out of her ass. Even the soldiers were embarrassed.

Embarrassments and anxieties aside, what a privilege to go on these trips with Dave, a privilege to personally thank the men and women who put their lives on the line for us.

* * *

As I approach my seventh decade of life, I must confess to some self-examination, to asking, as did Dionne Warwick, "What's it all about, Alfie?"

Naturally I am a believer in the spiritual properties of music. Music is my muse, my soul, and my salvation. Music pays my children's orthodontist. Music puts gas in the car, food on the table, and a smile on my face. Music lights my way—always has and always will—as I navigate life's tricky mazes. Music expresses feelings I cannot put into words. Plain and simple, music—music heard and music played—makes me feel good. Even the blues takes away my blues.

As demonstrated in these pages, my musical gods who jam atop Mount Olympus are many—many writers, players, producers, and singers in all styles. If God ever caught me, as Moses caught the children of Israel, worshipping a graven image, it would probably look a little like Felix Cavaliere of the Rascals.

I also worship at more traditional altars. I attend *shul.* I'm a member of an Orthodox congregation where my son Will is scheduled to celebrate his bar mitzvah a few years from now. That's important to me. It was important to both me and Cathy that she convert to Judaism before we married. My faith, and the tradition that informs it, is a vital part of my life.

Here's something quirky about my relationship to modern Orthodox Judaism. As you might expect, it involves music. At my current *shul,* most of the traditional centuries-old prayer melodies—the same melodies I learned and loved as a child in Thunder Bay—are being replaced by melodies written by Rabbi Shlomo Carlebach. Carlebach, who died in 1994, was a gifted composer who gave a modern folksy spin to Hebraic music. Some have compared him to Dylan. His motifs became hugely popular among younger Orthodox Jews. In many *shuls* around the world, they have actually replaced the ancient melodic lines.

This doesn't thrill me. And though I know it sounds strange for me—lover of rock and roll and defender of all genres of pop music—to hold such a staunchly traditional view, I just want to hear the melodies I first heard when I entered the synagogue as a boy, those same melodies that filled the hearts of my ancestors. Today those melodies fill my heart with a love linked to the history of a people who have suffered and survived. I need for those haunting melodies to survive. I need those haunting melodies for strength.

* * *

When my mother fell ill in 1999, I needed a great deal of strength. By then my father had also fallen into an alarming decline. A few years earlier, Mom had told me, in her genteel way, "I'm afraid, dear, that your dad is losing his marbles a little bit." It turned out to be Alzheimer's.

That's probably why he broke the news the way he did.

I was in postproduction for *Blues Brothers 2000*. While not the same kind of blockbuster as its predecessor, the film was a wonderful experience for me. Dan Aykroyd made good on his promise to bring me back into the funky world of the Blues Brothers. To me, my presence in the second movie made up for my absence in the first. That meant a great deal to me. I got to produce Aretha doing "Respect" with yours truly on organ while the Queen played her soulful piano. I especially relished the spectacular ending where I led an all-star jam extravaganza that included Billy Preston, Isaac Hayes, Stevie Winwood, B.B.

King, Wilson Pickett, Bo Diddley, Dr. John, Jimmie Vaughan, Travis Tritt, and my old friend Eric Clapton.

Looking at early rushes of the film and coordinating the music, I was hard at work when Dad called. Looking back, our conversation felt like something out of Larry David's *Curb Your Enthusiasm*.

"How are you, Paul?" he asked.

"Fine, Dad."

"Just calling to check up on you."

"That's nice of you, Dad. The film's almost done."

"Can't wait to see it, son."

"I'll fly you and Mom out for the premiere."

"Mom may not be able to come."

"Why not?"

"Oh, well, because she's in the hospital."

"Mom's in the hospital! When did this happen?"

"A few weeks ago."

"And you never told me?"

"I didn't want to bother you."

"Not bother me! She's my mother! What's wrong with her?"

"Pneumonia."

"Will she be all right?"

"I'm not sure."

Cathy, the kids, and I flew up to Canada to see her. Her condition had stabilized, and the doctors were optimistic.

Back in New York, I called her every day. A week later, she sounded excited.

"They're letting me go home today," she said.

"Oh, Mom, that's wonderful."

"I can't wait to get back to my own bed."

"I can only imagine. Hey, Mom, I love you."

"I love you too, Paul."

Three hours later, my aunt Lorna called. "Your mother's dead."

"I just talked to her. What happened?"

"Her heart gave out."

Shirley Eleanor Wood Shaffer was seventy-seven.

* * *

Dad hung on for quite a few more years. But his decline was difficult. I'd fly home to see him often. Passionate about jazz singers his entire life, toward the end he only wanted to hear three: Nat Cole, Tony Bennett, and Sinatra. Later, only Nat and Frank sounded good to him. During his last days, three dwindled down to one: Dad only wanted to hear Sinatra. That's how he left this earth, listening to Frank. Bernard Shaffer was ninety.

* * *

I miss my parents every day of my life. I think of them every day. I feel great gratitude in my heart for the love they gave me. I forgive them for urging me to get a wig when my hairline started to recede. Rugsville? I don't think so.

Despite differences in our outlook on hair, I am the product of my parents' culture. When my culture began to move in a new direction, when rock and roll invaded my soul, Mom and Dad supported and encouraged me. They saw that my passion was genuine; they realized the music was worthwhile. Without their backing, I may well have wound up an unhappy barrister or a barista at Starbucks.

Instead, I'm a happy pianist. I'm happy to be the guy who backs up the singers, the strippers, the rockers, and the rollers.

I'm happy when I'm pumping the organ and Bruce Springsteen jumps on top of it while whipping up a frenzied "Glory Days." I still hear myself telling my mother, just as I told her when I was a kid falling in love with music, *"Ma, it's rock and roll."*

It's a party.

It's a life.

It's a dream.

It's a different dream than the one I imagined when I first came to New York through the kind auspices of composer Stephen Schwartz. When I first stayed with Stephen in his home in Connecticut, I knew that the vanilla suburbs were not for me. I had to have the city. I had to have the funk. I had to move to big-city beats. And yet here I am, decades later, one foot on Broadway and another in Westchester County with the wife and kids.

Yes, my people, I have a divided soul. I live a double life. And I like it.

My suburban life finds me fathering America's two greatest kids, Victoria and Will. I put on my *Father Knows Best* baby-blue Orlon cardigan sweater and attend parent conferences with their teachers. Cathy and I are absolutely aglow when we're told our children are achieving on a high level, as invariably they are. I have been known to barbecue in the backyard. I consult gardeners about crabgrass. I drive to the supermarket.

But two nights a week, after the Letterman show has wrapped, I'm back in the funk. I troll the city nightlife. I might fall by my favorite bar and restaurant, Caffe Cielo. And even though I do not drink—my migraines won't tolerate it—and even though I am a happily married man, I stand at the bar, like Jackie Gleason at Toots Shor's, and listen to the proprietor, my pal Joe, go on and on about the wonders of Brazilian women.

After that, I might hook up with Tom Leopold, the wittiest of writers, and go catch a Ben Vereen, a Tony Martin, or a Lynda Carter at an East Side cabaret. Or maybe catch Lew Soloff at a club in the Village where he's brewing up a hot pot of New York post-bop.

Yes, kids, it's a gas to be living in a city where I walk the streets to the harmony of a Henry Mancini jazz score. It's a gas to rock the Ed Sullivan Theater every weekday night with the baddest band in the land. A gas to walk through Manhattan at midnight when the skyscrapers are glowing neon and the streets shimmering like jewels.

If you stop by my apartment overlooking the moody Hudson River, you won't find me in front of a bank of high-tech synthesizers with the latest digital this and digital that. No, sir, you will find me at the tried-and-true Hammond B3, the one that belonged to Soul Brother Number One, Godfather James Brown. Hey, I just might favor you with a few of my best Jimmy McGriff or Dr. Lonnie Smith licks. I'll play the blues for you. I'll get you to thinking that you're in some semi-sleazy lounge where the waitresses wear cat suits and the patrons want their funk unfiltered.

This is where I began. This is where I am. This is where I'll be. And if I stop, it's only because we gotta take a short pause for the cause. We'll be back in a flash. We got one more set to go. And then, somewhere east of midnight, in those wee small ones, it'll be time to wrap it up. In the words of Sam Butera, "It's a pleasure to kill ourselves for you, ladies and gentlemen." We hate to go, but we got to go. So we leave you with the love and the sincerity and all good stuff. Please come back and see us.

We'll be here for the rest of our lives.

Credits

Insert, page 1, top, courtesy of the author.

Insert, page 1, bottom, courtesy of the author.

Insert, page 2, top, courtesy of the author.

Insert, page 2, middle, courtesy of the author.

Insert, page 2, bottom, courtesy of Universal Music Enterprises.

Insert, page 3, top, courtesy of NBCU Photo Bank.

Insert, page 3, middle, courtesy of Edie Baskin Studios, © Edie Baskin.

Insert, page 3, bottom, courtesy of NBCU Photo Bank.

Insert, page 4, top, courtesy of the author.

Insert, page 4, middle, courtesy of Chuck Pulin.

Insert, page 4, bottom, courtesy of HBO.

Insert, page 5, top, courtesy of the Rock and Roll Hall of Fame Foundation.

Insert, page 5, middle, courtesy of the author.

Insert, page 5, bottom, courtesy of NBCU Photo Bank.

Insert, page 6, top, courtesy of the author.

Insert, page 6, bottom, courtesy of Canada's Walk of Fame.

Insert, page 7, top, courtesy of the author.

Insert, page 7, bottom, courtesy of CBS Photo: JP Filo.

Insert, page 8, top, courtesy of the author.

Insert, page 8, bottom, courtesy of Kimberly Butler/Kimberly Butler Photography.

ABOUT THE AUTHORS

Paul Shaffer is one of America's enduring musical icons. He is the musical director of *Late Show with David Letterman* as well as the co-composer of "It's Raining Men."

David Ritz has co-written memoirs with, among others, Ray Charles, Aretha Franklin, and Don Rickles. He also co-wrote "Sexual Healing."